Cyberbullying and Online Harms

T0386490

Cyberbullying and Online Harms identifies online harms and their impact on young people, from communities to campuses, exploring current and future interventions to reduce and prevent online harassment and aggression.

This important resource brings together eminent international researchers whose work shines a light on social issues, such as bullying/cyberbullying, racism, homophobia, hate crime, and social exclusion. The text collates into one volume current knowledge and evidence of cyberbullying and its effect on young people, facilitating action to protect victims, challenge perpetrators and develop policies and practices to change cultures that are discriminatory and divisive. It also provides a space where those who have suffered online harms and who have often been silenced in the past may have a voice in telling their experiences and recounting interventions and policies that helped them to create safer spaces in which to live in their community, study in their educational institutions and socialise with their peer group.

This is essential reading for researchers, academics, undergraduates and postgraduates in sociology, psychology, criminology, media and communication studies, as well as practitioners and policymakers in psychology, education, sociology, criminology, psychiatry, counselling and psychotherapy, and anyone concerned with the issue of bullying, cyberbullying and online harms among young people in higher education.

Helen Cowie is Emerita Professor at the University of Surrey, Fellow of the British Psychological Society and a Chartered Counselling Psychologist. Currently, she is collaborating with the European Commission through the Network of Experts working on the Social Dimension of Education and Training (NESET) to develop preliminary recommendations for promoting well-being, enhancing mental health resilience and preventing bullying at school throughout Europe.

Carrie-Anne Myers is Associate Dean for Education in the School of Policy and Global Affairs at City, University of London, and Reader in Criminology, with special reference to Victimology. She has extensive research experience in a number of key areas including Youth Criminality, School Violence and Bullying, Cyberbullying Across the Educational Lifespan and Victimisation Processes. She has published widely in these key areas, and her research has attracted both national and international acclaim and has fed into policy initiatives globally.

Cyberbullying and Online Harms

Preventions and Interventions from Community to Campus

Edited by Helen Cowie and Carrie-Anne Myers

Routledge
Taylor & Francis Group

LONDON AND NEW YORK

Designed cover image: © Getty Images

First published 2023
by Routledge

4 Park Square, Milton Park, Abingdon, Oxon OX14 4RN
and by Routledge

605 Third Avenue, New York, NY 10158

Routledge is an imprint of the Taylor & Francis Group, an informa business

British Library Cataloguing-in-Publication Data
A catalogue record for this book is available from the British Library

Library of Congress Cataloging-in-Publication Data
Names: Cowie, Helen, editor. | Myers, Carrie-Anne, editor.
Title: Cyberbullying and online harms : preventions and interventions from
   community to campus / edited by Helen Cowie and Carrie-Anne Myers.
Description: Abingdon, Oxon ; New York, NY : Routledge, 2023. |
   Includes bibliographical references and index.
Identifiers: LCCN 2022052023 (print) | LCCN 2022052024 (ebook) |
   ISBN 9781032193113 (hbk) | ISBN 9781032193090 (pbk) | ISBN
   9781003258605 (ebk)
Subjects: LCSH: Cyberbullying—Prevention. | Bullying—Prevention.
Classification: LCC HV6773.15.C92 C9362 2023 (print) | LCC
   HV6773.15.C92 (ebook) | DDC 302.34/302854678—dc23/
   eng/20230227
LC record available at https://lccn.loc.gov/2022052023
LC ebook record available at https://lccn.loc.gov/2022052024

ISBN: 978-1-032-19311-3 (hbk)
ISBN: 978-1-032-19309-0 (pbk)
ISBN: 978-1-003-25860-5 (ebk)

DOI: 10.4324/9781003258605

Typeset in Bembo
by Apex CoVantage, LLC

Contents

vi   *Contents*

Contributors

Dr Christopher P. Barlett is a social psychologist in the Department of Psychological Sciences at Kansas State University. His research focuses on understanding the antecedents and consequences of aggression (broadly defined) and has recently focused on understanding the psychological processes germane to cyberbullying perpetration. Dr Barlett has created and validated the only cyberbullying theory unique to the online world, an intervention that focuses on cyberbullying perpetration, and published many research articles, book chapters and a book on cyberbullying perpetration. His aim is to better understand cyberbullying to inform intervention efforts to reduce this antisocial behaviour.

Professor James Barnes is Associate Director at Fatima College of Health Sciences in Abu Dhabi. He completed his PhD at Kings College at the University of London and was previously Head of School of Psychology at the University of Bedfordshire and Oxford Brookes University. He is Chartered Psychologist and Associate Fellow of the British Psychological Society (BPS). James has worked in the area of neuropsychology for more than 20 years and has research interests focusing on the neuropsychological aspects of visual hallucinations, psychosis and deviant behaviours in both clinical patients and the general population. He has been involved in a variety of projects working with individuals with Parkinson's disease, dyslexia and PTSD and was a research professor at the National Centre of Cyberstalking Research (NCCR) examining risk factors for stalking violence and stalker motivational behaviour.

Dr Sheri Bauman is Professor Emerita of counselling at the University of Arizona. She earned her PhD in counselling psychology from New Mexico State University in 1999. Before then, she worked in K–12 schools for 30 years, as a teacher and school counsellor. In those roles, she was passionate about student well-being and worked to support students who struggled academically, personally or socially. Dr Bauman conducts research on peer victimisation including bullying and cyberbullying, and is currently co-PI on a funded project to study the effects of teacher practices on peer victimisation and defending behaviours. She is a frequent presenter on these topics at local, state, national and international conferences. She is the sole author/editor or first author of six books and third author of another book and has over 65 publications in peer-reviewed journals, 32 book chapters, three training DVDs and numerous publications in non-scholarly outlets. She is the former editor of the *Journal for Specialists in Group Work* and has co-edited three special issues related to bullying and cyberbullying. Dr Bauman is currently on the editorial board of two scholarly journals. She was honoured with the Eminent Career Award from the Association for Specialists in Group Work in 2018. She has been the recipient of two research grants from the National Science Foundation. She is on the board of trustees of DitchtheLabel.org, an anti-bullying charity based in the UK, and serves as their research consultant.

Dr Leah Burch is Lecturer at Liverpool Hope University in the School of Social Sciences. Her research interests are largely situated within the fields of disability studies and hate studies. Her ESRC-funded PhD project explored disabled people's experiences and understandings of hate crime within the context of their everyday life. She continues to build on this research by paying attention to the ways that disabled people navigate and resist hate crime experiences and is currently leading a steering group to develop a disability hate crime toolkit with disabled people. Leah is a member of the British Society of Criminology Hate Crime Network and leads on ECR and PGR events. Leah runs a PGR and ECR hate studies discussion group, which provides a safe, online space for researchers to present their findings and share methodological dilemmas. Leah is a core member of the Centre for Culture and Disability Studies at Liverpool Hope University. Leah has recently co-led a Ministry of Justice-funded qualitative research project that aims to better understand the support needs of disabled victim-survivors of rape and sexual violence.

Dr Marilyn Campbell is Professor at the Queensland University of Technology. She is a registered teacher and a registered psychologist. Before this, Marilyn supervised school counsellors and has worked in infants, primary and secondary schools as a teacher, teacher-librarian and school counsellor. Her main clinical and research interests are the prevention and intervention of anxiety disorders in young people and the effects of bullying, especially cyberbullying in schools.

Wanda Cassidy is Professor in the Faculty of Education and Director of the Centre for Education, Law and Society at Simon Fraser University. She researches and writes in the areas of social justice education, legal literacy, the ethic of care, vulnerable youth and cyberbullying at K-12 and post-secondary schools.

Carmel Cefai, PhD, FBPS, is the Director of the Centre for Resilience and Socio-Emotional Health, and Professor at the Department of Psychology, at the University of Malta. He is Honorary Chair of the European Network for

Social and Emotional Competence, joint founding editor of the *International Journal of Emotional Education* and a coordinating member and expert of the European Commission Network of Experts on Social Aspects of Education and Training. He has led various local, national, European and international research projects in social and emotional learning, mental health in schools, children's voices, and resilience and well-being in children and young people. His research interests include the well-being and resilience of children and young people, mental health in school, children's voices, and social and emotional education. He has published extensively with numerous books, research reports, journal papers and book chapters.

Helen Cowie is Emerita Professor at the University of Surrey in the Faculty of Health and Medical Sciences. She is Fellow of the British Psychological Society and a Chartered Counselling Psychologist. In 2019, she was given a Lifetime Achievement Award by the European Network for Social and Emotional Competence (ENSEC). She has researched and published widely in the field of anti-bullying interventions at school and university, as well as on the emotional health and well-being of children and young people, to include *From Birth to Sixteen (second edition)* (2019), *A School for Everyone* (2021) (with Ffion Jones and Harriet Tenenbaum) and the Monograph *Peer Support in Schools* (2020) www.um.edu.mt/cres/our research/ourpublications. Currently, she is a member of an expert group of the European Commission Network of Experts on Social Aspects of Education and Training, advising the European Commission on the promotion of well-being, enhancement of mental health and resilience, and the prevention of bullying in schools throughout Europe. She co-edited *School Bullying and Mental Health: Risks, Intervention and Prevention*, published by Routledge in 2018 as the first in a new series entitled *The Mental Health and Well-being of Children and Adolescents*. She also co-authored (with Carrie-Anne Myers) *Bullying Among University Students*, Routledge, 2016.

Jordan Daly is co-founder and Director of Time for Inclusive Education (TIE), a charity founded to address the prejudice and bullying that LGBT young people can experience at school with an educational approach. He won Young Scot of the Year and the Enhancing Education Award in 2018 for his work to ensure future generations do not have the same experiences of homophobia at school that he did.

Christopher Dietzel, PhD, (he/him), is a research associate on the iMPACTS Project. Dietzel's research explores the intersections of gender, sexuality, health, safety and technology. Recently, his interests have focused on issues of consent and sexual violence, particularly related to mobile apps and LGBTQ+ people.

Dr Kathy Evans has taught in a number of different Special Schools, known as Social, Emotional and Behavioural Difficulties (SEBD) Schools. She then moved on to research and write a doctorate at Bristol University, and then to teach at the University of South Wales, where she ended up being the Course Manager of the MA in Child and Adolescent Mental Health. She is now retired and works as a volunteer in the United Kingdom and France. She has a son who works in the same field, and a very new grandson.

Chantal Faucher (PhD, Criminology, Simon Fraser University) is a criminal justice instructor at Langara College, Vancouver, BC. She is also the coordinator for the Centre for Education, Law and Society at Simon Fraser University, Canada, where she is involved in research projects on cyberbullying at the post-secondary level.

Johannes Nilsson Finne, PhD, is Associate Professor at the Norwegian Center for Learning Environment and Behavioral Research, University of Stavanger, Norway. His research focuses on bullying, moral disengagement, social competence and the development of learning environment in school, and also how these different perspectives can contribute in reducing harmful effects of bullying in the follow-up work after bullying has been stopped.

Lynn Gazal has taught in a variety of settings, including primary, secondary and special needs, and in her capacity as an environmental educator and CIC (Community Interest Company) director. Lynn has an MA in Education (Special Needs), and she is AMBDA trained (Associated Member of British Dyslexia Association). Lynn has two primary-age children and a niece and nephew of secondary age. She has seen the dangers and multiple consequences of cyberbullying first hand and believes this is an area in pressing need of more understanding and research.

Ram Herkanaidu is an IT security researcher and educator and is currently a research fellow with the University of Plymouth. His PhD was titled 'Effective Online Safety Awareness for Young People in Less Developed Countries'. He has extensive experience in the IT field, including support, sys admin, consultancy and training. He has created and delivered a number of courses in both a voluntary and professional capacity.

Nathan Hudson is Research Director at the National Centre for Social Research (NatCen). With expertise in interdisciplinary study of poverty, violence and inequality, he has extensive experience leading research on the prevention of crime and victimisation. As a mixed-methods researcher, Nathan is experienced in both qualitative and quantitative methods. This includes expertise in undertaking qualitative research with vulnerable groups (such as victims of crime), as well as stakeholder research, particularly with voluntary and community sectors. Having led and delivered several projects for government departments and non-departmental bodies, Nathan's main area of expertise is LGBT+ equality. This research has explored a range of issues including recruitment discrimination, non-binary gender identities and transgender awareness in education and training. Most recently, Nathan has been as Principal Investigator on an Economic and Social Research

Council (ESRC)-funded project exploring UK LGBT+ communities' experiences of the COVID-19 pandemic.

Margaret Jackson is Professor Emerita in the School of Criminology at Simon Fraser University, Director of FREDA, an SFU research centre focusing upon gender-based violence against women, and past Director of the School of Criminology. In addition to bullying/cyberbullying issues, other research areas include justice policy and family/criminal law case decision-making.

Loraleigh Keashly (PhD U of Saskatchewan) is Professor, Department of Communication, Associate Dean, Curricular and Student Affairs, College of Fine, Performing and Communication Arts and Distinguished Service Professor, Wayne State University, Detroit. She is also the chair of the university campus climate study group. Her research and consulting focus on quality of work relationships, particularly the amelioration of uncivil, hostile and bullying behaviours, an area in which she has worked for almost 30 years. She has a particular interest in developing bystander efficacy to address negative work relationships and build constructive work relationships. Most recently, she has focused her attention on problematic behaviours in academic environments and works with universities on these issues.

Kaelyn Macaulay is a BCL/JD student at McGill University and a legal research assistant with iMPACTS. Prior to law school, she received a BA in English with distinction from the University of Calgary, where she also worked as a Digital Humanities research assistant. Kaelyn's work often examines the intersections between feminism, social media and Canadian law. She is currently the Co-Executive Editor of McGill's Indigenous law publication, Rooted, and a summer student with McCarthy Tétrault.

Renata Miljević-Riđički, PhD, was Full Professor of Developmental Psychology and Education for Development at the Faculty of Teacher Education of the University of Zagreb, Croatia. In the European Network for Social and Emotional Competence (ENSEC), she was the chair responsible for research for seven years (until 2018). She was one of two chairs and organisers of the 4th ENSEC Conference held in Zagreb in July 2013. She was the project team leader for Croatia of the international LLP – Comenius project RESCUR – A Resilience Curriculum for Early and Primary Schools in Europe (2012–2015). The Curriculum has been published in seven languages (Croatian, English, Maltese, Portuguese, Swedish, Italian and Greek) and has been in use ever since. She presented her papers at numerous international conferences and is the author of various books and papers published in relevant scientific journals. Main topics of her interest are preschool education, education for development, developmental psychology, child psychology, child and human rights. She is a member of the Crisis Intervention Team of the Society for Psychological Assistance in Croatia.

Dr Leah Mutanu Mwaura is currently a full-time faculty at the United States International University – Africa in the department of computing. She has a special interest in Software engineering and Information Systems Research. Her research activities include designing Early Warning Systems and Autonomous Computing solutions for development, with related publications in these areas. She has over 15 years' research and teaching experience in academia. Leah holds a PhD in Computer Science and a Master of Science degree in Managing Information Systems.

Dr Carrie-Anne Myers is the Associate Dean for Education in the School of Policy and Global Affairs at City, University of London, and a Reader in Criminology with special reference to Victimology. She has extensive research experience in a number of key areas including Youth Criminality, School Violence and Bullying, Cyberbullying Across the Educational Lifespan and Victimisation Processes. She has published widely in these key areas including two co-edited collections (with Helen Cowie): *School Bullying and Mental Health: Risks, Intervention and Prevention*, published by Routledge in 2018 as the first in a new series entitled *The Mental Health and Well-being of Children and Adolescents* and *Bullying Among University Students*, also by Routledge, in 2016. Her research on Cyberbullying at University considers the intersections between Criminological and Psychological theory, gaps in policy and the legal boundaries that need to be acknowledged with this particular age group (those over 18). Her research has attracted both national and international acclaim and has fed into policy initiatives globally.

Dr Joshua Rumo Arongo Ndiege has over 17 years of university experience, including five years heading the Departments of Computing at United States International University – Africa (three years) and the University of Eastern Africa, Baraton (two years). Currently, Ndiege is an Assistant Professor of Information Systems at United States International University, Africa. Ndiege's research interest is largely in the areas of Knowledge Management, Development Informatics, ICT4D, SMEs, IT Adoption and Business Informatics. He has authored and co-authored a number of refereed journal articles and conference papers. He is a reviewer for a number of academic journals. Ndiege has supervised a number of postgraduate students and acts as an external examiner for master's degree and PhDs for a number of universities in South Africa and Kenya. He has been a member of several university-wide committees such as the Senate, Educational Effectiveness Committee and Academic Standards Committee amongst others. Ndiege holds a PhD in Information Systems, a master's degree in Commerce (Information Systems) and a master's degree in e-Commerce.

Dr Holly Powell-Jones is the founder of OnlineMediaLaw.co.uk, specialising in research, training and consultancy on media law and ethics for the digital age. She is a broadcast journalist and lecturer in media and criminology. Her

PhD explores teenagers' constructs of law, criminality and responsibility on social media (City, University of London).

She has designed and delivered large-scale police-commissioned projects educating tens of thousands of children in schools and has contributed to several research projects related to youth, crime, victimisation, law, human rights and online safety. Holly is also the Online Law Leader for the Global Equality Collective (GEC) and received a Violent Crime Prevention Board award for her work with young people in 2020.

Dr Gella Richards is Senior Lecturer in Psychology at Roehampton University and an HCPC counselling psychologist. She has given presentations internationally on multicultural psychology, including at Xi'an University, Sha'anxi Province, China, and taught related topics on difference and unconscious bias to professional staff. Gella is involved with the UKCP as – Professional Research Network Lead. Additionally, Gella has a background in experimental methods and the NHS. She has been involved in research into memory in animals and brain scanning in older people. She has taught various aspects of neuroscience, psychology and psychiatry at both undergraduate and postgraduate levels. In the field of neuropsychology and neuroscience, Gella's main interest is in neurodegenerative disorders and technology, especially dementia. As part of a team, she was a co-finalist for an Alzheimer's Society award.

Ian Rivers is Associate Principal and Executive Dean of the Faculty of Humanities and Social Sciences at the University of Strathclyde. For 30 years, his research has focused on understanding and challenging LGBT bullying in schools and understanding its long-term effects. He is a recipient of the British Psychological Society's Award for Promoting Equality of Opportunity in the United Kingdom and is a Fellow of the American Psychological Association, British Psychological Society, the Academy of Social Sciences and the Royal Society of Edinburgh.

Sara Sanabria is a BCL/JD candidate at McGill University's Faculty of Law and a research assistant with the iMPACTS project. Her most recent work has focused on 'stealthing', sexual harassment on virtual reality platforms and sexual violence legislation in Quebec. She has a dual BA in International Relations and Political Science from SciencesPo Paris and the University of British Columbia. She was formerly involved in Education and Employment research at UBC.

Shaheen Shariff is a James McGill Professor at McGill University in the Faculty of Education. She is also Associate Member of McGill's Law Faculty and its Center for Human Rights and Legal Pluralism. She is an ongoing Affiliate Scholar at Stanford University's Center for Internet and Society. Her research on the intersection of law and education is focused on prevention and responses to sexual and domestic violence; technology-facilitated violence, diversity, inclusion and pluralism; and leadership, and impacts of intersectional and systemic discrimination on public policy and educational practice. Professor Shariff has served as an expert witness for Canadian and Quebec legislative committees and advisory boards and continues this work on Quebec Minister Lacombe's advisory board. Two of her five books on cyberbullying are translated and used in Brazilian and Italian schools. She received a *Queen's Diamond Jubilee Medal* for her contributions to public policy and an award from the *International Alliance for Women* for her academic and community service to facilitate access to women's education under the *Economic Empowerment of Women* category.

Dr Emma Short is a psychologist based at London Metropolitan University and specialises in cyberpsychology. She is a Chartered Health Psychologist and HCPC registered as a practitioner in Health Psychology. She has conducted research in the area of cyber harassment and technology-facilitated abuse since 2005, working with partners in the third sector, Higher Education, Police and Government bodies. In 2011, Emma was a co-founder of the National Centre for Cyberstalking Research and has been working to represent the impact of technological evolutions within harassment, stalking and fixated abuse since that time. She has published widely and is a media contributor on the subject.

Ruthaychonnee Sittichai works at the Faculty of Humanities and Social Sciences, Prince of Songkla University. She is the Deputy Director of the Research Center for Kids and Youth Development and the Research Center for Educational Innovations and Teaching and Learning Excellence. She is an ISSBD Coordinator in Thailand. Her research interests include cyberbullying, bullying, cyberhate, polyvictimisation, e-cigarette behaviour and behaviour science mainly in adolescents.

Ida Risanger Sjursø, PhD, is Associate Professor at the Norwegian Center for Learning Environment and Behavioral Research in Education, University of Stavanger. Her research focuses on traditional bullying, cyberbullying and victimisation, in addition to the role of teachers in tackling bullying. Her field of interest runs from bullying in kindergarten to higher education.

Peter K. Smith is Emeritus Professor of Psychology at Goldsmiths College, University of London. He has researched extensively in aspects of children's social development, and in 2015 was awarded the William Thierry Preyer award for Excellence in Research on Human Development, by the European Society for Developmental Psychology, and in 2018 the Student Wellbeing and Prevention of Violence Award, from Flinders University, Australia. He has authored, co-authored or co-edited 38 books, and over 200 journal articles. His most extensive research has been on bullying and violence in schools, where he has led many research projects including a COST Action on cyberbullying.

Recent book publications include *The Psychology of School Bullying*. London: Routledge (2018), *Making an Impact on School Bullying: Interventions and Recommendations*. London: Routledge (2019), and (with James O'Higgins Norman) *The Wiley Blackwell Handbook of Bullying: A Comprehensive and International Review of Research and Intervention* (2 Vols.). Chichester: Wiley-Blackwell (2021).

Dr Barbara A. Spears is (Adjunct) Professor of Education and Social Development, at the University of South Australia: Education Futures. A former Primary school teacher, she was awarded the May Mills Scholarship for Women (Flinders University) to explore girls' bullying behaviours for her PhD in the 1990s. With over 100 publications, she is recognised nationally and internationally for work on youth voice, cyber/bullying, sexting, mental health, well-being, and the role of technology in young people's social relationships. With a particular interest in pre-service teacher education and knowledge mobilisation of research to policy and practice, she has led the following key projects: review of the National Safe Schools Framework, A Public Health Approach to Sexting, Youth Exposure to and Management of Cyber-Bullying Incidents in Australia, and the Safe and Well Online Study for the Young and Well Cooperative Research Centre. She is an inaugural member of the Child Development Council of SA and recent Chair of the Australian Universities Anti-Bullying Research Alliance (AUARA).

Francesca Stevens is currently a PhD candidate and Graduate Teaching Assistant at City, University of London, where her research focuses upon online harms in the workplace. She has also worked as a Research Assistant since 2021 at University College London, where her research explores technology-enabled domestic abuse. Her interests include online abuse, victimisation, gender and mental health.

Liam Stevenson is co-founder and Director of Time for Inclusive Education (TIE), a charity founded to address the prejudice and bullying that LGBT young people can experience at school with an education approach. In 2018, Scotland became the first country in the world to advance LGBT Inclusive Education in schools as a result of the campaigning efforts of TIE, meaning young people will now learn about LGBT history, role models and rights at school.

Dr Carmel M. Taddeo is Senior Lecturer, Research Methods and Postgraduate Supervision: Education Futures, University of South Australia. Carmel has expertise in technology initiatives and change processes, particularly related to youth online safety and well-being. She has been involved in the education sector for over 30 years, in primary and tertiary settings and was awarded a postdoctoral research fellow by the Young and Well Cooperative Research Centre and the University of South Australia. Carmel's research interests include online research methods/design, change processes, youth well-being and the potential of technology to facilitate positive outcomes, in both learning settings and broader life contexts. Carmel has worked on several significant Australian research projects which have informed Australian policy and legislation.

Zoe Vaill is an Australian researcher with a PhD in the area of anti-bullying policy in educational institutions and has multiple publications on this topic. Zoe has a background in psychology, moving from practice to research to try and find prevention and intervention options before students end up needing to see a psychologist, and to create a larger impact on mental health in education. Zoe has also worked with universities and related organisations to help improve the content and dissemination of information and policies relating to behaviours which may negatively impact student mental health and well-being.

Jorge J. Varela is a psychologist and Master in Educational Psychology, Pontificia Universidad Católica de Chile and Master and Doctor of Psychology and Education, University of Michigan. He is U.S. Associate Professor and Director of the Center for Studies in Welfare and Social Coexistence, Faculty of Psychology, Universidad del Desarrollo. Varela has also conducted research on school climate, aggression, citizen security, and prevention, with several scientific articles, books and book chapters, with Conicyt (ANID) projects. He has also been a consultant for the IDB and government agencies, such as Minister of Education and the Ministry of the Interior. He received Fulbright scholarship for doctoral studies in the United States, CONICYT – Chile scholarships for doctoral studies abroad in 2012, and Stanley E. and Ruth B. Dimond Best Dissertation Award, College of Education, University of Michigan in 2012.

Fiona Waye worked for over 25 years in the education sector at both secondary and higher education levels as a teacher, lecturer, researcher and in policy development. She is now retired from Universities UK (UUK), where she was the Policy Manager working with universities to address all forms of harassment and hate at Universities. During her career, she played a pivotal role in higher education policy development, including funding, student support, quality, admissions and social mobility, and was a driving force behind the Changing the Culture Initiatives within UK HE.

Preface

Our engagement with the digital world, as well as the electronic communication technologies it brings, is now ubiquitous. Around 5 billion people, nearly two-thirds of the world's population, are regular internet users; most of these engage with some form of social media (Statista, 2022). Electronic communication technologies bring many benefits. For example, engagement with social media can support critical developmental tasks in adolescence, including identity development and peer engagement. It can also increase self-esteem and social capital, and develop support networks for young people (Uhls et al., 2017). However, these same technologies also provide opportunities for perpetration of and exposure to 'online harms', including sexual harassment, hate crime, disablist bullying, cyberbullying, cyberstalking and microaggressive behaviours. In the United Kingdom, an online safety bill – designed to establish new regulations to address illegal and harmful content and activity online – is in the process of being passed (H M Government, 2022). The development of equivalent forms of legislation is also evident elsewhere in the world. The publication of this edited collection on cyberbullying and online harms is therefore extremely timely.

The first thematic set of chapters focuses on the nature and impact of cyberbullying and online harms. Sheri Bauman begins with a chapter summarising the literature on cyberbullying and online harassment in the context of higher education, including prevalence, correlates and predictors of involvement, and coping strategies. This chapter is particularly welcome, given that the traditional focus of work on these issues has been children and adolescents of school age. Christopher P. Barlett and colleagues continue the theme of moving beyond the status quo in their chapter, adopting a lifespan perspective on the effects of cyberbullying from childhood into late adulthood, and also moving beyond the predominant Western evidence base. Carrie-Anne Myers and colleagues' chapter reports research on bullying and cyberbullying in UK universities, arguing that this presents a continuation of related behaviours throughout the education system (e.g. sexual violence and dating violence in schools), emphasising the need for both a lifespan approach and early intervention.

The second thematic set of chapters focuses on the social and cultural contexts which facilitate or challenge cyberbullying and online harassment. This section brings new insights by moving beyond the individual aspects of online harm to explore the social contexts in which it occurs. Wanda Cassidy and colleagues begin by exploring the role of leadership in supporting or inhibiting cyberbullying and online harms in educational institutions, illustrating their arguments with illustrative case studies from post-secondary settings in Canada. Gella Richards' chapter follows, exploring how 'crafty' (e.g. subtle microaggressions) racist cyberbullying is perpetrated and how this impacts on racialised-minority students. Ian Rivers and colleagues' chapter examines the findings of a national survey of LGBTQI+ young people's experiences of homophobic and transphobic online harassment during the COVID-19 pandemic. Worryingly, though not altogether surprisingly, given the literature on exposure to victimisation among gender and sexual minority groups, the authors report that LGBTQI+ young people were at significantly increased risk of bullying and harassment. Chapters by Ruthaychonnee Sittichai and Ram Herkanaidu (cyberbullying and online hate speech in Thailand), Francesca Stevens (workplace-based sexual harassment in the post-#MeToo/Time's Up era) and Leah Burch (online disablism and cyberbullying) round out the section, exploring different social contexts and international perspectives.

The third thematic set of chapters considers the legal consequences of online harassment and related activities. It is an important section which highlights the legal complexities that characterise cyberbullying and online harms. Shaheen Shariff and colleagues' chapter indicates how toxic behaviours such as misogyny can be so prevalent in online communities, how this affects users (including how victims from marginalised communities may be particularly impacted, why current online safety measures are inadequate and what legal regulations currently exist, with a particular focus on virtual reality environments. The authors use their chapter as an opportunity to call for social media companies to implement measures to make such environments safer for their users. Emma Short and James Barnes' chapter charts our path, exploring how the crime of stalking has evolved into the digital world and some of the challenges this brings in the context of higher education.

The fourth thematic set of chapters turns our attention to how we respond to cyberbullying and online harms, and in particular, approaches to prevention and intervention. Carmel M. Taddeo and Barbara A. Spears' chapter discusses the importance of fostering social connectedness as a protective factor to help young people cope when they are exposed to online harms. This chapter is particularly welcome as it illustrates how the same technologies that are used to perpetrate cyberbullying and online harms can also be used to great benefit of young people's well-being. Helen Cowie and Carrie-Anne Myers' chapter follows, in which the authors argue how bystanders – those who witness instances of online harms – can be encouraged to speak out and intervene. This work has its roots in research on bystander intervention in 'traditional' (e.g. face to face) cases of bullying and harassment, illustrating the parallels between the digital and non-digital. Johannes Nilsson Finne and Ida Risanger Sjursø's chapter continues the implicit theme of peers as protective resources, arguing that a caring and supportive peer ecology can help to prevent further harm from victimisation and promote the development of prosocial behaviour and well-being among students. Kathy Evans and Lynne Gazal conclude the section, with a chapter that explores current and evolving strategies to challenge bullying and online harassment in the context of schools.

The final thematic set of chapters builds on the previous one by focusing on effective policies to counteract bullying and online harassment. Zoe Vaill and Marilyn Campbell get us started with their chapter on policies to address cyberbullying in schools and higher education settings. The authors bemoan the lack of research on the effectiveness of such policies and highlight the lack of accurate, usable and consistent policies in higher education in particular. Loraleigh Keashly's chapter follows, providing a thought-provoking take on cyberbullying of academic staff in higher education settings, and one which illustrates the importance of context in interpreting behaviour that may ultimately be viewed as cyberbullying. Carmel Cefai's chapter shifts our focus back to students, and in particular, a group who have traditionally experienced inequitable processes and outcomes: those from refugee or migrant backgrounds. The author uses a social justice lens to build a policy proposal whose aim is to provide equitable access to higher education within a safe, inclusive and empowering learning environment. Chapters by Joshua Rumo Arongo Ndiege and Leah Mutanu (cyberbullying in higher education in developing countries) and Renata Miljević-Riđički (the development of #MeToo-type movements in three Eastern European countries) draw the section to a close, serving as compelling examples of one of the key strengths of this collection: the truly international body of authors.

In sum, this edited collection is particularly welcome as it adopts an integrated approach, spanning a range of social contexts (e.g. school, college, workplace, community), and with content that will be of interest and relevant to a range of actors, including researchers, practitioners, policymakers, digital experts, criminologists and educators. Critically, it also provides a space for the voice of those who have suffered online harms to be heard. The editors have assembled a group of eminent authors from around the world, bringing a range of perspectives from East to West, and North to South. It will be an essential resource for those working in this space for years to come.

Professor Neil Humphrey
(Sarah Fielden Chair, Psychology of Education: University of Manchester)

References

HM Government. (2022). *Online safety bill.* https://publications.parliament.uk/pa/bills/cbill/58-03/0121/220121.pdf

Statista. (2022). Global digital population as of April 2022. *Statista.* www.statista.com/statistics/617136/digital-population-worldwide/ (Accessed 13 September 2022).

Uhls, Y. T., Ellison, N. B., & Subrahmanyam, K. (2017). Benefits and costs of social media in adolescence. *Pediatrics, 140*(Suppl_2), S67–S70. https://doi.org/10.1542/peds.2016-1758e

Theme 1

The nature and impact of cyberbullying and online harassment

1 Cyberbullying and online harassment

The impact on emotional health and well-being in higher education

Sheri Bauman

The context: emerging adulthood

When we think about cyberbullying in higher education, it is necessary to frame the inquiry within a developmental framework. The college (or university) years are an important period of life that occurs at the juncture of adolescence and adulthood. However, Arnett (2000) proposed that there actually is an intervening stage between adolescence and adulthood that he called *emerging adulthood*. He proposed that individuals between the ages of 18 and 25 (typical ages for traditional college students) are at this stage in industrialised countries. Although Erikson (1950) did not specify a stage analogous to emerging adulthood, he noted that adolescent identity exploration continues and intensifies in young adulthood, while the commitments and responsibilities characteristic of adulthood are deferred (career, marriage, childbirth). Erikson's theory describes the central conflict of adolescence as identity versus confusion, and in adulthood the conflict is intimacy versus isolation. The tasks of developing a coherent identity and forming serious romantic attachments seem intertwined in contemporary society. This is reflected in the increasing age of first marriage and first birth all over the world (Arnett, 2000; Halim & Rivera, 2020). During emerging adulthood, college students experiment with intimate relationships, work and careers, defining and refining their worldviews and religious and political beliefs. This process often includes an increase in risky behaviours, such as substance use, sexual experimentation and unsafe driving. I propose that cyberbullying is also a risky behaviour – that for some is part of the search for social status and an enduring identity.

Cyberbullying at university

Just as research on offline bullying initially focused on children and adolescents, the same is true for cyberbullying (Balakrishnan & Norman, 2020; Condeza et al., 2019; Kota et al., 2014; Kowalski et al., 2016; Peled, 2019; Rivituso, 2014). Perhaps it is that the term 'bullying' conjures the image of the stereotypical schoolyard bully – the menacing lout who preys on defenceless children. While there are undoubtedly such bullies, the past 50 years of research

DOI:10.4324/9781003258605-2

has deepened our understanding of this troublesome behaviour. We know that bullying happens in schools, and in workplaces, neighbourhoods, politics, and online. Bullying behaviour does not suddenly cease when adolescents leave high school; often the behaviours continue or even increase at university (Larrañaga et al., 2019). There is ample evidence that cyberbullying occurs in colleges and universities (Blaya, 2019), perhaps due to the need to establish social status in a large environment, where high school social rankings do not automatically transfer. College students are still at risk for cyberbullying and its associated harms. In fact, there are studies that found that college students tend to replicate the roles they enacted in high school (cyberbully, cyber-victim, etc.) in the university setting and that even the methods used (devices and tactics) tend to remain constant. However, not all college victims of cyberbullying were bullied in their previous schools; as many as a third had their first experience of cyberbullying in college, and for 60% who had been bullied earlier in their education, the worst experience occurred in college (Blaya, 2019; Kowalski et al., 2012). The problem is not trivial.

Today's college students are true digital natives. Digital devices have always been an integral part of their lives to the degree that their offline and online interactions are interwoven. College students are among the highest users of digital technology, and the college environment provides little adult oversight of their online activity (Kota et al., 2014). The positive uses of the internet for college students are many: the ability to access information online, the capability to take courses online (particularly during the pandemic), to socialise, and to stay current on university activities and opportunities. For those just entering college, and perhaps living independently for the first time apart from family, the ability to keep in touch with high school classmates may soften the feelings of loneliness and isolation that often accompany such a major life change (Wang et al., 2019). On the other hand, it is clear that cyberbullying is one of the risks for college students online, who are seeking to establish their social position in a new context when access to the internet is ubiquitous, especially since innovations made smartphones available and affordable. Social media allow college students to express ideas and refine their identity, and gain status with peers, via feedback from other users. It is when some students choose to use these platforms to attack others, perhaps thinking that aggressive behaviour enhances their status, that the harmful effects occur and proliferate.

Digital divide

Digital connectivity varies around the world, and the digital divide is vast. However, although internet access is increasingly available around the world, developing countries continue to lag behind in infrastructure necessary to support access. In 2019, significant increases in broadband coverage were made in South Asia and sub-Saharan Africa. A 2020 report by World Bank (2020) was based on data from 170 countries in 2019. The data showed that even where access has expanded, barriers such as literacy and digital literacy gaps, and income disparities (which may be exacerbated by the economic costs of the pandemic) maintain the inequality of access in many places.

Social media now have global reach. According to Dean (2021), there are 4.48 billion active users of social media worldwide (49% of the world population) – an increase of 13% over the previous year, including 63% of the population over age 13. Virtually all social media users access their sites from a mobile phone, with 78% using mobile phones exclusively to access social media. In the United States, 84% of 18–29-year-olds use social media. The countries with the largest increase in social media users (in descending order) were India, China, Indonesia, Brazil, Iran, and the United States (Dean, 2021). Social media use has also grown in many countries in Africa (e.g. Cilliers, 2021, Pachawo, 2017, South Africa; Makori & Agufana, 2020, Kenya; Gondwe et al., 2021, Zambia), and data show recent large increases in social media in Ghana (Kemp, 2021a) and Nigeria, Uganda, Zambia, Zimbabwe, Cameroun, Tunisia, Morocco and Kenya (Ephraim, 2013). Dean (2021) reports that social media growth from 2019 to 2020 was 13.92% in Africa, with Asia the only region to exceed that rate.

Inequities in access to broadband connections exist between countries, but there are also gaps within countries, with people in rural areas less likely to use the internet than those in urban locations. Furthermore, access to tertiary education varies among countries around the world. As with digital access, these proportions are rising everywhere, but inequalities remain. The most recent data from the World Bank (2019/2020) show glaring discrepancies. The average worldwide ratio of total enrolment in tertiary education, regardless of age, to the population of the age group that officially corresponds to the level of education was 40%; Tanzania had the lowest percentage in 2020 (7.8%), the highest were above 100% (many non-traditional age students attending) and included Greece, Australia, Turkey, Uruguay, and Macao. Data are also compiled by region: Sub-Saharan Africa reported 9.5%, the Middle East and North Africa are at 41%, East Asia and the Pacific increased to 51% in 2020, Latin America and the Caribbean are at 54%. Europe and Central Asia are reported to have 75% rates of college enrolment, while the Euro area is a bit higher at 80%. North America is at 87% (World Bank, 2021).

Some student groups appear to be more at risk than others (e.g. high-profile students such as athletes and student leaders, fraternity and sorority members, LGBT students (MacDonald & Roberts-Pittman, 2010), and students with disabilities; Kowalski et al., 2016). Involvement in cyberbullying has been linked to a variety of mental health disorders, with depression and anxiety being most commonly reported (see later).

When digital communication, or ICT, became widely available and more affordable, aggression in these media also emerged. Innovations such as instant messaging, texting, online gaming, and social networks provided exciting new affordances, each of which also became an opportunity for aggressive behaviour. The precise definition of cyberbullying is still unclear, as is the question of whether cyberbullying is another form of bullying or a qualitatively different phenomenon. Experts do agree that cyberbullying is a form of digital aggression, in which harmful actions are directed towards another person. Repetition is a defining attribute of bullying, and there are some who argue that because online content is easily shared, forwarded, re-posted, etc., even one malicious digital attack can be viewed by a very large audience and is thus repeated. The power imbalance characteristic of offline bullying is also somewhat vague in the cyber context. It may be that the perpetrator has social status that renders them more powerful overall, but it has also been argued that greater proficiency with digital tools also creates a power imbalance, regardless of social standing offline.

Mental health in university students

The consequences of exposure to cyberbullying are frequent symptoms of mental health disorders. Mental health disorders are diagnosed in college students at the same rate as in non-students the same age (Hunt & Eisenberg, 2010). Pedrelli et al. (2015) point out that this is also a time when the onset of some serious psychological disorders occurs: 75% of people who ever have a mental health disorder had their first episode before age 25. Pre-existing mental health conditions may be intensified by the additional stressors of adjusting to college and to greater independence from parents. In recent years, more effective therapies and medication have made it possible for young adults to manage serious psychological disorders while attending college, when in the past that was less likely. For example, Harrison (2015) surveyed 396 college-age women and examined the association between social media (Facebook) and eating disorders. She found that participants who had low and mean scores on the measure of Facebook activity had the highest levels of scores on a measure of eating disorders when they experienced verbal cyberbullying. A similar result was obtained for social cyberbullying.

A survey of 274 college counselling centre directors found that 88% believed there had been a notable increase in students with more severe psychological problems in recent years (Hunt & Eisenberg, 2010; Kitzrow, 2003; Pedrelli et al., 2015). Hartrey et al. (2017) noted that the frequency of psychopathology in college students has increased by a factor of 5 over the last 50 years. Kitzrow (2003) noted that this increase has been accompanied by an increase in the number of students wanting counselling services without a concomitant increase in resources to increase the capacity to provide those services. Given that in the last several years, the students have been coping with the pandemic, it is likely that the prevalence would be higher today.

It is unfortunate that many college students experiencing stressors such as cyberbullying and developing symptoms of mental health disorders do not seek help even when it is available (Hubbard et al., 2018), with women seeking services more than men. These scholars suggest that the low rate of help-seeking might be the perception that doing so displays weakness, fear of stigma, and a lack of understanding of what counselling is.

Research on college students

In this section, I review some of the existing literature on the impact of cyberbullying on well-being and mental health. I selected papers that came from around the world to demonstrate that researchers everywhere are interested in this line of inquiry and that although the review is not exhaustive, the findings are very similar.

Research on cyberbullying in college is relatively sparse. College students are still at risk for cyberbullying and its associated harms. In fact, there are studies that found that college students tend to replicate the roles they enacted in high school (cyberbully, cyber-victim, etc.) in the university setting and that even the methods used (devices and tactics) tend to remain constant. However, not all college victims of cyberbullying were bullied in their previous schools; as many as a third had their first experience of cyberbullying in college, and for 60% who had been bullied earlier in their education, the worst experience occurred in college (Blaya, 2019; Kowalski et al., 2012). The problem is not trivial.

In addition to the focus on adolescents (students in middle school and high school) in research, many of the studies to date have been conducted in Western countries although cyberbullying is a global problem that merits attention in countries around the world (Anonymous, 2019; Balakrishnan & Norman, 2020). Cultural context may affect the prevalence and nature of cyberbullying (see later). Furthermore, in developing countries, those relatively few who are able to go to university because they have the resources to do so are usually an elite and privileged group, likely to have digital devices and connectivity even when most people in their countries do not.

It is widely accepted that cyberbullying is harmful and that as a result of increasing digitisation in many countries, the risk for negative outcomes, particularly mental and emotional health symptoms, is high. An understanding of various aspects of this form of aggression may lead to the development of effective strategies to reduce the risk and better prepare individuals and institutions to respond.

Cultural factors in cyberbullying at university

Cyberbullying occurs within a cultural context. Two examples from the literature highlight the importance of culture in understanding research findings. Musharraf and Al-Haque (2018) described Pakistani culture as patriarchal with a strong value for family honour, which is tied to the behaviour of the women in the family. In conservative areas of the country, women who damage the family honour are subject to honour killing. Thus, their finding that while cybervictimisation is associated with increased anxiety in males and females, the steep slope for females suggests that females are at greater risk for anxiety if they are cyberbullied. Considering the potential of extreme responses if their victimisation was understood to bring dishonour to the family, the high rate of anxiety is understandable. Overall, they found that in their sample of 508 university students, cybervictimisation was associated with poor mental health (depression, anxiety, and stress) and negatively correlated with a measure of well-being.

A study of cybervictimisation of a sample of Ghanaian students, including 476 university students (53% female), also illustrates the importance of culture. Sam et al. (2018) explain that face-to-face bullying is accepted in Ghana, and it is considered to be entertainment for older students. The preferred parental style in Ghana is authoritarian and normative. Ghana is also the most religious country in the world; research on bullying would be remiss if this characteristic of the cultural context is ignored.

Sam et al. (2018) reported that 93.3% of university students had been vic-timised at least once in the previous six months, which is similar to the rate for high school and higher than that of junior high school. No gender differ-ences were detected among university student participants. Overall, the most common experience was receiving a nasty text message, and being targeted by e-mail was the least common. Compared to the younger students, univer-sity victims had significantly higher scores on the psychological symptoms and somatic symptoms measures and anxiety, with medium effect sizes, and a small effect size for the difference in psychological well-being. The authors observed that although Ghana compares favourably to other African countries in access to and use of the internet, the rate of cyberbullying was quite high. They also noted that although there were small to moderate effect sizes of differ-ences in outcomes between victims and non-victims, this might be due to the normality of bullying in that culture. Ghanaian females typically ignore rude sexual comments they frequently hear in daily activities; perhaps this extends to cyberbullying as well.

Global prevalence and consequences of cyberbullying and mental/emotional health and well-being

The concept of emerging adulthood serves as a backdrop for understand-ing how aggression online (cyberbullying and cyber-harassment) affects the emotional and mental health of college students. The dramatic changes in the environment, along with the absence of adult oversight of many aspects of life and the social need to belong in the new (college or university) setting, set the stage for online misbehaviour to emerge. College students are vul-nerable to becoming involved in cyberbullying (as bully, victim or bystander) and given high rates of mental health symptoms and diagnoses, this should elevate our concerns. In some cases, college students who are cyberbullied have pre-existing mental disorders, which can be exacerbated by cyber-victimisation. In other cases, cyberbullying is one more stressor at a very stressful time in their life, and that can lead to mental and emotional health problems in those who had not experienced any such problems prior to college. For example, Seilkie et al. (2015) investigated the link between cybervictimisation in a sample of 265 female undergraduate students in the United States and concluded that involvement in cyberbullying was linked to depression; bullies had elevated risks of depression and problematic alcohol use, and bully/victims had the highest risk of depression. They also found that depression was most likely among those who had experienced unwanted sexual advances via digital means. Musharraf and Anis-ul-Haque (2018) analysed the impact of cyberaggression and victimisation on well-being and mental health of 208 Pakistani university students (Musharraf and Anis-ul-Haque (2018). Being the target of cyberaggression was associated with lower well-being and an increase in mental health problems (depression, anxiety and stress). In addition, results indicated that victimised females were more likely to report anxiety than males who were targeted (Musharraf & Anis-ul-Haque, 2018). An additional study conducted during the pandemic lockdown with 5,551 college and university students in Bangladesh (ages 18–25) found that problematic social media use was associated with high levels of anxiety and depression. This study utilised a measure that assesses social media use using the components of an addiction model (Islam et al., 2021).

In a study conducted in the United Kingdom, the most frequently reported consequence of being cyber-victimised in college was the loss of confidence, diminished self-esteem, and harm to emotional and mental well-being (O'Brien & Moules, 2010). Nigerian researchers reported that 4% of their sample of 850 undergraduates described that their purpose for using social media was to cyberbully others (Tayo et al., 2019). Researchers in Hong Kong found that 55% of their sample of 312 college students engaged in cyberbullying others, and of those, 68% also were victimised. Both were negatively correlated with life satisfaction (Leung et al., 2017). In China, Wang et al. (2019) surveyed college students from Shantou and discovered that perpetrators with low levels of neuroticism and higher levels of cyberbullying others had had significantly higher levels of depression.

Seven hundred and twelve university students in Malaysia completed a questionnaire, which revealed that 66% of participants had been cyberbullied and that Malays were victimised online more than any other ethnic group (Chinese, Indian, Indigenous students from Borneo and others). Victimised students reported negative impacts on their emotional and mental health. The effects included becoming over-sensitive to their environments, experiencing emotional changes, feeling insecure online, avoiding interpersonal interactions and digital devices. Some indicated that they experienced sleep disorders, changes in appetites and suicide attempts. Findings from a study of 606 Vietnamese university students were consistent with the many other studies that found positive relations between cybervictimisation and depressive symptoms. However, they also reported that relation was partially mediated by parental support, and other support was also protective against depressive symptoms (Ho et al., 2020). Emotional reactions to cybervictimisation in a sample of 6,740 Egyptian university students were described as anger, hatred and sorrow (Arafa & Senosy, 2017).

A Canadian study (Mishna et al., 2018) of 1,350 diverse students from three Canadian universities who completed an online survey followed by nine focus groups and eight individual interviews added depth to the survey results. Among the notable findings were the rate at which participants had been victimised in the previous six months, about 25% by sharing a private image or video and 29% who were victimised by receiving upsetting and threatening messages. The largest group of perpetrators was a friend of the victim (50%), another student (20%), or intimate partner (18%). The rates at which participants acknowledged perpetrating cyberbullying were lower than those who were victimised. Importantly, of 1,669 comments to an open-ended question about the impact of cyberbullying experience, one-third reported mental health symptoms such as stress, anxiety, fear, discomfort, insecurity and reduced self-esteem. This is similar to the findings of other Canadian researchers (Faucher et al., 2014), in that 25% of male victims and 47% of female victims of cyberbullying reported experiencing mental health problems, including anxiety depression and emotional outbursts when they were cybervictimised.

Researchers investigated the prevalence and effects of cyberbullying in a prestigious Chilean university with highly competitive admission requirements. They indicated that 12.5% of participants reported being bullied in the past year, with 2.4% saying they were being bullied at the time they completed the survey. Responses to an item enquiring about the impact of those experiences identified feeling physically or emotionally threatened (51.7%), having mental health problems (52.5%), along with academic and social difficulties. In France, Blaya (2019) conducted a two-part study: the first utilised 1,125 valid surveys, and the second study involved interviews with 20 students who had taken the survey. Data analysis revealed that more than half of the respondents had been victims of cyberbullying during the academic year, with 40% classified as pure victims, 14% as pure bullies and 12% as cyberbullies/victims. Their data also indicated that male students were more likely to be perpetrators. An interesting finding was that 54% believed their victimisation was caused by friendship disputes. On the other hand, the perpetrators indicated the most common motivation was because they were annoyed at their victims, followed by getting revenge on a former romantic partner. Another unique aspect of this study was the inclusion of online gaming as a context for cyberbullying. This was more common among males, who described being targeted for their (poor) performance in the game. In terms of impact of victimisation, many cited low self-esteem, depression and damage to relationships.

A team of researchers in Spain surveyed 1,328 university students (M_{age} = 21.65) and discovered that 18.6% had been cyberbullied in the previous two months. Almost three-fourths of the victims had high levels of anxiety, depression and stress. Their data showed a strong association between victimisation and suicidal ideation and suicide attempts.

It is clear from previous studies that cyberbullying has a negative impact on the well-being of college students, with anxiety and depression being the most commonly documented. The findings were similar although the studies were conducted in very different settings. This suggests that perhaps researchers around the world can jointly find solutions and evaluate their effectiveness empirically.

Solution: what can we do?

Solutions to this pervasive problem have been proposed by several experts, although very few have been evaluated empirically. An innovative tool created by Lee and Jung (2018) is an app called DeStressify, which they tested in a randomised trial. The app uses mindfulness as guiding principle. Participants in the experimental group were asked to use the app five days per week for four weeks. Results demonstrated that the use of the app was associated with reduced trait anxiety and improved general health, energy and emotional well-being.

Blaya's (2019) survey included an open-ended question about the potential for university intervention. Ten per cent of respondents did not think the university should have any role. A larger proportion of responses mentioned instituting peer mediation and support programmes and emphasised the importance of involving students in developing strategies. Pedrelli et al. (2015) emphasised the stress level (academic and psychosocial) experienced by most college students and recommend making energetic outreach efforts to ensure students who are having substance abuse or psychological disorders are appropriately referred for help. They also suggest involving the parents in treatment (which in the United States could not be done without the student's consent) and enlisting parental help in ensuring continuity of care during college breaks. Kitzrow (2003) encourages counselling centre directors to understand the importance of this situation and advocate for increased funding for mental health services. She noted that 13% of college counselling centres charge a fee for service to offset the increased expenditure. She also pointed out that counselling centres could seek alternative ways to deliver services (e.g. evening appointments, online counselling and increased use of group counselling). Although college students are young adults, the university still has a duty of care, which includes making genuine efforts to implement effective strategies, programmes and services to reduce the harm from cyberbullying. There should be explicit campus policies on cyberbullying and that universities need to incorporate education about cyberbullying in introductory courses or freshman orientation programmes or both.

I add my own recommendations here. First, I strongly agree that all universities need a specific cyberbullying policy, created with input from students, faculty and administrators. The policy should be disseminated in a way that students are likely to read. Second, counselling centres are a critical component of any solution: increased resources, additional personnel and use of technology to increase availability are essential. Given the high rates of anxiety and depression among those victimised by cyberbullying, I suggest that anyone who is diagnosed with either disorder, even at sub-clinical levels, should be queried about their experiences in cyberspace. Conversely, when students present with cybervictimisation as the problem, they should be screened for anxiety, depression, suicidal behaviours and stress.

My third recommendation is based on the importance of stress in the dynamics of cyberbullying. I suggest that an educational unit on identifying and managing stress be incorporated into required experiences for incoming students and made available to any student who would like to get such information. That information should include a list of available resources, where students might go for assistance.

Future research

We have seen that cyberbullying at university is not unknown and has serious impacts on students' well-being and mental and emotional health. We have also noted that the research that has been done has had representation from many countries. Further research on apps like DeStressify (and others not yet developed) is needed as smartphone-based tools that can be done independently might appeal to university students' digital engagement.

However, there are persisting problems that researchers must strive to overcome. Most of the studies referenced in this chapter are cross-sectional. The findings are informative, but there is a need for longitudinal studies that can identify directional relationships.

While we are slowly building a body of literature on cyberbullying in college, researchers use primarily convenient non-representative samples. Efforts should be made to replicate the findings in large representative samples. In addition, when researchers use different scales to assess the construct of interest, it is impossible to compare results across studies. It is also essential to report psychometric properties in the current sample and to conduct confirmatory factor analyses to determine whether the scale demonstrates factorial invariance. In addition, there are differences in the reference period used. We would expect very different outcomes from reports asking about the last month, last year, in college, etc. Finally, when surveys are translated, the translation process should be carefully documented.

It would be ideal to have an international think tank of cyberbullying researchers to come to consensus about what is needed, what questions needed to be investigated and how we can best aim to answer those questions. This book is a step in the right direction.

References

Anonymous. (2019). Preface. In W. Cassidy, C. Faucher, & M. Jackson (Eds.), *Cyberbullying at university in international contexts* (p. ix). New York: Routledge.

Arafa, A., & Senosy, S. (2017). Pattern and correlates of cyberbullying victimization among Egyptian University students in Beni-Suef. *Journal of Egyptian Public Health Association, 92*(2), 107–115. https://doi.org/10.21608/epx.2017.11244

Arnett, J. J. (2000). Emerging adulthood: A theory of development from the late teens through the twenties. *American Psychologist, 55*(5), 469–480. https://doi.org/10.1037//0003-066X.55.

Balakrishnan, V., & Norman, A. A. (2020). Psychological motives of cyberbullying among Malaysian young adults. *Asia Pacific Journal of Social Work and Development, 30*(3), 181–194.

Blaya, C. (2019). Cyberbullying among university students in France: Prevalence, consequences, coping, and intervention strategies. In W. Cassidy, C. Faucher, & M. Jackson (Eds.), *Cyberbullying at university in international contexts* (pp. 9–22). New York: Routledge.

Cilliers L. (2021). Perceptions and experiences of cyberbullying amongst university students in the Eastern Cape province, South Africa. *The Journal for Transdisciplinary Research in South Africa, 17*(1), 2–6. http://doi.org/10.4102/td.v71i1.776.

Condeza, R., Gonzelo, G., & Pérez, P. R. (2019). In W. Cassidy, C. Faucher, & M. Jackson (Eds.), *Cyberbullying at university in international contexts of cyberbullying at a Chilean university: the voices of students* (pp. 36–52). New York: Routledge.

Dean, B. (2021, October 10). *Social network usage and growth statistics: How many people use social media in 2022?* https://backlinko.com/social-media-users#social-media-penetration-by-country

Ephraim, P. E. (2013). African youths and the dangers of social networking: A culture-centered approach to using social media. *Ethics and Information Technology, 15*, 275–284. https://doi.org/10.1007/s10676-013-9333-2

Erikson, E. (1950). *Childhood and society*. New York: WW Norton.

Faucher, C., Jackson, M., & Cassidy, W. (2014). Cyberbullying among university students: Gendered experiences, impacts, and perspectives. *Education Research International, 2014*. Article ID 698545, 10 pgs. http://dx.doi.org/10.1155/2014/698545

Gondwe, G., Muchangwe, R., & Mwaya, J. E. (2021). Motivations for social media use and consumption in Zambian online platforms. *Advances in Social Networking and Online Communities*, 204–215. https://doi.org/10.4018/978-1-7998-4718-2.CH011

Halim, D., & Rivera, S. (2020, February 14). Love, marriage, and development: 4 observations. *World Bank Blog*. https://blogs.worldbank.org/opendata/love-marriage-and-development-4-observations

Harrison, K. R. (2015). *Cyberbullying on Facebook: How does it influence the risk for eating disorders* [Unpublished master's thesis], University of Houston.

Hartrey, L., Denieffe, S., & Wells, J. S. (2017). A systematic review of barriers and supports to the participation of students with mental health difficulties in higher education. *Mental Health & Prevention, 6*, 26–43.

Ho, T. T. Q., Li, C., & Gu, C. (2020). Cyberbullying victimization and depressive symptoms in Vietnamese university students: Examining social support as a mediator. *International Journal of Law, Crime and Justice, 63*, 100422.

Hubbard, K. Reohr, P., Tolcher, L., & Downs, A. (2018). Stress, mental health symptoms, and helpseeking in college students. *Psi Chi Journal of Psychological Research, 23*(4), 293–304. https://doi.org/10.21839/2325-7342.JN23.1.2

Hunt, J., & Eisenberg, D. (2010). Mental health problems and help-seeking behavior among college students. *Journal of Adolescent Health, 46*(1), 3–10.

Islam, M. S., Sujan, M. S. H., Tasnim, R., Mohona, R. A., Ferdous, M. Z., Kamruzzaman, S., . . . & Pontes, H. M. (2021). Problematic smartphone and social media use among Bangladeshi college and university students amid COVID-19: The role of psychological well-being and pandemic related factors. *Frontiers in psychiatry, 12. JMIR Mental Health, 5*(1), e2, 1–16. https://doi.org/10.2196/mental.8324

Karyotaki, E., Cuijpers, P., Albor, Y., Alonso, J., Auerbach, R. P., Bantjes, J., . . . & Kessler, R. C. (2020). Sources of stress and their associations with mental disorders among college students: Results of the world health organization world mental health surveys international college student initiative. *Frontiers in Psychology, 11*, Article 1759.

Kemp, S. (2021a). *Digital 2021: Ghana*. https://datareportal.com/reports/digital-2021-ghana

Kemp, S. (2021b). *Digital 2021: Nigeria*. https://datareportal.com/reports/digital-2021-nigeria

Khan, H., & Malik, A. (2021, February). Academic use of smartphones among medical students in Pakistan. *Information Development, 36*(2), 3–5.

Kitzrow, M. A. (2003). The mental health needs of today's college students: Challenges and recommendations, *NASPA Journal, 41*(1), 167–181, https://doi.org/10.2202/1949–6605.1310

Kota, R., Schoohs, S., Benson, M., & Moreno, M. A. (2014). Characterizing cyberbullying among college students: Hacking, dirty laundry, and mocking. *Societies, 4*(4), 549–560.

Kowalski, R. M., Giumetti, G. W., Schroeder, A. N., & Reese, H. H. (2012). Cyber Bullying among college students: Evidence from multiple domains of college life. In L. A. C. Wankel, C. (Eds.) *Misbehavior online in higher education (Cutting-edge technologies in higher education, Vol. 5)* (pp. 293–321). Bingley: Emerald Group Publishing Limited. https://doi.org/10.1108/S2044-9968(2012)0000005016

Kowalski, R. M., Morgan, C. A., Drake-Lavelle, K., & Allison, B. (2016). Cyberbullying among college students with disabilities. *Computers in Human Behavior, 57*, 416–427.

Larrañaga, E. L., Yubero, S., Navarro, R., & Ovejera, A. (2019). In W. Cassidy, C. Faucher, & M. Jackson (Eds.), *Cyberbullying at university in international contexts* (pp. 99–11, ix). New York: Routledge.

Lee, R. A. A., & Jung, E. (2018). Evaluation of an mHealth app (DeStressify) on university students' mental health: Pilot trial. longer period and in university staff and faculty.

Lipson, S. K., Speer, N., Brunwasser, S., Hahn, E., & Eisenberg, D. (2014). Gatekeeper training and access to mental health care at universities and colleges. *Journal of Adolescent Health, 55*(5), 612–619.

MacDonald, C. D., & Roberts-Pittman, B. (2010). Cyberbullying among college students: Prevalence and demographic differences. *Procedia-Social and Behavioral Sciences, 9*, 2003–2009.

Makori, A., & Agufana, P. (2020). Cyberbullying among learners in higher educational institutions in sub-Saharan Africa: Examining challenges and possible mitigations. *Higher Education Studies, 10*(2), 53–65. https://doi.org/10.5539/hes.v10n2p53

Mishna, F., Cook, C., Gadalla, T., Daciuk, J., & Solomon, S. (2010). Cyber Bullying Behaviors Among Middle and High School Students. *The American Journal of Orthopsychiatry, 80*, 362–74. https://doi.org/10.1111/j.1939-0025.2010.01040.x.

Musharraf, S., & Anis-ul-Haque, M. (2018). Impact of cyber aggression and cyber victimization on mental health and well-being of Pakistani young adults: The moderating role of gender. *Journal of Aggression, Maltreatment & Trauma, 27*(9), 942–958.

O'Brien, N., & Moules, T. (2010). *The impact of cyberbullying on young people's mental health. Final report*. East Anglia: Anglia Ruskin University. https://arro.anglia.ac.uk/id/eprint/702456/1/O'Brien_Moules_2010.pdf

Pachawo, T. P. (2017). *Probing cyber-bullying experiences of first year university students at a rural university in South Africa* [Unpublished master's thesis]. University of Venda.

Pedrelli, P., Nyer, M., Yeung, A., Zulauf, C., & Wilens, T. (2015). College students: Mental health problems and treatment considerations. *Academic Psychiatry, 39*(5), 503–511.

Peled, Y. (2019). Cyberbullying and its influence on academic, social, and emotional development of undergraduate students. *Heliyon, 5*(3), e01393.

Rivituso, J. (2014). Cyberbullying victimization among college students: An interpretive phenomenological analysis. *Journal of Information Systems Education, 25*(1), 71–75.

Sam, D. L., Bruce, D., Agyemang, C. B., Amponsah, B., & Arkorful, H. (2019). Cyberbullying victimization among high school and university students in Ghana. *Deviant Behavior, 40*(11), 1305–1321. https://doi.org/10.1080/01639625.2018.1493369

Selkie, E.M., Kota, R., Chan, Y.F., & Moreno, M. (2015). Cyberbullying, depression, and problem alcohol use in female college students: a multisite study. *Cyberpsychology Behavior Social Network, 18*(2), 79–86.

Syrluga, S., & Anderson, N. (2021, October 14). College students struggle with mental health as pandemic drags on. *Washington Post.* www.washingtonpost.com/education/2021/10/14/college-suicide-mental-health-unc/

'Tayo, S., Adebola, S. T., & Yahya, D. (2019). Social media: Usage and influence on undergraduate studies in Nigerian universities. *International Journal of Education and Development using Information and Communication Technology, 15*(3), 53–62.

Wang, W., Xie, X., Wang, X., Lei, L., Hu, Q., & Jiang, S. (2019). Cyberbullying and depression among Chinese college students: A moderated mediation model of social anxiety and neuroticism. *Journal of Affective Disorders, 256*, 54–61.

World Bank (2021, September). *School enrollment, tertiary (% gross).* https://data.worldbank.org/indicator/SE.TER.ENRR

World Bank, GSMA. (2020). *The poverty reduction effects of mobile broadband in Africa: Evidence from Nigeria.* www.gsma.com/mobilefordevelopment/wp-content/uploads/2020/12/The-Poverty-Reduction-Effects-of-Mobile-Broadband-in-Africa-Evidence-from-Nigeria.pdf

2 A review of cyberbullying perpetration research

A lifespan perspective

Christopher P. Barlett, Peter K. Smith and Jorge J. Varela

The internet allows for the near-instantaneous exchange of ideas and information, has influenced almost every aspect of life and is used extensively. Indeed, results from survey data collected in 2021 show that 93% of US adults use the internet (Pew Research Center, 2021). We contend that although the internet has yielded mostly positive consequences to society (e.g. banking, education, shopping and dating), there are, unfortunately, negative outcomes that are associated with the internet. The focus of the current chapter is on one such negative internet behaviour: cyberbullying, defined as intentionally and repeatedly harming another using the internet (Englander et al., 2017). Cyberbullying has emerged as an important societal issue across the world. Indeed, survey data shows that 17% of respondents across the world report online harassment, and 10% reported being bullied online (Microsoft, 2021).

Cyberbullying perpetration is important to empirically study and prevent because of the deleterious effects observed for those who are cyber-victimised, such as anxiety, depression, low self-esteem, and suicidal ideation (Kowalski et al., 2014). We believe that it is imperative to better understand the psychological processes and moderators germane to cyberbullying so that intervention efforts can be adapted or created to prevent cyberbullying perpetration and victimisation. Thus, the purpose of the current chapter is to discuss and review the relevant literature on cyberbullying perpetration from a developmental perspective.

Cyberbullying perpetration in context

The scientific study of cyberbullying is young, compared to the much larger and storied body of research testing traditional bullying and aggression. Much of the early work on cyberbullying was largely atheoretical and descriptive – focusing on prevalence rates (e.g. Kowalski & Limber, 2007), sex differences (e.g. Li, 2006) and the degree of overlap with traditional bullying (e.g. Beran & Li, 2007). This research was incredibly important for alerting parents, doctors, academics, school officials and others about the 'cyberbullying problem'. Since then, research has exponentially expanded. Indeed, Smith and Berkkun (2017) examined the Abstracts of all journal articles on cyberbullying. They searched

DOI:10.4324/9781003258605-3

the period from 2000 (no articles were found prior) up to 2015 on a yearly basis, obtaining a total of 538 eligible abstracts over the 16 years, an average of 33.6 per year. Results showed a small number of articles from 2000 to 2006 (range 0 to 5 per year); from 2007 to 2011, a substantial but still modest number of articles (range 14 to 38 per year); and from 2012 on, a very large number of articles (range 85 to 131 per year by 2015; and up to 188 by 2017).

The myriad empirical studies focused on understanding cyberbullying perpetration have answered many questions related to (a) the variables that predict cyberbullying perpetration and victimisation, (b) the consequences of cyberbullying others or being cyber-victimised, (c) intervention efforts aimed at reducing cyberbullying perpetration, (d) perceptions and definitions of what does (and does not) constitute cyberbullying, (e) differences between cyber and traditional bullying, and (f) demographic (e.g. sex, age, ethnicity) differences in either types of cyber-behaviour. This burgeoning research is welcomed. Indeed, an understanding of the psychological processes germane to cyberbullying perpetration can help inform theory and subsequent intervention efforts to help reduce this antisocial behaviour. However, one criticism levied against the early research – and even some recent work – is the atheoretical nature of the research (Barlett, 2017) and variation in quality (Selkie et al., 2016). Although many theories have been applied to the study of cyberbullying, much more theoretical attention, adaptation and creation is needed. Our aim is to discuss cyberbullying perpetration research using developmental perspective and theory to help understand the genesis and maturation of cyberbullying perpetration. We will review this perspective by focusing on the research examining differences across age groups before delving into research on the learning-based theoretical mechanisms germane to the development of cyberbullying perpetration. Finally, we will end with intervention implications and future directions.

Developmental perspective

Unlike other theoretical lenses by which cyberbullying can be viewed, a developmental perspective emphasises (a) age differences across different periods of human development – from childhood to late adulthood, (b) the moderating influence that age has in the relationship between other cyberbullying perpetration predictors and subsequent behaviour, and (c) the learning-based mechanisms that increase the likelihood that cyberbullying perpetration will occur. We will discuss each of these.

Age differences

First, meta-analytic work shows that age and cyberbullying perpetration are weakly, albeit significantly, correlated ($r = .07$; Kowalski et al., 2014). This weak correlation may be expected, considering that meta-analyses aggregate data across studies that sample populations of various ages – usually youth into adulthood – and meta-analytic tests assume a linear relationship between variables. Thus, the .07 effect size indicates that across all populations sampled in the primary literature, older participants are more likely to cyberbully than younger participants. This interpretation is plagued by issues regarding range restriction, given that too few studies sample populations older than emerging adulthood. The primary literature shows similar linear trends. Smith et al. (2008) showed that cyberbullying perpetration was lowest for youths aged 11–12, and then increased for youths aged 14–16. Furthermore, Kowalski and Limber (2007) showed that prevalence rates for being a bully and a bully/victim were higher for a sample of US youths in 8th grade compared to their younger 6th-grade peers. Finally, an analysis of over 181,000 children (aged 11–15) across 42 countries across the world showed that the median estimate of cyberbullying increased slightly with age (especially for boys; Craig et al., 2020).

There are several reasons to explain the increase in cyberbullying perpetration across age in youth populations. For instance, survey data show that most youths get their first cellular phone in middle school (Lenhart, 2010). Research has shown that US youths (aged 8–11 years) are more likely to be cyberbullies if they own a cellular phone (Englander, 2018). Further, results from a longitudinal study of South Korean youths showed that parental supervision was negatively related to cyberbullying perpetration (Song et al., 2020), and data from the Pew Research Center in the United States has shown that online parental supervision also decreases with age (Anderson, 2016).

Second, retrospective research findings suggest that physical and verbal bullying frequency decreases from high school into college (Curwen et al., 2011) – information that begets a common myth that cyberbullying perpetration follows the same trajectory. However, research has shown such a myth to be false. Indeed, research with college-aged participants in the United States suggests that cyberbullying is prevalent and increases from first to fourth year (Zacchilli & Valerio, 2011). Further, research has also found that cyberbullying perpetration is a problem in the workplace and is associated with job dissatisfaction (Kowalski et al., 2017). Finally, data collected through online data collection websites show mean levels of cyberbullying perpetration akin to adolescents and emerging adults (e.g. Schodt et al., 2021).

We are aware of only two studies that examined mean-level cyberbullying perpetration differences across a lifespan. In the first, Ševčíková and Šmahel (2009) sampled participants from the Czech Republic aged 12–88 years and classified them into cyberbullies, cyberbully/victims and cyber-victims based on a response to a single item, and showed that the likelihood of being a cyberbully or cyberbully/victim decreased with age. However, this study was limited by using a non-validated questionnaire and separating participants into cyberbullying categories, rather than retaining the scores on the cyberbullying measure as continuous. To fix these issues, Barlett and Chamberlin (2017) sampled participants aged 11 to 75 from the United States and assessed cyberbullying perpetration frequency with a valid scale. Results showed a significant quadratic effect of age on cyberbullying – a finding which may explain why the meta-analytic correlation between age and cyberbullying was weak ($r = .07$). Examination of the trends showed that cyberbullying perpetration increased from the 11–17 age group (middle to late adolescence) to the 18–26 age group (emerging adulthood), which remained relatively stable for the 27–35 age group (early to middle adulthood) until a substantial decrease to the 36–49 and 50+ age groups (middle to late adulthood).

Age as a moderator

While testing direct age differences in cyberbullying perpetration is important, we believe age to be better theoretically situated to be a moderator in the relationship between other variables and cyberbullying perpetration. However, examining the moderating role of age often requires participants of varying ages in a single study or meta-analytic moderation test of age. Here, we will discuss several of these variables.

The first relationship that age has shown to moderate is sex differences in cyberbullying perpetration. Some studies find that females cyberbully more than males (i.e. being a cyberbully/victim; Pettalia et al., 2013), others find that males cyberbully more than females (Barlett & Gentile, 2012), and some show no reliable sex differences in cyberbullying perpetration (Barlett, 2015). Such varied research findings were the impetus for a meta-analysis that showed males cyberbully more than females; however, this effect was moderated by age (Barlett & Coyne, 2014). Moderation analysis confirmed that (a) females engaged in more cyberbullying than males at young ages, (b) no difference between males and females in cyberbullying in early to late adolescence, and (c) males cyberbullied more than females during emerging adulthood.

The second relationship that age may moderate is the effect of parental mediation and cyberbullying perpetration. Parental mediation often includes restrictive mediation (e.g. checking websites; Mesch, 2009), evaluative mediation (e.g. having rules about media time and content; Mesch, 2009), and co-using mediation (e.g. participating with child). Such mediation has been shown to have mixed effects. For instance, Navarro et al. (2013) sampled Spanish youth and found that evaluative parental mediation lowered the odds of children reporting being cyber-victimised. Further, Mesch (2009) showed that evaluative parental mediation was negatively related to cyberbullying perpetration in a sample of US youth. On the other hand, results from a longitudinal study with Singaporean youth showed that restrictive mediation negatively predicted cyberbullying but not evaluative mediation (Chng et al., 2014). However, the success or failure of parental mediation techniques to change cyberbullying likely depends on the participant's age. Indeed, results from a meta-analysis showed that age moderated the negative relationship between evaluative parental mediation and cyberbullying perpetration – the effect was stronger for children than for adolescents (Ho et al., 2017). Perhaps with more autonomy granted to children as they age, parental mediation is less effective because children may disclose less of their online behaviours.

Finally, the relationship between several traditional bullying variables and cyberbullying perpetration may be moderated by age. Examination of the Kowalski et al. (2014) and Guo (2016) meta-analyses show that several aggression-related variables significantly predict cyberbullying perpetration, such as traditional bullying, internalising problems, narcissism and others. However, it is likely that age moderates such effects. Indeed, a meta-analysis of cyberbullying predictors showed that age moderated the relationship between traditional bullying and cyberbullying perpetration, such that the effects were significantly larger for adolescents ($r = .40$) and adults ($r = .50$) than for children ($r = .14$; Chen et al., 2017).

Learning and theory

In addition to investigating the direct or moderating influence of age on cyber-bullying perpetration, the developmental perspective also relies heavily on high-quality theorising to predict how individuals develop the psychological mechanisms germane to such antisocial behaviour. Broader aggression theories often incorporate learning-based developmental theoretical postulates and have been used to predict cyberbullying perpetration, such as the General Aggression Model (Anderson & Bushman, 2002). However, while these theories are useful and valid for predicting cyberbullying perpetration, one criticism is that these theories do not adequately differentiate cyber from traditional bullying. This is important because quality theory that guides intervention efforts aimed at reducing cyberbullying perpetration should uniquely and significantly reduce cyberbullying incrementally from traditional bullying (cf. Barlett, 2019). Moreover, despite the overlap in traditional and cyberbullying (Kowalski et al., 2014), research has identified several differences that negate the oversimplification of equating both types of bullying. For instance, data suggest the following key differences: (a) anonymity perceptions are higher in the online environment, (b) there is no physical aggression involved in cyberbullying, (c) the bullying is not confined to school and can take place anywhere due to the online nature of the harm, (d) the physical attributes that often help bullies inflict harm (i.e. physical size) is rendered irrelevant in the online world, (e) the meaning and recognition of 'intention to harm' germane to the definition of (cyber)bullying is vaguer online and (f) the roles of bystanders and peers vary according to the medium through which cyberbullying occurs (Dooley et al., 2009; Kowalski et al., 2012; Vandebosch & Van Cleemput, 2009). Thus, while several existing theories that focus on the development of bullying and aggression can validly predict cyberbullying perpetration frequency and processes, it is important for theory to differentiate both types of bullying due to these, and other, differences.

We will focus our theoretical discussion on the Barlett Gentile Cyberbullying Model (BGCM) (Barlett & Gentile, 2012), because it currently is the only valid cyberbullying-focused theory that clearly differentiates cyber from traditional bullying and takes a developmental approach. The BGCM is a learning-based

social-cognitive theory that posits how early cyberbullying experiences eventually lead to long-term automatic cyberbullying behaviours. After an individual
cyber-aggresses against another person, they are likely to perceive themselves to
be anonymous and believe that anybody, no matter their physical stature, can
harm others online. Recall, these two perceptions and beliefs differentiate cyber
from traditional bullying. Continued cyber-aggressive behaviours further reinforce these perceptions and beliefs, which will eventually lead to the development
of positive cyberbullying attitudes. Finally, continued cyberbullying behaviours
automatise these attitudes, beliefs and perceptions to eventually predict automatic
and consistent cyberbullying behaviour (see Barlett, 2017 for review).

Evidence for the validity of the BGCM has been found in youth (Barlett,
2015), emerging adult (Barlett & Gentile, 2012) and older adult (Barlett et al.,
2019) populations. From a developmental perspective, there are several important aspects of the BGCM that warrant discussion and future research. First,
the BGCM posits that the perceptions, beliefs and attitudes that are germane
to cyberbullying perpetration take time to develop. Currently, there is no published research testing the number of cyber-aggressive trials that are needed to
make cyberbullying automatic, and, therefore, it is unclear how long or how
many cyberbullying learning trials are needed to automatise the BGCM processes. Second, the role that positive reinforcement has in developing cyberbullying behaviour and underlying mechanisms is non-trivial. Research has shown
that reinforcement to engage in cyberbullying behaviours predicted online bullying (Shadmanfaat et al., 2020). Thus, as youths are beginning to engage in
cyberbullying behaviours, the extent to which they are positively reinforced
either by others or by their own self-satisfaction is incredibly important to
developing cyberbullying attitudes and behaviours later.

Invention implications

The discussion of the research and theorising regarding the developmental
perspective germane to cyberbullying perpetration is moot without application to intervention efforts aimed at reducing the perpetration of online harm.
Indeed, intervention efforts should be derived based on theory, solid empirical
validation evidence and careful consideration of moderating factors that could
change the likelihood that any intervention is successful. We believe that age
may moderate intervention success; however, there is a paucity of research
examining such conclusions.

First, we want to explicate that research has shown cyberbullying interventions to have some success, depending on many factors, including the nature
of the program and the cultural context (Menesini et al., 2021). Meta-analytic
findings have shown significant mean level decreases in cyberbullying from a
pre-test to post-test for participants randomly assigned to an anti-cyberbullying curriculum, compared to participants in a control condition (e.g. Gaffney
et al., 2019). Furthermore, other interventions have been shown to be effective
and devoid of changes in mean-level cyberbullying perpetration. For instance,

Barlett et al. (2020) failed to show mean changes in cyberbullying perpetration in a sample of emerging adults in their 'You're not Anonymous' cyberbullying program; however, this intervention was successful by showing that participants in the intervention condition, compared to control groups, had a decrease in self-reported anonymity perceptions immediately following the intervention, which predicted cyberbullying perpetration two months later. Finally, meta-analytic findings have shown a few moderators that influence the degree of success for cyberbullying intervention programs, such as who delivers the intervention (Ng et al., 2022), the type of research design employed (Gaffney et al., 2019) and whether the program specifically targeted cyberbullying or more general violence (Polanin et al., 2021). However, none of these meta-analyses reported the moderating role of age.

However, there is corollary evidence to suggest that age may moderate the success of cyberbullying programs. Examination of meta-analyses of traditional bullying interventions shows that anti-bullying programs are effective (Gaffney & Farrington, 2021); however, the effectiveness decreases for older participants (Yeager et al., 2015). Research has shown cyberbullying interventions to be successful for child participants (e.g. Chaux et al., 2016) and emerging adult participants alike (e.g. Doane et al., 2016). Perhaps there is good reason for not fully understanding whether age across a lifespan moderates intervention success. For example, cyberbullying intervention programs are likely administered differently, focus on different aspects of cyberbullying and employ different curriculum delivery methods than traditional bullying interventions – and even those methods likely vary across age and developmental period. Indeed, interventions aimed at emerging adults are often delivered online (e.g. Doane et al., 2016), whereas interventions developed for youth audiences are often delivered in person (e.g. Chaux et al., 2016). Other differences besides who delivers the intervention abound but are expected. For instance, it may be developmentally inappropriate to teach young school-aged children about the legal ramifications of cyberbullying using an online video format, whereas it may be equally ineffective to have adults use empathy-based scenarios to role-play. However, these, and other, differences make comparing youth-based to adult-based cyberbullying intervention curricula problematic. Although meta-analytic techniques can offer some evidence by using standardised effect size calculations, we are unaware of any study sampling participants that vary on age across the lifespan using the same intervention curricula and then testing age as a moderator.

Future research

Although we have delved into summarising the existing literature on cyberbullying perpetration via a developmental lens, there are several additional research questions that have not adequately been asked and tested that we believe can, and should, be examined in future research. Next, we will summarise several potential questions.

The first unanswered research question is whether age moderates the success of cyberbullying interventions. To do this, however, researchers need to develop a cyberbullying intervention curriculum that can be understood by participants of any age and delivered in the same format (e.g. mode of delivery, content and language used). As we argued previously, currently such an intervention does not exist; however, this does not suggest that such interventions would be unwelcome. For instance, the 'You're not Anonymous' intervention (Barlett et al., 2020) could be adapted to be longer and delivered online across multiple sessions for youth and adults alike. Theoretically, we would expect age to moderate the success of the YNA intervention. Recall that the BGCM posits that cyberbullying is a learning-based process that requires cyberbullying experiences to eventually lead to the development of cyberbullying-related knowledge structures (e.g. anonymity perceptions and attitudes) to yield subsequent cyberbullying behaviour. Thus, emerging adults who presumably have more experiences being victimised and perpetrating harm online should have greater success with the YNA program than youth who presumably have fewer cyberbullying experiences. Other interventions, besides the YNA curriculum, could also be adapted for varying age groups and delivery methodologies.

The second unanswered research question is to examine whether the mediating processes that drive the decision to cyberbully are moderated by age. For instance, the BGCM posits that positive reinforcement is paramount for youth to develop cyberbullying knowledge structures – especially in the early learning stages, which may not be as important for those who have already been cyberbullying frequently. On the other hand, cyberbullying attitudes may not have fully developed (or started to develop) for youth compared to adults who may have more online harm experiences (as either the perpetrator or victim). In other words, it would be interesting to test cyberbullying theory across a lifespan and test which mediating processes are moderated by participant age.

The third unanswered research question pertains to the number of learning trials that are important to develop cyberbullying-related knowledge structures. For instance, does it take 3, 13 or 30 times cyberbullying another to internalise anonymity perceptions and BIMOB, according to the BGCM? This question has not been answered because to fully answer this question, researchers must identify a population of people who have never cyberbullied another and then monitor their cyberbullying behaviours across time. Indeed, Barlett et al. (2021a) explicated the importance and difficulty in conducting such a study – especially since research has shown that youth as early as nine years old cyberbully others (Englander, 2018).

Fourth, researchers should examine the development of cyberbullying cross-culturally (Smith et al., 2019). Although scholars have demonstrated that cyberbullying perpetration is a worldwide phenomenon (Craig et al., 2020), the processes germane to the psychological mediators and moderators likely differ cross-culturally. For instance, Barlett et al. (2021b) showed that the processes germane to the BGCM are similar across emerging adults from seven countries (United States, Brazil, Singapore, Japan, China, Germany and Australia). While these findings offer an interesting perspective on cyberbullying process, none of these studies sampled youth or sampled populations of varying ages to allow for tests of the moderating influence of age cross-culturally in the development of cyberbullying perpetration.

Conclusion

Cyberbullying perpetration has emerged as a worldwide negative consequence of increased internet accessibility and usability. Here, we offered a review of the literature that seeks to understand cyberbullying from a developmental perspective. It is our hope that more high-quality research that allows for tests of development can be conducted to inform high-quality interventions to, hopefully, reduce cyberbullying perpetration and cybervictimisation.

References

Anderson, C. A., & Bushman, B. J. (2002). Human aggression. *Annual Review of Psychology, 53*, 27–51, https://doi.org/10.1146/annurev.psych.53.100901.135231

Anderson, M. (2016). How parents monitor their teen's digital behavior. www.pewresearch.org/internet/2016/01/07/how-parents-monitor-their-teens-digital-behavior/ on 1/20/2022.

Barlett, C. P. (2015). Predicting adolescent's cyberbullying behavior: A longitudinal risk analysis. *Journal of Adolescence, 41*, 86–95. https://doi.org/10.1016/j.adolescence.2015.02.006.

Barlett, C. P. (2017). From theory to practice: Cyberbullying theory and its application to intervention. *Computers in Human Behavior, 72*, 269–275. https://doi.org/10.1016/j.chb.2017.02.060.

Barlett, C. P. (2019). *Predicting cyberbullying: Research, theory, and interventions.* San Diego, CA: Academic Press

Barlett, C. P., & Chamberlin, K. (2017). Examining cyberbullying across the lifespan. *Computers in Human Behavior, 71*, 444–449.

Barlett, C. P., & Coyne, S. M. (2014). A meta-analysis of sex differences in cyber-bullying behavior: The moderating role of age. *Aggressive Behavior, 40*, 474–488. https://doi.org/10.1002/ab.21555.

Barlett, C. P., & Gentile, D. A. (2012). Attacking others online: The formation of cyberbullying in late adolescence. *Psychology of Popular Media Culture, 1*, 130–135. https://doi.org/10.1037/a0028113.

Barlett, C. P., Bennardi, C., Williams, S., & Zlupko, T. (2021a). Theoretically predicting cyberbullying perpetration in youth with the BGCM: Unique challenges and promising research opportunities. *Frontiers in Psychology, 12*, 708277.

Barlett, C. P., Heath, J. B., Madison, C. S., DeWitt, C. C., & Kirkpatrick, S. M. (2020). You're not anonymous online: The development and validation of a new cyberbullying intervention curriculum. *Psychology of Popular Media Culture, 9*(2), 135–144. https://doi.org/10.1037/ppm0000226.

Barlett, C. P., Seyfert, L. W., Simmers, M. M., Chen, V. H. H., Cavalcanit, J. G., Krahe, B., Suzuke, K., Warburton, W. A., Wong, R. Y. M., Pimentel, C. E., & Skowronski, M. (2021b). Cross-cultural similarities and differences in the theoretical predictors of cyberbullying preparation: Results from a seven-country study. *Aggressive Behavior, 47*, 111–119. https://doi.org/10.1002/ab.21923

Beran, T., & Li, Q. (2007). The relationship between cyberbullying and school bullying. *The Journal of Student Wellbeing*, 1(2), 15–33.

Chaux, E., Velasquez, A. M., Schultze-Krumbholz, A., & Scheithauer, H. (2016). Effects of the cyberbullying prevention program Media Heroes (Medienhelden) on traditional bullying. *Aggressive Behavior*, 42, 157–165. https://doi.org/10.1002/ab.21637

Chen, L., Ho, S. S., & Lwin, M. O. (2017). A meta-analysis of factors predicting cyberbullying perpetration and victimization: From a social cognitive and media effects approach. *New Media and Society*, 19(8), 1194–1213. https://doi.org/10.1177/1461444816634037

Chng, G. S., Liau, A., Khoo, A., & Li, D. (2014). Parental mediation and cyberbullying – a longitudinal study. *Annual Review of Cybertherapy and Telemedicine*, 199, 98–102.

Craig, W., Boniel-Nissim, M., King, N., Walsh, S., Boer, M., Donnelly, P. D., Harel-Fisch, Y., Malinowska – Cieslik, M., Gaspar de Matos, M., Cosma, A., Van den Eijnden, R., Vieno, A., Elgar, F. J., Molcho, M., Bjereld, Y., & Pickett, W. (2020). Social media use and cyber-bullying: A cross-national analysis of young people in 42 countries. *Journal of Adolescent Health*, 66, S100–S108.

Curwen, T., McNichol, J. S., & Sharpe, G. W. (2011). The progression of bullying from elementary school to university. *International Journal of Humanity Social Sciences*, 1, 47–54.

Doane, A. N., Kelley, M. L., & Pearson, M. R. (2016). Reducing cyberbullying: A theory of reasoned action-based video prevention program for college students. *Aggressive Behavior*, 42, 136–146. https://doi.org/10.1002/ab.21610

Dooley, J. J., Pyzalski, J., & Cross, D. (2009). Cyberbullying versus face-to-face bullying: A theoretical and conceptual review. *Journal of Psychology*, 217(4), 182–188.

Englander, E. (2018). Cell phone ownership and cyberbullying in 8–11 year olds: New research. *Pediatrics*, 142(1_meetingabstract), 724. https://doi.org/10.1542/peds.142.1MA8.724

Englander, E., Donnerstein, E., Kowalski, R., Lin, C. A., & Parti, K. (2017). Defining cyberbullying. *Pediatrics*, 140, S148–S151. https://doi.org/10.1542/peds.2016.1758U

Gaffney, H., & Farrington, D. P. (2021). A review of systemic reviews and meta-analyses of the effectiveness of school-based anti-bullying programs. In P. K. Smith & J. O'Higgins Norman (Eds.), *The Wiley Blackwell handbook of bullying: A comprehensive and international review of research and intervention, volume 2* (pp. 676–706). Chichester: Wiley.

Gaffney, H., Farrington, D. P., Espelage, D. L., & Ttofi, M. M. (2019). Are cyberbullying intervention and prevention programs effective? A systematic and meta-analytic review. *Aggression and Violent Behavior*, 45, 134–153

Guo, S. (2016). A meta-analysis of the predictors of cyberbullying perpetration and victimization. *Psychology in the Schools*, 53(4), 432–453. https://doi.org/1-.1002/pits.21914

Ho, S. S., Chen, L., & Ng, A. P. Y. (2017). Comparing cyberbullying perpetration on social media between primary and secondary school students. *Computers and Education*, 109, 74–84.

Kowalski, R. M., Giumetti, G. W., Schroeder, A. N., & Lattanner, M. R. (2014). Bullying in the digital age: A critical review and meta-analysis of cyberbullying research among youth. *Psychological Bulletin*, 140(4), 1073–1137. https://doi.org/10.1037/a0035618

Kowalski, R. M., Limber, S. E., & Agatston, P. W. (2012). *Cyberbullying: Bullying in the digital age* (2nd ed.). Wiley-Blackwell

Kowalski, R. M., & Limber, S. P. (2007). Electronic bullying among middle school students. *Journal of Adolescent Health*, 41(6), S22–S30. https://doi.org/10.1016/j.jadohealth.2007.08.017.

Kowalski, R. M., Toth, A., & Morgan, M. (2017). Bullying and cyberbullying in adulthood and the workplace. *Journal of Social Psychology*, 158(1), 64–81.

Lenhart, A. (2010). Is the age at which kids get cell phones getting younger? www.pewre-search.org/internet/2010/12/01/is-the-age-at-which-kids-get-cell-phones-getting-younger/ (Accessed 20 January 2022).

Li, Q. (2006). Cyberbullying in schools: A research of gender differences. *School Psychology International, 27*(2), 157–170. https://doi.org/10.1177/0143034306064547

Menesini, E., De Luca, L., Palladino, B. E., & Nocentini, A. (2021). In P. K. Smith & J. O'Higgins Norman (Eds.), *The Wiley Blackwell handbook of bullying: A comprehensive and international review of research and intervention, volume 2* (pp. 469–489). Chichester: Wiley.

Mesch, G. S. (2009). Parental mediation, online activities, and cyberbullying. *CyberPsychology and Behavior, 12*(4), 387–393. https://doi.org/10.1089/cpb.2009.0068

Microsoft (2021). *Civility, safety and interaction online* (5th ed.). www.microsoft.com/en-us/online-safety/digital-civility?activetab=dci_reports%3aprimaryr3

Navarro, R., Serna, C., Martinez, V., & Ruiz-Oliva, R. (2013). The role of Internet use and parental mediation on cyberbullying victimization among Spanish children from rural public schools. *European Journal of Psychological Education, 28*, 725–745. https://doi.org/10.1007/s10212-012-0137-2

Ng, E. D., Chua, J. Y. X., & Shorey, S. (2022). The effectiveness of educational interventions on traditional bullying and cyberbullying among adolescents: A systematic review and meta-analysis. *Trauma, Violence, and Abuse, 23*(1), 132–151. https://doi.org/10.1177/1524838020933867

Pettalia, J. L., Levin, E., & Dickinson, J. (2013). Cyberbullying: Eliciting harm without consequences. *Computers in Human Behavior, 29*, 2758–2765. https://doi.org/10.1016/j.chb.2013.07.020

Pew Research Center (2021). Internet/broadband fact sheet. www.pewresearch.org/internet/fact-sheet/internet-broadband/ on 1/20/2022.

Polanin, J. R., Espelage, D. L., Grotpeter, J. K., Ingram, K., Michaelson, L., Spinney, E., Valido, A., El Sheikkh, A., Torgal, C., & Robinson, L. (2021). A systematic review and meta-analysis of interventions to decrease cyberbullying perpetration and victimization. *Prevention Science, 22*, 1–16. https://doi.org/10.1007/s11121-021-01259-y

Schodt, K., Quiroz, S. I., Wheeler, B., Hall, D. L., & Silva, Y. N. (2021). Cyberbullying and mental health in adults: The moderating role of social media use and gender. *Frontiers in Psychology, 12*, 1–14. https://doi.org/10.3389/fpsyt.2021.674298

Selkie, E. M., Fales, J. L., & Moreno, M. A. (2016). Cyberbullying prevalence among US middle and high school-aged adolescents: A systematic review and quality assessment. *Journal of Adolescent Health, 58*(2), 125–133. https://doi.org/10.1016/j.jadohealth.2015.09.026

Ševčíková, A., & Šmahel, D. (2009). Online harassment and cyberbullying in the Czech Republic: Comparison across age groups. *Journal of Psychology, 217*(4), 227–229.

Shadmanfaat, S. M., Howell, C. J., Muniz, C. N., Cochran, J. K., Kabbiri, S., & Fontaine, E. M. (2020). Cyberbullying perpetration: An empirical test of social learning theory in Iran. *Deviant Behavior, 41*(3), 278–293. https://doi.org/10.1080/01639625.2019.1565513

Smith, P. K., & Berkkun, F. (2017). How research on cyberbullying has developed. In C. McGuckin & L. Corcoran (Eds.), *Bullying and cyberbullying: Prevalence, psychological impacts and intervention strategies* (pp. 11–27). Hauppauge, NY: Nova Science.

Smith, P. K., Görzig, A., & Robinson, S. (2019). Cyberbullying in schools: Cross-cultural issues. In G. W. Giumetti & R. M. Kowalski (Eds.), *Cyberbullying in schools, workplaces, and romantic relationships* (pp. 49–68). New York: Routledge.

Smith, P. K., Mahdavi, J., Carvalho, M., Fisher, S., Russell, S., & Tippett, N. (2008). Cyberbullying: Its nature and impact in secondary school pupils. *Journal of Child Psychology and Psychiatry, 49*(4), 376–385. https://doi.org/10.111/j.1469-7610.2007.01846.x

Song, H., Lee, Y., & Kim, J. (2020). Gender differences in the link between cyberbullying and parental supervision trajectories. *Crime and Delinquency, 66*(13–14), 1914–1936. https://doi.org/10.1177/0011128720912371

Vandebosch, H., & Van Cleemput, K. (2009). Cyberbullying among youngsters: Profiles of bullies and victims. *New Media and Society, 11*(8), 1349–1371.

Yeager, D. S., Fong, C. J., Lee, H. Y., & Espelage, D. L. (2015). Declines in efficacy of anti-bullying programs among older adolescents: Theory and three-level meta-analysis. *Journal of Applied Developmental Psychology, 37*, 36–51. https://doi.org/10.1016/j.appdev.2014.11.005

Zacchilli, T. L., & Valerio, C. Y. (2011). The knowledge and prevalence of cyberbullying in a college sample. *Journal of Scientific Psychology, 5*, 11–23.

3 'It was only a bit of fun' – when bullying and cyberbullying becomes harassment and sexual violence among university students – findings from the Violence at University Project

Carrie-Anne Myers, Helen Cowie, Nathan Hudson, Holly Powell-Jones, Emma Short and Fiona Waye

Introduction

Tackling violence, harassment and hate crime is high on the agenda for UK universities. Since 2010 the National Union of Students has conducted surveys that evidence problematic behaviours within university settings, including sexual harassment and unwanted sexual advances amongst the student population (NUS, 2010; NUS, 2014). Further research also provides evidence of staff sexual misconduct and predatory behaviours (NUS, 2018), as well as racial and homophobic harassment, prejudice and (cyber)-bullying (Wertans & Chakraborti, 2020; EHRC, 2019; Formby, 2017; Myers & Cowie, 2017).

The impact that violence, harassment and experiences of hate crime has on any age, but especially young people, is considerable. Studies suggest not only long-term damage to self-esteem, emotional health and well-being (Cowie & Myers, 2016) but also increased propensity to contemplate suicide or self-harm, develop an eating disorder and engage in substance abuse (Stenning et al., 2013). Evidence also suggests that experiences of violence can negatively impact students' academic attainment, as well as damage universities' institutional reputation and negatively affect student retention and recruitment.

In light of this growing body of evidence, Universities UK (UUK) in 2016 launched 'Changing the Culture', a strategic framework to support universities to prevent and respond to violence against women, harassment and hate crimes affecting university students. Follow-up reports in 2017 and 2019 demonstrate that, although some progress has been made, as the then UUK's President, Prof Julia Buckingham, stated, 'there is much more to be done, with progress still variable across the higher education sector' (UUK, 2017, 2019).

One of the key gaps in understanding the prevalence of violence at university is sector-wide data collection. This is an area that universities in both Australia and the United States are more advanced in, but within the UK higher education sector, existing research is piecemeal at best but highlights some key

DOI:10.4324/9781003258605-4

themes that need to be included, for example, Homophobic and Transphobic Aggression (Rivers, 2016); Cyberbullying and Rape Culture (Shariff & DeMartini, 2016); Cyber-aggression (Simmons et al., 2015) and the need to unpack the nature, prevalence, impacts and policy of cyberbullying in post-secondary institutions in a global context (Cassidy et al., 2018) due to the international nature of the higher education market. Many of these areas are discussed in this volume in relation to online harms. The only way that a full understanding of violence, in all its forms, from the online to the offline, and the physical to the psychological, within universities and higher education providers can be understood is to design a survey, which can then be rolled out across the sector, once the exact measurements/definitions of violence have been established and piloted.

The research project – violence at university

For this chapter, we report findings from the Violence at University Project (Myers et al., 2022), a quantitative pilot research project that ran from November 2020 until December 2021. The survey was designed by City, University of London, in collaboration with Universities UK (UUK), University of Surrey, De Montfort University and the National Centre for Social Research (NatCen). It was a feasibility study to investigate the possibility of measuring violence, in all its forms, within the HE sector and was not a prevalence study. It did not ask for rates or frequency of violence; it was designed to ascertain whether it would be possible to measure violence in all its forms, picking up both subtle and unsubtle events.

The questionnaire comprised 34 questions, with each core sub-section having an open-text qualitative question to record further thoughts and observations. In line with victimisation surveys and the need for anonymity, it was not possible to work out who had written the open free text and, consequently, the quotations given are completely anonymised but give depth to observations gleaned from the breadth of the statistics.

It was designed and disseminated by Qualtrics and even though the Covid-19 pandemic could have been a factor for unsuccessful data collection, not being able to carry out supplementary interviews was the only setback the project faced. In total, there were n = 263 responses to the questionnaire, with n = 188 of the respondents being in the 18–25 age category. It is also relevant to note that not all participants answered every question since there was the option to move on through the questionnaire if a respondent did not want to answer in a particular area of questions. (For a full breakdown of the demographics and the results of the survey, see the report Violence at University Pilot Project, Student Experiences of Violence Harassment and Discrimination, 2022.)

This chapter discusses the subset of questions that considered bullying, cyberbullying, online harms and their relation to sexual and dating violence among university students. It also reports the link to protected characteristics and how identity characteristics (actual or perceived) are linked to experiencing victimisation. This is to draw out the findings from existing bullying and cyber-bullying research within the sector, although it must be stressed that the prevalence of bullying and cyberbullying was not the remit of the research project.

Broad experiences of violence and related behaviours

This question was answered by 252 of the 263 respondents and was where many different forms of violence were unpacked. Students reported experiencing bullying both in person and online. It took a number of forms, n = 36 experienced verbal abuse; n = 35 reported emotional or psychological abuse; n = 27 suffered from persistent unwanted behaviour that caused fear or distress in the form of harassment/stalking; n = 18 experienced bullying; n = 14 had threats levelled at them, including threats of violence; n = 12 reported tracking/monitoring or surveillance causing anxiety or stress (harassment/stalking); n = 16 had been victimised by upsetting online content or behaviour, such as trolling flaming or abuse; and n = 13 had suffered from silent, hoax or abusive phone calls. This range of reported behaviours is demonstrated in previous research and is also consistent with chapters presented in this volume. It also demonstrates that universities need to begin to address and deal with these broad experiences and the emerging evidence base that bullying and cyberbullying happens across the lifespan of education (Pörhölä, 2015; Myers & Cowie, 2019).

Broad experiences happened online more than other forms of violence that are discussed later, with n = 30 detailing that they had occurred in the digital environment via mobile, messaging or social media. Also, the perpetrators were unknown, with n = 33 reporting that they did not know who had carried out the behaviour. This could be one of two things, that online violence is emerging as a 'weapon of choice' for stranger and acquaintance violence, or it could be the Covid effect. Future research would need to explore this further, but the self-report section gave two opposing accounts, both highlighting the danger of online forms of violence.

On the one hand, the fear and consequence of victimisation were highlighted:

> It has destroyed the illusion of law and order and presumed safety – violence without cause or consequence is common in our society.

And on the other hand, how it is used as a tool to commit the behaviours:

> There was an Instagram account pretending to be me to scam people into getting their money. It wasn't and I had to prove my innocence when I had done nothing wrong.

Sexual violence and related behaviours

The question on sexual violence asked about experiences while students were at university across a range of online and in-person scenarios; the idea was to determine what had occurred whilst away at university in comparison to 'home' life. Respondents could answer as many times as they wanted to report all behaviours they had experienced. In total, 481 incidents were recorded. Regarding online harms and behaviours, n = 12 had experienced sexual bullying or harassment, in that it was repeated behaviour; n = 19 had been sent sexually explicit emails, text messages or other communication; n = 30 reported repeated or inappropriate advances over email, social media, text message or other communication; and n = 5 had had inappropriate video, photos or commentary about them distributed digitally (via social media, email or messaging service) without consent. Concerning the location of the experiences, the online environment accounted for 13% of the student experiences, with the majority of incidents happening in physical social spaces. The self-report section where participants were able to expand and reflect highlighted alarming narratives and the perception that when sexual violence was happening online, it was not perceived as serious as physical forms of sexual violence. As one respondent detailed:

> The uni I go to has a rape culture on campus, with a Facebook group dedicated to posting photos and videos of other students on there kissing and undertaking sexual acts. People then comment on them, rating people or making comments about their appearance, often tagging their profiles. Rape is seen as a joke, so a lot of the comments joke about a video showing rape, people having 'rape eyes' or running a 'rape train'. This group has been active for 6+ years and the uni is trying to pretend it doesn't exist. Joking about rape is common around campus too, and I have several friends who have been sexually assaulted, reported it and never heard anything back.

Such observations tie in with Shariff's (2016) argument that such beliefs are commonplace on many university campuses and are rooted in a misogynistic culture, which reflects attitudes in society.

There are still unanswered questions as to why the presence of such sites is acceptable and normalised. This also ties in with observations about cyberbullying among university students and the idea that such behaviours are often passed off as 'banter' or a 'bit of fun'. Non-consensual sharing of digital sexual content may be 'justified' by teenagers as a 'joke', particularly if the abuse is perpetrated by peers (Powell-Jones, 2018b). However, more needs to be done to understand the victims' perceptions, too. Research shows teenagers frequently expect little or no consequences for cyber-enabled abuse from authorities, such as education institutes or police – and that this belief becomes *more common* among *older* students (Powell-Jones, 2018b). This is likely to be a key factor in victims under-reporting of incidents.

Identity-based violence and related behaviours

The research team wanted to explore how students experienced identity-based violence and in particular wanted to unpack violence that was motivated due to the individual's identity or perceptions of identity. Once again respondents were able to report all experiences and in total 409 instances were detailed. Out of all the questions, this one demonstrated that both traditional bullying and cyberbullying were commonplace among the student population. In terms of traditional in-person bullying, n = 34 reported being excluded or ignored in a social, work or group situation; n = 26 experienced direct derogatory name-calling, insults and slurs and n = 29 reported these behaviours indirectly. The subtle indirect nature was also reported in terms of insensitive/offensive comments, toxic 'jokes' or rhetoric with n = 43 disclosing this form of experience and n = 29 having such behaviours presented to them directly. Subtle or nuanced hostile behaviours, such as microaggressions, were recorded by n = 29 respondents. Labelling the behaviour as bullying or harassment in terms of repeated behaviour was highlighted by n = 21 students. With regard to cyberbullying and online harms, n = 14 reported exposure to offensive material, messages, comments, images or displays and n = 13 highlighted receiving hostile, hateful or offensive digital communications via email, social media and text messages. Therefore, this form of violence was predominantly carried out in person, either directly or indirectly, and the research into recognising and responding to harassment based on an individual's identity or perceived identity is urgently needed across the sector.

The other key finding to note in this area is the negative treatment that individuals received after raising concerns or speaking up, with n = 27 reporting victimisation after drawing attention to identity-based violence. This is often an observation made within the victimology literature about a survivor's unwillingness to report for fear of repercussions, not being taken seriously or suffering secondary victimisation. Again, to understand and prevent such behaviours the voice of the victim really needs to be understood.

The self-reported identity characteristics (perceived or actual) that were catalysts for identity-based violence were overwhelmingly linked to protected characteristics set out in the Equality Act (2010). Gender, for example, sexism and misogyny was the highest reported characteristic, n = 44; followed by racism (e.g., ethnicity, nationality or skin colour) with n = 33; sexual orientation (e.g. homophobia) was reported by n = 20 and disability (ableism) by n = 16, which among this age group and the intersections with hate crime legislation is alarming and a cause for concern. Initiatives being introduced in the HE sector are somehow not getting an adequate message across. Several respondents also detailed the relevance of their background or accent, for example, classism. The number for this characteristic was n = 23, suggesting that the class-based bias of universities is still very much in existence and is an area that requires further exploration.

The location of these identity-based experiences was in a range of physical spaces, both on and off campus, but interestingly within this study it was predominantly online, with n = 29 reporting the digital environment such as via mobile, messaging or social media as the space for the violence. This could be an example of the Covid effect as the research was carried out during lockdown so it would be interesting in future research to see if this is still the case.

The main perpetrators of identity-based violence were fellow students at the same university, with n = 41 reporting. This was closely followed by someone known to them in their social group, with n = 37 identifying the perpetrator. Research shows proximity and relationship between perpetrators and victims can influence the extent to which teenagers may consider the behaviour 'problematic' (or not) – including for digitally enabled violence (Powell-Jones, 2018b). Interestingly n = 34 did not know the offender, but this again could be linked to the unique situation of the pandemic and requires further unpacking in future work. At one level, the results confirm existing findings on face-to-face bullying, where the perpetrator is often known, and cyberbullying, where the perpetrator often is not (Cowie & Myers, 2017). However, it must be remembered this was not a survey exclusively about bullying. To unpack such nuanced findings, subset questions would need to be developed but this does demonstrate the complex relationships there are around understanding students' experiences of both the offline and online world.

As before, analysis of the qualitative responses gave some insight into what students had experienced in terms of identity-based violence. The complexity of the intersections among the protected characteristics is summed up by the following response which details sexism, classism and homophobia:

> The most common perpetrators are men in these situations, I'm extremely privileged as I am white so I have never experienced any form of racism. I have experienced sexism and misogyny almost on a daily basis. I am also from a northern working-class town which doesn't seem to go down well at university, I've been relentlessly tore down and made fun of because of my accent and made to feel like I'm stupid. I also have been tormented because I am bisexual, told that I'm not gay enough or called a homophobic slur or that I'm only going out with women for male attention.

Responses such as this demonstrate that there is not a clear-cut solution. We suggest that perhaps understanding these behaviours would be a way forward for the university sector to engage with.

The following account gives another example, this time around racism:

> I'm only a quarter Korean, but I still look semi or like a mix. I've had people make fun of my eyes by them asking me what was wrong with them, I've been called slurs such as ch★nk and "slit eyed".

This is an example of name-calling, which would be passed off as bullying but is a racially motivated derogatory comment. Previous research into bullying at university highlights the diffusion that using the bullying label can achieve when it is against a protected characteristic. However, uncertainty over what constitutes an offence (e.g. a hate crime) online – or what characteristics are protected by law – is likely to be a barrier to tackling these issues among young people (Powell-Jones, 2016). It is also a pattern that continues across the lifespan of education.

The final example gives an account of homophobia:

> The person in question insinuated that people from the LGBTQ+ community only get into uni so the uni can seem more diverse and not because of their individual skills etc.

Alongside demonstrating a slur on a protected characteristic, this is an example of indirect bullying that occurs on campus. Claiming that students are playing a 'card' to advance them in the higher education system is something that was also reported in terms of gender, race and ableism. Not only would this form of victimisation be distressing to those concerned, but the assumption is also simply not true and is only based on perception rather than evidence. This could be an important aspect that the sector could highlight by educating students on their conduct, attitudes and behaviours on campus, an intervention that is already established within schools and further education colleges. The HE sector should continue to learn from this work with younger students. It should not be taken for granted that, because an individual is 18, he/she is not in need of reminding about the consequences of their actions and the impact of throw-away comments or microaggression on fellow students. Research shows teens may be quicker to recognise and label online incidents as 'racist' than 'homophobic' (or biphobic, transphobic, misogynistic, etc.), which suggests that education on key definitions, protected characteristics and legal rights may benefit student communities too (Powell-Jones, 2018b).

Conclusions

This chapter provides a snapshot of just some of the themes and findings uncovered in the violence at university project that can be used to understand incidents of bullying and cyberbullying amongst university students. What is interesting is the links to protected characteristics and the fact that in online violence the perpetrators are predominantly unknown or acquaintances.

As previous research has demonstrated, there is still an urgent need to unpack harassment in all its forms across the sector (Wertans & Chakraborti, 2020). Research that focuses on one aspect only, for example, gender-based violence and harassment (Bull et al., 2022), simply raises more questions and highlights failings rather than providing answers.

The idea of looking at patterns of behaviour across the lifespan of education and in different cultural contexts is elaborated in the present volume. There is a clear need to take account of university students' previous experiences at school, college and in the community and the workplace since these experiences and the attitudes that evolve from them have a powerful impact on their lives and on the ways in which they relate to other people.

Overall, the feasibility study reported here asks more questions than it answers, but the redesign and upscaling of this project could lead to sector-wide benchmarking and an evidence base that can be built upon. For example, the research has the potential to be scaled to a sector-wide, annual survey, like the NSS but with a focus on student experiences of violence. By this means, universities can identify how HEIs can make better use of research, evidence and data to understand better the needs of the students in their care and improve services and outcomes. Perhaps then useful interventions can be developed to lower the incidence of violence, as well as promote opportunity and reduce adversity for students in the future. There is still a long way to go but a decade ago none of the themes discussed in this chapter was on the radar of the HE sector. It has moved at pace and hopefully will continue to do so.

Bibliography

Bull, A., Duggan, M., & Livesey, L. (2022). Researching students' experiences of sexual and gender-based violence and harassment: Reflections and recommendations from surveys of three UK HEIs. *Social Sciences*, *11*(8), 373–391.

Cassidy, W., Faucher, C., & Jackson, M. (2018). *Cyberbullying at university in international contexts*. London: Routledge.

Cowie, H., & Myers, C.-A. (2016). *Bullying among university students: Cross-national perspectives*. London: Routledge.

Cowie, H., & Myers, C.-A. (Eds.) (2017). *School bullying and mental health: Risks, intervention and prevention*. London: Routledge.

EHRC (2019). Tackling racial harassment: Universities challenged (available at Tackling racial harassment: Universities challenged | Equality and Human Rights Commission (equalityhumanrights.com) (Accessed 24 September 2022).

Equality Act (2010). The Equality Act and protected characteristics | Local Government Association (Accessed 24 September 2022).

Formby, E. (2017). How should we 'care' for LGBT+ students within higher education? *Pastoral Care in Education*, *35*(3), 203–220

Myers, C.-A., & Cowie, H. (2017). Bullying at university: The social and legal contexts of cyberbullying among university students. *Journal of Cross-Cultural Psychology*, *48*, 1172–1182.

Myers, C.-A., & Cowie, H. (2019). Cyberbullying across the lifespan of education: Issues and interventions from school to university. *International Journal of Environmental Research and Public Health*, *16*(7), 1217

Myers, C.-A., Cowie, H., Hudson, N., Powell-Jones, H., Short, E., & Waye, F. (2022). *Violence at University Pilot Project: Student experiences of violence, harassment and discrimination*. London: City University of London.

National Union of Students Education (2010). *Hidden marks: A study of women students' experiences of harassment, stalking, violence and sexual assault*. London: NUS.

National Union of Students Education (2014). Education beyond the straight and narrow. In *LGBT students' experience in higher education*. London: NUS.

National Union of Students (NUS) (2018). *Power in the academy: Staff sexual misconduct in UK higher education*. London: NUS.

Pörhölä, M. (2015). Do the roles of bully and victim remain stable from school to university?: Theoretical considerations. In H. Cowie & C.-A. Myers (Eds.), *Bullying among university students* (pp. 35–47). London: Routledge.

Powell-Jones, H. (2016). *Online and social media law and ethics – Final report* 2015/16 (see also: 2013, 2014). Surrey: Eagle Radio Ltd. and the Office of the Police and Crime Commissioner.

Powell-Jones, H. (2018a). 'Bullying and social media. In H. Cowie & C.-A. Myers (Eds.), *School bullying and mental health: Risks, intervention and prevention* (pp. 115–129). London: Routledge.

Powell-Jones, H. (2018b). *How do young people interpret and construct risk in an online context?* [Unpublished Doctoral thesis], City, University of London. https://openaccess.city.ac.uk/id/eprint/22557/

Rivers, I. (2016). Homophobic and transphobic bullying in universities. In H. Cowie & C.-A. Myers (Eds.), *Bullying among university students* (pp. 48–60). London: Routledge.

Shariff, S., & DeMartini, A. (2016). Cyberbullying and rape culture in universities: Defining the legal lines between fun and intentional harm. In H. Cowie & C.-A. Myers (Eds.), *Bullying among university students* (pp. 172–190). London: Routledge.

Simmons, J., Sheri, B., & Ives, J. (2015). Cyber-aggression among members of college fraternities and sororities in the United States. In H. Cowie & C.-A. Myers (Eds.), *Bullying among university students* (pp. 93–109). Routledge: London

Stenning, P., Mitra-Kahn, T., & Gunby, C. (2013). Sexual violence against female university students in the UK: A case study. *Rivista di Criminologia, Vittimologia e Sicurezza, 7*(2), 100–119.

Universities UK (UUK). (2016). *Changing the culture: Report of the Universities UK Taskforce examining violence against women, harassment and hate crime affecting university students.* London: UUK.

Universities UK (UUK). (2017). *Changing the culture: One year on – an assessment of strategies to tackle sexual misconduct, hate crime and harassment affecting university students.* London: UUK.

Universities UK (UUK) (2019). *Changing the culture – tackling gender-based violence, harassment and hate crime: Two years on.* London: UUK.

Wertans & Chakraborti (2020). *A catalyst for change: Recognising and responding to students' experiences of harassment.* Leicester: Centre for Hate Studies (available at Research | The Centre for Hate Studies | University of Leicester) (Accessed 24 September 2022)

Theme 2

The social and cultural contexts which facilitate or challenge cyberbullying and online harassment

4 Leadership as a double-edged sword

The social, cultural and institutional contexts of cyberbullying and online harassment

Wanda Cassidy, Chantal Faucher, and Margaret Jackson

Introduction

The presence of bullying and cyberbullying in elementary, middle and secondary schools around the world is well known (Cassidy et al., 2013; Hinduja & Patchin, 2012; Smith et al., 2018). Increasingly, a picture is being revealed about related behaviours also occurring in post-secondary educational institutions (Cassidy et al., 2019; Cowie & Myers, 2016; Hollis, 2012). This chapter looks at the role of leadership in promoting or curtailing bullying and cyberbullying in the university setting. We begin with an examination of the literature pertaining to educational leadership, particularly in relation to school and university cultures that promote or prevent these behaviours. We then present cases from our own research, examining the role leadership plays in cyberbullying in universities.

Educational settings, bullying and cyberbullying

In the K-12 setting, school culture is seen as central to addressing bullying and cyberbullying in a meaningful way (Hinduja & Patchin, 2012; Roberge, 2011; Smith et al., 2012). Approaches that involve the whole school community in the development, implementation and evaluation of policies and programs show much more promise in reducing negative behaviours (Farrington & Ttofi, 2009; Hinduja & Patchin, 2012; Roberge, 2011; Smith et al., 2012), than do zero-tolerance responses and reactive punitive measures.

At the university level, the hierarchical structure of the institution, the focus on individualism and competitiveness, the tenure process and the use of academic freedom to justify unsavoury behaviours provide a fertile environment for bullying activity (Driver, 2019; Miller et al., 2019; Tiamboonprasert & Charoensukmongkol, 2020; Twale, 2018). It can be relatively easy for a 'bully culture' to set in, exacerbated by inadequate responses by university administrators and opaque policies that tend to protect the bully, rather than those who are bullied (Twale, 2018).

DOI:10.4324/9781003258605-6

Further, these settings exist within a broader societal culture where bullying and cyberbullying behaviours are normalised. Examples abound of celebrities and politicians who use their platforms to tear down others. Cyberbullying and online harassment are frequently seen in the context of friendships and intimate relationships, among acquaintances, between strangers in anonymous social media platforms and/or in virtual games (Cassidy et al., 2014; Faucher et al., 2014; Leisring, 2019). Often, these interactions further the sexism, racism, classism, ableism and heterosexism pervasive throughout society (Cénat et al., 2015; Jackson et al., 2010; Lampman, 2012; Mishna et al., 2018; Navarro & Jasinski, 2013; Rivers, 2016).

Bullying and cyberbullying negatively impact those targeted, their associates and even the institutions as a whole (Cassidy et al., 2013, 2019; Hollis, 2012; Wright, 2016). Those targeted may experience physical and mental health effects, disengagement from their work or studies, concern for their safety or fractured personal and professional relationships. Institutions may see a loss of productivity, loss of collegiality and negative repercussions with respect to their public image. Some also argue that the harms associated with cyberbullying are particularly persistent due to the potential reach and permanence of online posts, as well as the anonymity and lack of ability to respond as one might do in face-to-face interactions (Twale, 2018, pp. 78–80). These effects are compounded when the targets feel unsupported by inadequate institutional responses to the behaviour (Cassidy et al., 2017; Hollis, 2012; Twale, 2018).

The pivotal role of leadership

Leaders drive the organisational culture of an institution (Hollis, 2012). As noted by Page and colleagues (2021, p. 29), 'leadership matters'. Poor leadership can overtly or inadvertently promote negative behaviours, whereas good leadership can do the opposite (Hollis, 2012).

Poor leadership may also take the form of a lack of leadership, where leaders have their 'heads in the sand' or are 'in denial' to the problems or adopt a 'laissez-faire' approach to solving problems (Cassidy et al., 2012; Twale, 2018). In such instances, these 'leaders' fail to show leadership, and as a result bullying and cyberbullying can flourish. There is also a leadership style that is authoritarian, destructive and abusive, that both models and promotes bullying behaviour in institutions (Twale, 2018).

On the other hand, leadership can be transformational and serve to create a healthy, supportive and inclusive environment; build relational trust and capacity among all members of the community; implement and uphold policies; set the tone and role model the desired behaviours; and hold people accountable when their behaviour is harmful (Hollis, 2012; Page et al., 2021; Sergiovanni, 2005; Twale, 2018). As Sergiovanni (2005) notes: 'The heartbeats of leadership . . . are strengthened when word and deed are one' (p. 112). Leaders must do more than talk the talk; they must walk the walk.

Types of leadership

The literature on educational leadership is vast and beyond the scope of this chapter to review. However, certain leadership styles emerge as particularly noteworthy in relation to curtailing bullying and cyberbullying in schools and academic workplaces. Transformational and ethical leadership are described as effective models for creating an ethical and caring environment within which negative behaviours have no place (Begley & Stefkovich, 2007; Branson, 2014; Page et al., 2021; Tiamboonprasert & Charoensukmongkol, 2020). Ethical leaders 'lead with ethics' and put 'ethics in the foreground of all activities' (Tuana, 2014, p. 153), although they do not act in isolation. Instead, ethical leadership requires a whole community commitment, where all stakeholders (students, instructors, staff, administrators) are engaged and enact the ideals. According to Shapiro and Stefkovich (2016, pp. 10–27), ethical leadership includes attention to the ethics of justice, critique, care and the profession.

Starratt (2011) advocates a form of transformative leadership, which not only is supportive, nurturing and inclusive but also has an equity and social justice focus aimed at identifying and overcoming those obstacles that create disadvantage and vulnerability. Starratt, like others (Begley & Stefkovich, 2007; Branson, 2014; Noddings, 2006; Twale, 2018), purports that ethical leadership must also be authentic, meaning that it begins with self-knowledge, demonstrates sensitivity to others, is perceived as having moral integrity and being fair, responds to issues using multiple ethical lenses and allows for transparency in decision-making.

What these perspectives share is the notion that leadership is not a title or role that is given or bestowed from above. Rather, leadership is a position that rests on one's ability to generate a following and is supportive of others. The leader cannot control everything. Their power lies in their ability to influence the group to attain collective goals, and this is influenced by the leader's perceived openness, transparency, inclusiveness, trustworthiness and fairness (Branson, 2014, pp. 446–450).

Ethical leadership and intersectionality

In the school or university setting, ethical leaders who seek to address problems of bullying and cyberbullying must attend to the intersectional vulnerabilities faced by many students, staff, teachers, faculty and administrators. Angoff and Barnhart (2021, p. 275) quote that 'intersectionality is a conceptual framework that considers how multiple aspects of *identity* (e.g., race/ethnicity, gender, sexual orientation) that are formed by socio-cultural forms of privilege and oppression (e.g., racism, homophobia) interact to impact one's health and life experiences' inequitably. Ethical leadership directs its attention to these inequities and their intersections in determining a path of leadership that serves the best interests of those being led – not the leader's own best interests, nor even those of the organisation (Branson, 2014).

In post-secondary settings, women, racial and ethnic minorities; LGBTQ+ students and faculty; and younger, untenured faculty are more likely to be targeted and to experience harsher forms of cyberbullying as well as more severe impacts (Cassidy et al., 2014, 2016; DeSouza, 2011; Faucher et al., 2014; Lampman, 2012; Rivers, 2016; Sallee & Diaz, 2012; Snyder-Yuly et al., 2021; Taylor, 2012; Veletsianos et al., 2018). Although universities may be viewed by some as beacons of edification, where the brightest minds can be found and where learners go to open their minds to new perspectives, Snyder-Yuly et al. (2021) posit that 'the reality can be that universities mirror, rather than challenge, the same attitudes and generalities about cultural, gender, and racial differences that plague the larger society' (p. 249). This process is accomplished in part through hegemonic civility, where racist, sexist, heterosexist and other discriminatory ideas can be conveyed, while their 'conveyors' are able to maintain a façade of 'niceness' (see also Cole & Hassel, 2017, and Gilmour et al., 2012, on sexism and racism, respectively, in post-secondary education settings).

Culture of care

In many jurisdictions, K-12 schools are required to have anti-bullying policies (Campbell, 2016; O'Connor et al., 2018; Smith et al., 2012). However, policy buy-in from all key stakeholder groups in the school community is not a given and can be facilitated by strong school leadership (Låftman et al., 2017, p. 1233). In schools that have positive ratings of leadership, enact an ethic of care (Noddings, 2005) and create a better school climate, fewer online behavioural problems are experienced (Hinduja & Patchin, 2012; Låftman et al., 2017).

Similarly, in post-secondary institutions, students, faculty and staff can thrive when leaders create a culture of civility, community belonging and trust through values such as equity, fairness, collaboration, service, sensitivity, innovation, commitment, social justice and partnership (Hollis, 2012, p. 108; Page et al., 2021). Such environments can serve to promote well-being and openness to change, and also curtail 'othering' behaviours such as bullying and incivility, including racism, sexism and classism.

When the university culture is not one of caring and belonging but rather one that promotes competition, power-mongering, egotism and insecurity, negative behaviours such as incivility, bullying and cyberbullying flourish (Hollis, 2012; Miller et al., 2019; Page et al., 2021). Additionally, when those who are targets of these negative behaviours perceive a lack of response or inadequate response by the university, the impacts of these behaviours are further exacerbated (Ferber, 2018; Page et al., 2021).

Permutations of bullying and cyberbullying may involve members of the campus community being targeted by anonymous persons, students targeting other students, students targeting faculty or staff and faculty targeting students, staff, each other or members of the administration. Top-down forms of harassment are more easily understood, where one uses their power to intimidate those hierarchically ranked below them. However, the notion of contra-power harassment (DeSouza, 2011; Lampman, 2012) suggests that those with ostensibly less power may use bullying behaviours as a way to exert power over those hierarchically positioned above them. Students harassing instructors in relation to teaching style or grades are not uncommon (Cassidy et al., 2014; Faucher et al., 2019; Lampman, 2012). Heffernan and Bosetti (2021) conducted a study of deans who had experienced various forms of incivility (including bullying and cyberbullying behaviours) from faculty members and staff within their divisions leading to grave impacts and an unwillingness to continue in their administrative role.

Ferber (2018) describes attacks by members of the public on scholars who teach in areas that the alt-right (far-right white nationalists) opposes and attacks grounded in sexism, racism and other 'isms' where there may be a perceived threat to white male privilege. While such attacks are not new, social media have amplified the reach of these messages. Most respondents in Ferber's study felt they had little to no support from their university when they were abused in this way, despite the threat to their academic freedom and the efforts to silence them as scholars and experts in their fields. Such a lack of response is a failure on the part of universities to perform their leadership role within society (Ferber, 2018), as well as a failure of universities to protect or provide training and resources to those targeted (Veletsianos et al., 2018). We have certainly seen examples of academics from a range of ideological perspectives who have faced significant backlash, counterattacks, bullying, and threats due to their ideas. Central to these cases has been the universities' failure to support, or even assist, the scholars employed by them.

University study findings related to leadership

The authors conducted a large study of cyberbullying at four post-secondary institutions across Canada that included a policy scan, student surveys, faculty surveys, student focus groups, faculty interviews and policymaker interviews. Many of the findings from this study have been reported elsewhere (Cassidy et al., 2014, 2016, 2017; Faucher et al., 2014, 2015). We present here a brief overview of findings related to the theme of leadership followed by two case studies that emerged from the faculty interviews conducted at two different universities. In the student focus groups, participants were asked: *What role should the faculty and university administration play in the solutions [to cyberbullying]?* and *How important is modelling [to preventing and curtailing cyberbullying]?* both of which yielded responses relating to leadership. In the faculty interviews, participants were also asked about modelling. Questions were also asked to both groups about the importance of policy and the role that policymakers play in preventing or curtailing cyberbullying.

The students in the focus groups emphasised the importance of peer leadership. 'The university' was characterised as being out of touch with the digital world and needing to 'get caught up'. As such, students needed to be involved in policymaking at the university, in addition to being role models for one another as to acceptable forms of online conduct.

In the policymaker interviews, some reference was made to leadership. For example, respondents at all four universities believed that leadership training was deeply needed for chairs, who might be exceptional academics but do not necessarily have the experience to deal with interpersonal and professional conflict.

> I think the role the administration needs to play is to ensure that the people who are called upon to be the leaders in those departments, i.e. the chairs, are properly trained to be able to deal with on a day-to-day basis those issues when they arise . . . so that they're able to bring leadership to bear when those kinds of differences of opinion start to crystallize.
>
> (Policy maker interview 140521_001, University A)

One respondent argued that administrative fairness should be a cornerstone of that training. Others discussed openness, transparency and timely responses to issues that arise. Several respondents also said that some department chairs may be conflict-averse and prefer to ignore problems rather than dealing with them immediately and directly, leading to bigger problems and negative repercussions as the issue spins out of control.

> I'm dealing with one case right now that if the Dean had acted on the request of the faculty member a while ago, he would be in a much better mindset right now. And I've let that be known because there's more complications that have come out of that.
>
> (Policymaker interview 140819_002, University B)

Respondents also referred to the role played by the administration in determining the culture of the university:

> I think the administration has the responsibility to provide a workplace that is a harassment-free, safe, pleasant place to work and if you're running a good university, I think you ought to be, not just be content with . . . meeting the strict requirements of the law, but actually would try to promote a workplace that is for everybody, is a good place to work.
>
> (Policymaker interview 140509_001, University A)

The faculty interviews made the most direct references to the theme of leadership and its importance in preventing and curtailing cyberbullying. Several decried the denial and inaction they had observed on the part of so-called leaders at their universities, using terms like 'head in the sand', 'a tendency to want to sweep it under the carpet', and 'shirking of responsibility by management'.

> I think it is still the obligation of leadership in organizations whether that's a university, a high school, or an elementary school. It's the responsibility

of the leadership to not be wilfully blind about this, to choose to take it seriously, to have policies and procedures that are clear, and to following through on those. . . . it's not about the punishment, it's about stopping.

(Faculty interview 130624_01, University B)

Faculty members were also strong proponents of modelling as a way to prevent and curtail cyberbullying – modelling by chairs and deans, and of instructors towards students.

I think it's really important for people who are in leadership roles at this institution to model always, like respectful forms of interaction with each other. It's really important and, you know, you should never, no matter how tempted you are, no matter how aggressive and horrible an email you may have just received, you should always respond in a very polite, respectful way.

(Faculty interview 140414_001, University D)

We turn now to two cases highlighted in the faculty interviews.

University case study 1

This case was mentioned by two colleagues at University B in separate interviews with two of the study's researchers. The first interviewee identified herself as Debbie, the second as Molly (both pseudonyms). Both were female faculty members who had been at their university for over ten years. They were two of five female colleagues who eventually filed a group personal harassment grievance against a male colleague (pseudonym Kevin) who persistently bullied and cyberbullied them over the course of several years. At the time of the interview, the grievance was under investigation and Kevin was off work for medical reasons.

Debbie explained that the harassment was an open secret for over a decade, but it was never discussed. The typical pattern was that a legitimate issue would be raised in a meeting and then followed up by Kevin in emails containing ad hominem attacks – accusations of lying, manipulating others, falsifying statistics about students and calling the women in the department incompetent and unprofessional. Molly recalled e-mails Kevin had written to students or other colleagues in cc implying that Molly had done something wrong, had not followed protocol, had made a huge mistake or a grave error in judgment, all of which were untrue according to Molly. Nonetheless, his e-mails made her look bad in front of students and colleagues. There were also threatening emails – a lengthy paper trail of evidence to support the allegations against Kevin.

A few years into this pattern, there was an attempt at a conflict resolution process, but it only made things worse – he used it as a weapon against them, stating that they had tried to get him fired and that he had to go to anger management counselling because of them. Kevin's behaviour went on for years.

Their direct superior (pseudonym Lucy) was repeatedly asked to intervene, although she was also being bullied by Kevin. Molly stated that Kevin was playing power games and going above Lucy's head. Molly said that Lucy also went to human resources, but that, too, led nowhere. Lucy's boss was asked to intervene to no avail. Kevin's behaviour went on for years. After another chain of revealing emails, Lucy's boss responded: 'well, we have to remember that we don't know Kevin's side of the story'. For Debbie, this was the final straw. And that was what led Debbie to finally file a grievance and she refused to accept or respond to any more emails from Kevin. As a result of years of negativity and lack of response, Debbie said: 'the energy in our department is completely frozen . . . no one is willing to bring forth new ideas for fear of being attacked, everyone has entered into self-protection mode'. Molly got to the point where the whole work climate was too much for her. It kept her from sleeping at night, left her feeling desperate, insecure and fearful. She contacted a lawyer who specialised in workplace harassment only to be told that they could not represent her as she was a member of a union and the collective agreement barred lawyers from being involved.

Neither Debbie nor Molly wanted Kevin to be fired. They merely wanted the harassment to stop, to have their complaints acknowledged and acted upon. Perhaps Kevin could have been given a different work assignment or offered early retirement. His presence in the department was clearly toxic. Looking back, Debbie remains angry about the failings of the leadership at her university.

> The administrator, my boss' boss . . . a lot of my anger has been directed towards her. She's now gone from the institution. But I still think that there were other senior managers that are still there that had least had some inkling of what was going on . . . they could choose to say this was a complete failure of leadership to allow this to escalate. . . . And we're going to change as a result of this.

For Molly, the fact that the university administration let this go on for so long without intervening is the worst part. 'Management could have intervened any number of years in the past before it even got to that complaint process.. . . But they didn't do anything, they swept it under the rug'. Molly stated that no offers of help, support or counselling were made by either the direct supervisor or human resources. 'It was a struggle to get it acknowledged that, hey, this is really happening. It was painful'.

University case study 2

The second case involves Jane (pseudonym), a professor and department chair at University D for 17 years. She was targeted by men's rights activists in her community due to her work on sexual violence and her public profile in speaking to the media about this issue.

Jane was involved in a university-community anti-rape social marketing campaign that involved some marketing materials and several media engagements where Jane explained the campaign. The campaign's slogan was interpreted as anti-male by some men's rights activists who manipulated it and produced a defamatory poster of Jane to post around town and created a blog where they called her a bigot. In addition, they sent her many nasty and threatening emails and took to social media to spread their message.

As a senior academic, Jane was able to see the situation in context of her work in social justice.

> I mean I think that . . . if you're a public person, and maybe if you deal with controversial topics, you might just always be a target of these kinds of things. I'm just not sure, I don't think that you can control the crazies of the world, right, so. . . . Um {Chuckle}. What was the impact? I mean in terms of these harassing emails, I have to say not much. . . . I think it's better not to take them too seriously . . . you're always gonna have those things happen to you. . . . I know it had an impact on my department because the support staff especially were quite concerned about the potential for someone to come into the building and to be disruptive or worse, so for a time our APO [administrative professional officer] made a decision to lock our door, so it did have an impact on my unit.

Jane, however, said that the response of the university's leadership was feeble, and they could have done much more to take a stand to support her and her work:

> It's awful but, so the university could have responded, you know. I got a lot of emails from people like the president or, you know, saying oh, this is terrible, let me know if I can do anything. But I think the university should have been willing to make a much more public statement saying that this was wrong, which they didn't.

Discussion and conclusions

Given the literature on leadership and its effect on those being led (Låftman et al., 2017; Page et al., 2021; Shapiro & Stefkovich, 2016; Starratt, 2011; Tiamboonprasert & Charoensukmongkol, 2020; Twale, 2018; among others), and from our own studies of the impact of educational leadership on cyberbullying behaviours of faculty, staff and students, what emerges is a clear relationship between the role of leadership in the educational environment and the experiences of bullying and cyberbullying within the institution.

If the leader is both personally and professionally ethical and serves as a role model in the leadership role, especially in their making of decisions in a transparent and fair manner when dealing with conflict, then faculty, staff and students are much more likely to feel they have been fairly treated and supported.

In fact, faculty themselves were strong proponents of modelling as a way to prevent and control cyberbullying. The ethical role-modelling of the leader also influenced students to act as role models of behaviour – for themselves as well as for each other.

Another takeaway point, and one consistent with the idea of role modelling ethical behaviour, is the need for the decision-making of the leader to occur within a collaborative school culture. Decisions should not reflect a one-way path, from the top down. The decision-making about settling both individual and collective intersectional conflict must also be secured within a collaborative culture of care. This process must begin with the collaborative development of policy and procedures for the collective whole, with input from both students and faculty alike. Such a development serves as the foundation for how decisions about conflicts such as bullying and cyberbullying are subsequently addressed.

The two case studies presented here in the university setting illustrate how situations can further deteriorate when appropriate leadership is not taken but also how positive outcomes can occur when problems are dealt with ethically, transparently and collaboratively, in a timely manner, and within a culture of care. Burying one's head in the sand or imposing a 'cone of silence' are ineffective responses. Especially in school/university settings, leaders have a legal and moral responsibility to provide a safe space not only for faculty and staff but also for students.

References

Angoff, H. D., & Barnhart, W. R. (2021). Bullying and cyberbullying among LGBQ and heterosexual youth from an intersectional perspective: Findings from the 2017 national youth risk behavior survey. *Journal of School Violence, 20*, 274–286.

Begley, P. T., & Stefkovich, J. (2007). Integrating values and ethics into post secondary teaching for leadership development: Principles, concepts, and strategies. *Journal of Educational Administration, 45*(4), 398–412. https://doi.org/10.1108/09578230710762427

Branson, C. M. (2014). If it isn't ethical, it isn't leadership. In C. M. Branson & S. J. Gross (Eds.), *Handbook of ethical educational leadership* (pp. 439–454). New York: Routledge. https://doi.org/10.4324/9780203747582

Campbell, M. (2016). Policies and procedures to address bullying at Australian universities. In H. Cowie & C.-A. Myers (Eds.), *Bullying among university students: Cross-national perspectives* (pp. 157–171). London: Routledge.

Cassidy, W., Brown, K., & Jackson, M. (2012). 'Under the radar': Educators and cyberbullying in schools. *School Psychology International, 33*(5), 520–532. https://doi.org/10.1177/0143034312445245

Cassidy, W., Faucher, C., & Jackson, M. (2013). Cyberbullying among youth: A comprehensive review of current international research and its implications and application to policy and practice, by invitation, in special international issue of *School Psychology International, 34*(6), 575–612. https://doi.org/10.1177/0143034313479697

Cassidy, W., Faucher, C., & Jackson, M. (2014). The dark side of the ivory tower: Cyberbullying of university faculty and teaching personnel. *Alberta Journal of Educational Research, 60*(2), 279–299.

Cassidy, W., Faucher, C., & Jackson, M. (2017). Adversity in university: Cyberbullying and its impacts on students, faculty and administrators. *International Journal of Environmental Research and Public Health*, *14*(8), e888. https://doi.org/10.3390/ijerph14080888

Cassidy, W., Faucher, C., & Jackson, M. (Eds.) (2019). *Cyberbullying at university in international contexts*. London: Routledge.

Cassidy, W., Jackson, M., & Faucher, C. (2016). Gender differences and cyberbullying towards faculty members in higher education. In R. Navarro, S. Yubero, & E. Larrañaga (Eds.), *Cyberbullying across the globe: Gender, family, and mental health* (pp. 79–98). Basel, Switzerland: Springer.

Cénat, J. M., Blais, M., Hébert, M., Lavoie, F., & Guerrier, M. (2015). Correlates of bullying in Québec high school students: The vulnerability of sexual-minority youth. *Journal of Affective Disorders*, *183*, 315–321. https://doi.org/10.1016/j.jad.2015.05.011

Cole, K., & Hassel, H. (Eds.) (2017). *Surviving sexism in academia: Strategies for feminist leadership*. New York: Routledge.

Cowie, H., & Myers, C.-A. (Eds.) (2016). *Bullying among university students: Cross-national perspectives*. London: Routledge.

DeSouza, E. R. (2011). Frequency rates and correlates of contrapower harassment in higher education. *Journal of Interpersonal Violence*, *26*, 158–188. https://doi.org/10.1177/0886260510362878

Driver, J. (2019). Faculty members who are bullies. In W. Cassidy, C. Faucher, & M. Jackson (Eds.), *Cyberbullying at university in international contexts* (pp. 212–214). London: Routledge.

Farrington, D. P., & Ttofi, M. M. (2009). Reducing school bullying: Evidence-based implications for policy. *Crime and Justice*, *38*, 281–345. https://doi.org/10.1086/599198

Faucher, C., Cassidy, W., & Jackson, M. (2019). Power in the tower: The gendered nature of cyberbullying among university students and faculty at Canadian universities. In W. Cassidy, C. Faucher, & M. Jackson (Eds.), *Cyberbullying at university in international contexts* (pp. 66–79). London: Routledge.

Faucher, C., Jackson, M., & Cassidy, W. (2014). Cyberbullying among university students: Gendered experiences, impacts, and perspectives. *Education Research International*. https://doi.org/10.1155/2014/698545

Faucher, C., Jackson, M., & Cassidy, W. (2015). When on-line exchanges byte: An examination of the policy environment governing cyberbullying at the university level. *Canadian Journal of Higher Education*, *45*(1), 102–121.

Ferber, A. L. (2018). "Are you willing to die for this work?" Public targeted online harassment in higher education. *Gender & Society*, *32*(3), 301–320. https://doi.org/10.1177/0891243218766831

Gilmour, R. J., Bhandar, D., Heer, J., & Ma, M. C. K. (Eds.) (2012). *"Too Asian?": Racism, privilege, and post-secondary education*. Toronto: Between the Lines.

Heffernan, T., & Bosetti, L. (2021). Incivility: The new type of bullying in higher education. *Cambridge Journal of Education*. Advance online publication. https://doi.org/10.1080/0305764X.2021.1897524

Hinduja, S., & Patchin, J. W. (2012). *School Climate 2.0: Preventing cyberbullying and sexting one classroom at a time*. Thousand Oaks, CA: Corwin.

Hollis, L. P. (2012). *Bully in the ivory tower: How aggression and incivility erode American higher education*. Wilmington, DE: Patricia Berkly LCC.

Jackson, M., Cassidy, W., & Brown, K. N. (2010). "you were born ugly and youl die ugly too": Cyber-bullying as relational aggression. *In Education*, *15*(2), 68–82.

Låftman, S. B., Östberg, V., & Modin, B. (2017). School leadership and cyberbullying – A multilevel analysis. *International Journal of Environmental Research and Public Health*, *14*, 1226–1235. https://doi.org/10.3390/ijerph14101226

Lampman, C. (2012). Women faculty at risk: U.S. professors report on their experiences with student incivility, bullying, aggression, and sexual attention. *NASPA Journal of Women in Higher Education, 5*, 184–208.

Leisring, P. L. (2019). Cyberbullying in romantic relationships: A review of research in the United States. In G. W. Giumetti & R. M. Kowalski (Eds.), *Cyberbullying in schools, workplaces, and romantic relationships: The many lenses and perspectives of electronic mistreatment* (pp. 135–149). New York: Routledge.

Miller, G., Miller, V., Marchel, C., Moro, R., Kaplan, B., Clark, C., & Musilli, S. (2019). Academic violence/bullying: Application of Bandura's eight moral disengagement strategies to higher education. *Employee Responsibilities and Rights Journal, 31*, 47–59. https://doi.org/10.1007/s10672-018-9327-7

Mishna, F., Regehr, C., Lacombe-Duncan, A. Daciuk, J., Fearing, G., & Van Wert, M. (2018). Social media, cyber-aggression and student mental health on a university campus. *Journal of Mental Health, 27*(3), 222–229. https://doi.org/10.1080/09638237.2018.1437607

Navarro, J. N., & Jasinski, J. L. (2013). Why girls? Using routine activities theory to predict cyberbullying experiences between girls and boys. *Women and Criminal Justice, 23*(4), 286–303.

Noddings, N. (2005). *The challenge to care in schools: An alternative approach to education* (2nd ed.). New York: Teachers College Press.

Noddings, N. (2006). Educational leaders as caring teachers. *School Leadership & Management, 26*(4), 339–345. https://doi.org/10.1080/13632430600886848

O'Connor, K., Drouin, M., Davis, J., & Thompson, H. (2018). Cyberbullying, revenge porn and the mid-sized university: Victim characteristics, prevalence and students' knowledge of university policy and reporting procedures. *Higher Education Quarterly, 72*, 344–359.

Page, M. B., Bishop, K., & Etmanski, C. (2021). Community belonging and values-based leadership as the antidote to bullying and incivility. *Societies, 11*, 29–36. https://doi.org/10.3390/soc11020029

Rivers, I. (2016). Homophobic and transphobic bullying in universities. In H. Cowie & C.-A. Myers (Eds.), *Bullying among university students: Cross-national perspectives* (pp. 48–60). London: Routledge.

Roberge, G. D. (2011). Countering school bullying: An analysis of policy content in Ontario and Saskatchewan. *International Journal of Education Policy and Leadership, 6*(5), 1–14. https://doi.org/10.22230/ijepl.2011v6n5a305

Sallee, M. W., & Diaz, C. R. (2012). Sexual harassment, racist jokes, and homophobic slurs: When bullies target identity groups. In J. Lester (Ed.), *Workplace bullying in higher education* (pp. 41–59). New York: Routledge.

Sergiovanni, T. J. (2005). The virtues of leadership. *The Educational Forum, 69*, 112–123.

Shapiro, J. P., & Stefkovich, J. A. (2016). *Ethical leadership and decision making in education: Applying theoretical perspectives to complex dilemmas* (4th ed.). New York: Routledge.

Smith, P. K., Kupferberg, A., Mora-Merchan, J. A., Samara, M., Bosley, S., & Osborn, R. (2012). A content analysis of school anti-bullying policies: A follow-up after six years. *Educational Psychology in Practice, 28*(1), 47–70. https://doi.org/10.1080/02667363.2011.639344

Smith, P. K., Sundaram, S., Spears, B. A., Blaya, C., Schäfer, M., & Sandhu, D. (Eds.) (2018). *Bullying, cyberbullying and student well-being in schools: Comparing European, Australian and Indian perspectives*. Cambridge: Cambridge University Press.

Snyder-Yuly, J. L., Patton, T. O., & Gomez, S. L. (2021). Welcome to academia, expect cyberbullying: Contrapower and incivility in higher education. In L. Ramos Salazar (Ed.), *The handbook of research on cyberbullying and online harassment in the workplace* (pp. 242–265). Hershey, PA: IGI Global.

Starratt, J. (2011). Preparing transformative educators for the work of leading schools in a multicultural, diverse, and democratic society. *Counterpoints, 409,* 131–136. www.jstor.org/stable/42981301

Taylor, S. (2012). Workplace bullying: Does tenure change anything? The example of a Midwestern research university. In J. Lester (Ed.), *Workplace bullying in higher education* (pp. 23–40). New York: Routledge.

Tiamboonprasert, W., & Charoensukmongkol, P. (2020). Effect of ethical leadership on workplace cyberbullying exposure and organizational commitment. *Journal of Behavioral Science, 15*(3), 85–100. https://so06.tci-thaijo.org/index.php/IJBS/article/view/243966

Tuana, N. (2014). An ethical leadership developmental framework. In C. M. Branson & S. J. Gross (Eds.), *Handbook of ethical educational leadership* (pp. 153–175). New York: Routledge. https://doi.org/10.4324/9780203747582

Twale, D. J. (2018). *Understanding and preventing faculty-on-faculty bullying: A psycho-social-organizational approach.* New York: Routledge.

Veletsianos, G., Houlden, S., Hodson, J., & Gosse, C. (2018). Women scholars' experiences with online harassment and abuse: Self-protection, resistance, acceptance, and self-blame. *New Media & Society, 20*(12), 4689–4708. https://doi.org/10.1177/1461444818781324

Wright, M. (2016). Cyber victimization on college campuses: Longitudinal associations with suicidal ideation, depression, and anxiety. *Criminal Justice Review, 41*(2), 190–203.

5   Racism on Campus

Gella Richards

'No Irish, No Blacks, No Dogs' was a typical sign in local establishments that people of ethnic minority backgrounds reported being 'greeted' with when they arrived in the UK last century (pre-1970s). This did not equate with the type of welcome large groups of migrants from African-Caribbean Commonwealth diaspora were expecting on their entry into the UK. They were responding to an invitation from the British Government to come to the motherland to help rebuild post-war 'broken Britain'. These groups saw it as their duty to act on a request to help rebuild the UK by contributing to its much-depleted workforce and perceived this invitation as coming from their then Queen. Hence, they expected to be welcomed, appreciated and accepted when they landed in the UK.

Fast forward to the 21st century, regardless of modern national legislation and universities' local diversity, inclusion and widening participation policies, African-Caribbean Black students and staff, like their migrant ancestors, are still subjected to racism. One major difference between the generations is that the variety of channels for indicating prejudice, distaste and even hostility directed towards a racial group has immensely increased and diversified. Unfortunately, the university campus is no different: *'Racism exists on our campuses . . .'* (#callitracism). This seems ironic since universities are typically seen as, not only a place of academic learning but also an opportunity for a broadening of the mind and fighting against social injustices. Campus life at university holds the promise for inspiration and an outstanding formative experience for young adults and the opportunity for staff to be part of that experience. Unlike school and other previous learning places which were typically chosen by individuals who were not the direct recipients of the service, students have personally selected their university to be their alma mater. Likewise, staff have trained and studied for long periods of time to be able to engage (even endure) many aspects of the selection process for an academic position at their chosen place of work. Students' motivations are heavily ignited and energised by the environment. Staff are excited about influencing developing minds, imparting their knowledge with students and having pleasant relationships with their colleagues. However, for a notable number of ethnic minority students and staff, their choice of higher education institution has exposed them to unexpected and unwanted

DOI:10.4324/9781003258605-7

encounters. Many of their feelings about their university are outstanding for the wrong reasons: racism on campus.

A UK government-funded project that responded to findings highlighted by an Equality and Human Rights Commission inquiry revealed that:

- *24% of students from an ethnic minority background said they had experienced racial harassment; 1 in 20 students said racism had made them leave their studies.*
- *More than a quarter of staff said they had experienced racist name-calling, insults and jokes; 3 in 20 said racial harassment caused them to leave their jobs.*

(AdvanceHE, 2020, p. 1)

Incidental observations and reports from ethnic minority (mostly Black) students and staff at various universities and different types of programmes provide additional personal testimonies on the ground. For instance, Black students have recalled that they specifically chose a university, not only because of its attractive programme but indications that it welcomed diversity and encouraged inclusion. Yet there is an underrepresentation of Black students in some of the coveted programmes such as STEM and medicine, especially at top-ranking universities. These are disciplines built on 'objectivity'. So, aspects of inclusivity may be seen as obscuring and distracting from the focus: 'facts', 'figures and 'QED'. However, consideration of factors such as the (racial) sample of patients involved in medical randomised controlled trials (RCTs) is typically under reported, which could have implications for the results or treatment protocol. Medical students are given the impression that treatment-resistant conditions are because of the patient, rather than the medication. Indeed, Nobel laureate, James Watson, discoverer of the DNA structure with Francis Crick, questioned the intelligence of Black people. Unsurprisingly, there are Black students who feel that the contributions of Black scientists, researchers and clinicians have been neglected in the teaching of STEM and medical programmes.

It could be expected that humanities and social sciences programmes, due to the nature of their topics, can escape the charge of contributing to racism on campus. Admittedly, there are specific programmes or modules that focus on subjects around race and seemingly unflinchingly deal with racism. Nevertheless, students on such programmes/modules have complained about the restricted consideration of such issues and the understocking in the library of (the few) relevant texts. Typically, books are expensive for students to purchase due to many originating from outside of the UK (e.g. America). Staff on such modules typically were visiting lecturers, making it difficult for students to have conversations with them outside of their paid hours. Ironically, modules that claimed to focus on diversity and injustice were many times 'taught' by permanent staff who were from a privileged racial position. Although 'well meaning', they were perceived by ethnic minority students as finding it difficult to facilitate group discussions when heated debates increased in relation to aspects of exclusion and racism were called out during the class. The inability to comprehend the impact of such discrimination based on race has the potential to generate a divided class, where the lecturer, by lack of appropriate intervention, is signalling to the class that nothing is wrong, and simultaneously marginalising the hurt and damage experienced by the Black students. It may be perceived that when ethnic minority students and staff highlight racism, they are using the 'race card' to gain them some favouritism, exception or simply 'attention'. Nevertheless, when an empathetic staff member from a different race, typically (though not always) white, highlights the injustice experienced by their ethnic minority students or colleagues, it is given more credence. However, white colleagues are not always able to recognise acts of racism, especially when they involve subtle microaggressions that are crafted so that ethnic minority recipients' identification of racism can be doubted or minimised.

Due to the consequences for campus perpetrators if they are caught, their 'signals' of racism may be more complex, compared to the blatant unchallenged racist messages and acts faced by previous ethnic minority generations. Hence, although the racists' aims remain the same in both eras, that is, to hurt, exclude, alienate or vilify, at university, both the different media and subtleties of expression have evolved. Universities are attractive because of their renowned ability to develop skills of sophisticated learning at the highest level. Therefore, it may come as no surprise, that the racist tactics are similarly subtle, complex, deceptive and indeed ambiguous. And as research has shown, this can often be 'passed off' as banter or a bit of 'fun' and not as serious an issue as is being alleged. Recipients of racism may even sometimes 'feel' it but not be able to articulate it in a way that is convincing to others. One of the reasons is that in many cases (crafty) racist acts have been honed prior to the perpetrators arriving on campus within the sector-wide Equality, Diversity and Inclusion (EDI) priorities. Nevertheless, eventually, ethnic minority students and staff do speak out but are aware not to make their complaints too passionate or too emotional since they are likely to be conveying their experience to an authority figure in the university who shares the same powerful racial group as the person they are complaining about. An academic institution acts on evidence-based facts' and not 'feelings'.

However, this would be a somewhat unbalanced and pessimistic commentary if it neglected what is being done to try to combat racism on campus. There are many initiatives, and some have arisen directly from the #MeToo, #Icantbreathe, #blacklivesmatter movements along with the more recent #callitracism that is championed particularly by the university community. The apparent recent flourishing of all these important movements, and others, could give the impression that a publicised movement is needed before action is taken. On the contrary, universities and their campuses have tried for many decades, including the past century, to tackle racism on their campuses, aiming to engender a rewarding learning experience for all their students. A cynic may add that the financial relevance should not be understated in these endeavours. Having personally experienced racism at a highly prestigious London public school from a young age and having been the only Black pupil in the whole of the school, it was refreshing to attend an event by another highly prestigious

London institution of academic learning. One of the reasons for this was simply that its event's title bluntly captured what many generations of Black students have been continuously asking universities up and down the country: 'Why Isn't my Professor Black?' I decided to select this talk by my own alma mater, University College London ('UCL'), to exemplify that academic and training institutions can only progress their fight against racism on campus if they address issues that their ethnic minority students and staff are asking. This in itself is different from the typical university that many witness where the universities answer their *own* posed questions and decide their own agendas about ethnic minority staff and students without giving those groups a seat at the table, thereby continuing to silence and ignore both knowledgeable Black professionals and 'experts by experience'. At the UCL event, every main panel member was Black, apart from one. Ironically the 'guest' of the panel was the representative of the overall UCL-hosted event – a white man who was UCL's provost and president. To some extent, this could be seen as a continuation of the power imbalance between white and Black academics within universities. However, it can also be welcomed as an example of attempts to recognise the impact of the support that a world-stage academic institution can have by supporting the importance of discussing racism on campus.

Of course, many non-ethnic minority staff in positions much lower in status than the president of UCL have relentlessly challenged discrimination based on race and formed partnerships with their ethnic minority peers and students to deal with such matters at local level. Indeed, some have even gone out on a limb to highlight campus injustices. Nevertheless, the hosting of the event by UCL signals one of their very public messages about dealing with racism on campus by gradually admitting their own part in this process and seeking the views of recipients to enable them to continue their strategy towards eradicating it (UCL, 2014). UCL recognises that they have a long way to go since their history is steeped in slavery and the legacy of institutionalised racism and unconscious bias. The debate was also exhilarating and enriching as it allowed the views of Black students to be heard and appreciated. This included the astonishment of one Black student when she became aware of a (female) Black professor (of which there were under 20) for the first time in her academic journey. Many simply stated how grateful they were for the debate and the recognition of the need to expose this as an important issue. Many participants were startled by a student who referred to herself using a derogatory racial slur to describe how unpalatable she was made to feel as a Black student. This video is an excellent teaching resource to engender debates on racism in academia and on campus or at the minimum, an opportunity to start a debate.

Since it is accepted that racism does exist on campus, much more needs to be done to combat this, not least because of the devasting effect it has on students and staff alike. The impact of racism on the mental health and well-being of ethnic minority staff and students has implications for their academic success and requires a safe place for them to share their experiences, and equally for these to be valued and believed. Additionally, it can have psychologically damaging consequences for non-ethnic minority colleagues and students. By observing such problems, they may divert a lot of their energies to addressing injustice or feel helpless to do anything, even though they recognise actions by others as distasteful and harmful. Some white students have disclosed that they feel angry that the racism they identify is reminiscent of their own previous experience of bullying and ostracism because they were 'different' and included cyberbullying and trolling – aspects of which are explored in this book. Other less-aware white students have not noticed any racial discrimination or perhaps it has not even occurred to them to think about race. It is universities' responsibility to provide equal opportunities for all its stakeholders (especially students and staff) and to enable them to feel safe. Neither students nor staff should feel compromised or worried that calling out racism on campus will result in any type of penalty. Perhaps these experiences might be used as a learning tool for the University and any perpetrators involved.

The chapters in this book provide refreshing, yet hard-hitting perspectives on racism and other forms of discrimination in higher education. They shine a light on some of the very important EDI areas that need addressing, especially since most staff and students who have experienced racial harassment do not report it (AdvanceHE, 2020). This under-reporting gives the wrong impression that the campus experience is devoid of barriers for racialised minority staff and students to achieve their full potential. It may explain a finding from AdvanceHE (2020) that many universities seriously underestimate the prevalence of racial harassment and are over-confident in their complaint-handling processes. Fortunately, taken together in this volume, the chapters spin the coin for both sides of the debate on the challenges of all forms of discrimination on campus, so revealing problems and sharing solutions that have worked, or have the potential to approach the problem head-on. Partly pessimistic, yes, but mostly a move to a future with a better experience for all students and staff on campus, and in some cases, beyond.

References

AdvanceHE (2020). Tackling racism on campus: Raising awareness and creating the conditions for confident conversations. www.advance-he.ac.uk/tackling-racism-campus (Accessed 31 July 2022)

University College London (UCL) (2014). Why isn't my professor Black? www.youtube.com/watch?v=mBqgLK9dTk4 (Accessed 31 July 2022)

6 Homophobic and transphobic online harassment

Young people in Scotland during the COVID-19 pandemic

Ian Rivers, Jordan Daly and Liam Stevenson

On Friday, 20 March 2020, all schools across the UK closed in an attempt to stem the rate of COVID-19 infection. In England, the decision to close schools had been announced in a televised broadcast only two days earlier by Prime Minister Boris Johnson. In Scotland, on 19 March, First Minister Nicola Sturgeon announced that schools would close the following day. This sudden closure of schools occurred at a time when students were preparing for key national examinations, and much has been written about the educational harms caused by the ensuing lockdown and the so-called pivot to online and remote learning for which the UK's educations systems were ill-prepared (Timmins, 2021).

The 'pivot' to online learning for many schools, colleges and universities did, of course, bring to the fore digital inequalities that are often obscured by other metrics. These digital inequalities are linked, undoubtedly, to the social and economic inequalities that exist within our communities, and we saw reports of teachers (particularly in primary schools) delivering worksheets to many pupils' homes to ensure that learning continued (Moss et al., 2020). We also saw the curtailment of learning in certain practical subjects (Physical Education, Drama, Music, Design and Technology, and Science) due to fears about the spread of COVID-19 (Howard et al., 2021). As well as the disruption to learning, it also became apparent that schools, colleges and universities had and continue to have a wider social role to play in supporting pupils, students and their families, and this supportive role was lost. Lockdown also threw into relief various other harms that affect particular sub-sets of young people, including sexual minority and gender diverse young people (i.e. those who identify as lesbian, gay, bisexual, trans, queer, intersex or those who identify as non-heterosexual, non-cisgender or asexual – hereafter referred to as LGBTQI+). At the beginning of the pandemic, many of these young people were left without the community resources, groups and support services that had been previously available to them. In the first few months of the pandemic, we saw a massive shift in these services too, moving from face-to-face to online outreach and support. For many organisations, this move was labour intensive and relied on the young people they supported having online access – again throwing into relief the digital inequalities that currently exist in our societies. For LGBTQI+ young

DOI:10.4324/9781003258605-8

people, many of the resources available to them pre-pandemic were provided by the third sector (charities and voluntary organisations) and its ability to move online was contingent on continued and, in some cases, enhanced funding from local authorities and national government agencies at a time when resources were being stretched and prioritised to meet the health crisis.

LGBTQI+ youth and COVID-19

The challenges young LGBTQI+ people faced during the pandemic are clearly demonstrated by AKT's (formerly the Albert Kennedy Trust) report on youth homelessness, published in 2021 (Bhandal & Horwood, 2021). Based upon data collected from 161 young LGBTQI+ people (aged 16–25 years) between July 2020 and January 2021, 20% reported having been threatened or frightened by a romantic partner before they became homeless, two-thirds (66%) reported being repeatedly belittled by family members and 61% reporting being frightened or threatened by family members before they left home. Of those who were aware of the social and community services that were available to them, only 49% of the homeless young people surveyed had sought housing support, 40% sought mental health services support, and 32% benefits and welfare support. Worryingly, 17% reported accessing no services or support at all whilst being homeless.

Homelessness is, of course, an extreme example of the repercussions of LGBTQI+ intolerance, however, US studies have shown that LGBTQI+ youth who lived in less-supportive households during COVID-19 reported increased mental health concerns (Hawke et al., 2021; Salerno et al., 2021). Additionally, those with intersectional identities such as young people of colour, those from low socio-economic backgrounds and homeless youth also found themselves without the necessary support services, including mental health services, they most needed (Ormisiton & Williams, 2022). According to Ormisiton and Williams, while the eventual reopening of schools, colleges and universities resulted in LGBTQI+ young people receiving the support they required (spending less time isolated from others and more time away from unsupportive families), it also saw the return of anxieties relating to 'school-based trauma' such as bullying and harassment (see Fish et al., 2020). Yet the question is posed, did school-based or rather school-related traumas such as bullying and harassment ever go away? Even before the pandemic, our increased reliance upon and access to electronic forms of communication at home and at school had already resulted in those behaviours that were once apparent in the schoolyard or in the corridors or hallways of school buildings finding expression through electronic forms of communication, such as mobile/cell phones and social media.

Online harassment: what we know

Technology as a medium for bullying or harassment has been a feature of our lives since we were first able to network computers, send email, or send text messages via mobile/cell phones (Rivers & Noret, 2010). Within education, it has been shown that, with internet connectivity and the increase in circulation of mobile/cell phones among young people, there was a concomitant increase in online bullying and harassment. For example, in a cross-cultural study of Australian and Swiss students (mean age 13.8 years), Perren et al. (2010) found a significant overlap in experiences of 'traditional' offline bullying and so-called cyberbullying. Notably, their findings also suggested that even when controlling for exposure to traditional forms of bullying, those students who had experienced cyberbullying also reported significantly higher rates of depressive symptoms, a finding that has since been replicated several times over.

In addition to Perren et al.'s (2010) cross-cultural study showing the impact of cyberbullying upon mental health, we have, over the years, seen several reports of young people attempting to take their own lives after experiencing online bullying or harassment, and especially LGBTQI+ young people (Cénat et al., 2015).

For LGBTQI+ young people, Hinduja and Patchin's (2020) study suggests that they are more likely to report both offline and online bullying when compared to their heterosexual and cisgender peers. For example, in 2019, they surveyed 4,500 students from across the United States and found that 87% of LGBTQI+ had been bullied at some point at school, with 52% reporting having been bullied online (the figures were 72% and 35%, respectively, for heterosexual and cisgender peers). When this data was broken down further, they found that 'non-heterosexual' males were most likely to report being bullied at school (73.9%) and online (30%). Among transgender young people, the rate of online bullying was slightly higher – 33.3%. Of course, Hinduja and Patchin's study asked participants to report on a 'global' estimate of being bullied at school and online, rather than provide a recent estimate (in the last school term, month/30 days, or week). Thus, while rates of bullying were higher than those reported in other studies, a distinct trend remained with LGBTQI+ young people far more likely to report having been bullied at school or online than their heterosexual or cisgender peers.

So, why is online bullying potentially much more damaging than other forms of bullying? First, there is the issue of isolation as well as the fact that messages convey a meaning that is often personal to the individual. Second, those messages can be received at any time – day or night – there is no respite, and they can be anonymous. Finally, the lack of social filters can intensify the behaviours of perpetrators, pushing them to more extreme threats of violence or abuse. Indeed, Hinduja and Patchin (2008) argued that virtual worlds are spaces where the rules governing the material world no longer apply and thus afford perpetrators licence to express implicit attitudes and beliefs that they would not normally air offline.

Bullying and the COVID-19 pandemic

The COVID-19 pandemic was a global public health crisis. At the time of writing this chapter, it was estimated that nearly 6 million people had died because of contracting COVID. In the UK, the death toll was nearly 161,000.

In 2020, as governments around the world began to understand the highly infectious nature of COVID, it became clear that the only way to slow or stem the rate of infection was to enter one or more periods of lockdown, where as many people as possible stayed at home, and schools, businesses (especially hospitality and travel) and recreational venues closed. Lockdown also saw a global shift in the usage of online platforms for communication to keep industry and education going. With the move online came the threat of an increase in online bullying as those social filters (mentioned previously) began to erode gradually.

Vaillancourt and colleagues studied the impact of COVID-19 on bullying among a sample of 6,578 Canadian students in grades 4 (9–10 years of age) to 12 (17–18 years of age). As one might expect, these students reported higher rates of physical, verbal and social bullying pre-pandemic. However, notably there was little change in rates of cyberbullying. Overall, Vaillancourt et al.'s data indicated that both pre-pandemic and during the pandemic, despite changes in prevalence, the same patterns of behaviour emerged. Girls reported bullying more than boys, younger students reported higher levels of bullying involvement than older students, with LGBTQI+ students reporting more experiences of bullying than their cisgender or heterosexual peers (Vaillanocurt et al., 2021). By way of contrast, Bacher-Hicks et al. (2021) found that both traditional forms of school bullying and cyberbullying reduced during the pandemic, though the reduction in cyberbullying was less pronounced. Like Ormisiton and Williams (2022), they too argued that the return to face-to-face teaching for some young people resulted in a return to pre-pandemic levels of bullying.

In India, Jain et al. (2020) compared and contrasted the experiences of offline and online bullying for 256 students before the pandemic hit (October 2019) with those of 118 students during lockdown (June 2020). Results indicated that, in October 2019 and June 2020 experiences of offline bullying, perceptions to others' opinions of self, and the frequency with which students made social media posts predicted online bullying. However, among students surveyed in October 2019, a tendency to interact with strangers online, the number of hours spent on social media and the propensity to start a relationship online were also significant contributing factors. Among those students surveyed in June 2020, several additional factors were highlighted. These included sharing opinions online, preferring to post social media content via Instagram, using gaming platforms and the number of games played. Two other factors also affected susceptibility to online bullying: age and sexual orientation. Overall, the authors argued that the pandemic had increased the likelihood of young people reporting online bullying as they spent more time interacting with others via social media and gaming platforms and sharing personal information.

LGBTQI+ young people in Scotland: online harassment during lockdown

As mentioned previously, while lockdown and the closure of schools, colleges and universities brought respite in terms of some forms of bullying that take place in physical spaces; it did not bring respite for those who experienced online bullying and harassment. From April to June 2020, TIE (Time for Inclusive Education), Scotland's inclusive education charity, undertook a national survey of young people (aged 12–24 years) to determine the impact of lockdown upon well-being and mental health. Across six weeks and with extensive networking and online campaigns through Facebook and Instagram, a questionnaire was distributed to young people through schools, youth organisations and networks, university and college societies and clubs, and parent and carer groups. Responses were received from young people living in all of Scotland's 32 local authorities. After data cleansing, 1,015 responses were useable (cleansing included identifying duplicates as well as spoof or spam responses). Additional care was taken to ensure the robustness of the data after a Twitter campaign to disrupt the survey and corrupt the data was uncovered, with any suspect responses being removed from the final dataset. Lastly, for the purposes of the final report (see Time for Inclusive Education, 2020), and this chapter, participants who requested that their data not be used for publication were also removed.

In terms of demographics, 59.3% of respondents identified as female and 35.7% as male with 2.9% identifying as non-binary and 1.8% preferring not to say. In terms of education, 74% were at secondary school, 18% at university or college and a further 8% reported no longer being in education. Finally, 52.1% of respondents identified primarily as heterosexual while 35% identified as LGBTQI+. A further 25 respondents indicated that their identities include secondary characteristics (e.g. transgender and bisexual), and 10.4% preferred not to disclose their sexual orientations and/or gender identities.

Overall, 47% of all respondents indicated that they had seen or experienced online bullying during lockdown, with over half reporting that they believed this was more than usual. Fifty-nine per cent reported that they had witnessed an increase in prejudice-based posts, comments, and/or attitudes online, with 45% having witnessed racism and 36% witnessing homophobia. Other forms of prejudice that appeared online included misogyny (21%), biphobia (17%), transphobia (26%), sexism (20%), the shaming of those with additional support needs (8%) or a disability (15%), abuse relating to religion or belief (13%), asylum/refugee status (6%), being Gypsy/Traveller (5%), or care experienced (4%). Other forms of abuse also reported included sectarianism (8%), body or appearance shaming (34%) and abuse relating to socio-economic status (13%). In terms of emotional well-being, 39% of respondents indicated that the closure of schools, colleges and universities had negatively affected them. Prior to lockdown, 64% of respondents said their emotional well-being had been positive, however, because of lockdown, this figure decreased to 27%.

When comparing the responses from heterosexual and LGBTQI+ young people (N = 352), prior to lockdown 16% of LGBTQI+ young people in Scotland reported experiencing bullying 'most days', with 37% reporting that it happened 'sometimes', and 26% reporting it happening 'once or twice'. Only a small number (3%) said it happened 'every day'; however, only 18% said that they had not been bullied at school, college or university. Among heterosexual young people in Scotland, 1% reported being bullied 'every day', 4% 'most days', 24% 'sometimes', 30% 'once or twice', with 41% reporting that there had never been bullied at school, college or university.

Once lockdown began, a very different picture began to emerge. Sixty per cent of LGBTQI+ respondents said they had experienced and/or seen online bullying during lockdown (30% had 'seen' online bullying, 19% had 'seen and experienced' it, 11% 'experienced' it, and 40% reported they had not witnessed any online bullying). Among heterosexual respondents, only 38% had seen and/or experienced online bullying (27% had 'seen' it, 7% had 'seen and experienced' it, and 4% had 'experienced' it). Seventy-six per cent of LGBTQI+ respondents felt that there had been more online bullying during lockdown; this compares with 49% of heterosexual respondents.

In terms of emotional well-being, during lockdown, 52% of LGBTQI+ respondents indicated that they had been affected negatively by school, college and university closures. Among heterosexual respondents, this figure was 34%. Prior to lockdown, 52% of LGBTQI+ respondents rated their emotional well-being as positive, with 22% reporting it as 'Ok'. However, after lockdown began only 13% reported their emotional well-being was positive and 18% said it was 'Ok'. Among heterosexual respondents, prior to lockdown 72% said their emotional well-being was positive, with 14% reporting it was 'Ok'. However, this too dropped during lockdown, with only 36% reporting their emotional well-being was positive and 24% saying it was 'Ok'.

Of the LGBTQI+ young people in Scotland who reported having witnessed an increase in prejudice-based posts, comments and/or attitudes online, overall 55% reported witnessing racism and 56% said they had seen homophobia. Other forms of prejudice they witnessed included misogyny (35%), biphobia (36%), transphobia (48%), sexism (32%), the shaming of those with additional support needs (11%) or a disability (18%), abuse relating to religion or belief (18%), asylum/refugee status (9%), being Gypsy/Traveller (6%) or care experienced (4%). Other forms of abuse also reported included sectarianism (18%), body or appearance shaming (45%) and abuse relating to socio-economic status (19%).

As a comparator, of those who identified as heterosexual, 41% reported witnessing racism and 25% said they had seen homophobia. In terms of other forms of prejudice, 16% reported seeing misogyny, 6% reported seeing biphobia and 14% transphobia. Thirteen per cent said they had seen sexism online, and 6% had witnessed the shaming of those with additional support needs or a disability (13%). Twelve per cent reported seeing abuse relating to religion or belief online and 4% saw abuse relating to asylum/refugee status, being Gypsy/Traveller, or care experienced. Reports of sectarianism were also recorded (7%), as were reports of body or appearance shaming (28%) and abuse relating to socio-economic status (10%).

On most measures, participants who identified as girls and young women witnessed much more online abuse than those who identified as boys and young men, except for homophobia where the rates were 36% and 37%, respectively.

As we noted earlier in this chapter, the move to online service provision by many of the organisations that supported LGBTQI+ youth during lockdown was a mammoth undertaking, and LGBTQI+ young people in Scotland were asked if they had accessed any of the online support services that were available. The results suggested a very low take-up of those services supporting health and well-being with 12% of LGBTQI+ young people reporting that they had tried to access them and 20% saying they had used them. Among heterosexual young people, the rates were 6% and 8%, respectively.

Overall, the findings indicate that there was a significant shift in young people's self-reported emotional well-being once lockdown began, with more young people indicating that their emotional well-being has suffered as a consequence of the closure of schools, colleges and universities, and the move to online service provision. Concomitantly, during lockdown, young people in Scotland reported that they had experienced and/or witnessed more online bullying than before and that such bullying included comments relating to a broad range of personal characteristics with race, sexual orientation, body shape and physical appearance being the most highly cited. However, it is notable that across the further and higher education sector (colleges and universities); we did not see dropout rates change significantly due to perceived increases in bullying or harassment: retention rates improved, possibly because of the lack of viable alternatives such as employment opportunities (HESA, 2022).

Among LGBTQI+ young people, in particular, reports relating to the types of online bullying they witnessed during lockdown were markedly different from heterosexual young people. This was particularly stark when it came to reports of homophobia (56% vs. 25%), biphobia (36% vs. 6%), transphobia (48% vs. 14%), misogyny (35% vs. 16%) and sexism (32% vs. 13%). It has been suggested that one of the reasons why there can be such a stark contrast in terms of reports of these and other personal characteristics (e.g. additional, support needs, disability, body shape or appearance, and even religion or belief) relates to the heightened sensitivity many LGBTQI+ young people have to prejudicial attitudes, social rejection and structural stigma (see Pachankis et al., 2014; Haztenbuehler, 2016; Russell & Fish, 2016). Furthermore, we know that the veil of humour or the label 'banter' often results in a failure by many people to attribute underlying sentiments as prejudicial or harmful, especially when they relate to sex and gender stereotypes (Pettett, 2007; Athanases & Comar, 2008; Mallet et al., 2016). Therefore, it should not be surprising that online posts or interactions that are perceived by LGBTQI+ young people as bullying and harassment or inappropriate use of language are not recognised or reported as such by others.

Recovering from the pandemic: implications for LGBTQI+ young people

The reopening of schools, colleges and universities threw into relief the harms that were caused by the pandemic. In addition to the significant loss of life, and the emergence of chronic conditions linked to COVID-19, it was apparent that there were wider social harms that were not just related to a loss of learning but also a loss of income for many families, and increased levels of anxiety as people began to interact with one another again. Recognising that the pandemic had an impact on the physical and mental health of Scotland's young people, the Scottish Government introduced a range of measures to assist young people, their families and teachers rebuild their physical well-being and, especially, their mental health through the *Mental Health Transition and Recovery Plan* (Scottish Government, 2020). This plan included support to ensure that local authorities were able to provide counselling to young people through schools, and dedicated support for those young people who were deemed vulnerable or had complex additional support needs. Support also included the provision of art-based therapies, and hybrid (offline/online) targeted youth work as well as enhanced working with child and adolescent mental health services. The Scottish Government also produced a resource for all school staff to support young people's mental health and well-being, which covered issues such as understanding trauma and adversity, sleep, the impact of digital technologies and social media, and also body image (www.cypmh.co.uk). Additionally, this resource also focused on understanding diversity and discrimination and creating a stigma-free school.

For LGBTQI+ young people in Scotland, just prior to the pandemic, the Scottish Government had committed to introducing LGBT-inclusive education, which was eventually implemented in 2021 across all of Scotland's schools, with a national training platform for teachers (https://lgbteducation.scot) delivered by Time for Inclusive Education. This resource provided a framework to address some of the challenges young LGBTQI+ people faced during lockdown. At the time of writing the chapter, the resource had been taken up by over 500 schools in Scotland – almost 20% of the total number of schools (there are currently 2,630 early learning centres, 2,001 primary schools, 357 secondary schools and 111 special schools in Scotland). Plans were also put in place early to assess the effectiveness of the initiative through both medium- and long-term evaluations.

The extended nature of lockdown and the rise in online abusive behaviour witnessed by many young LGBTQI+ people in Scotland also showed us that there was also a need for interventions that would help all young people re-apply those behavioural and attitudinal filters that were increasingly missing from online and social media interactions. Pre-pandemic, numerous initiatives were introduced to tackle LGBTQI+ intolerance in schools, colleges and universities across the UK (e.g. *Visible and Valued*) however, their effectiveness in changing behaviours was not well documented. Furthermore, those improvements made in changing educational cultures prior to COVID-19 were likely undone in some part by the pandemic. Ultimately, the pandemic did not provide any justification for increased bullying and intolerance towards LGBTQI+ people in Scotland or any in other part of the UK, or world for that matter.

More widely, as indicated by the research conducted by AKT at the height of the pandemic, there remains a need to better understand the correlates of

LGBTQI+ youth homelessness and particularly if and how experiences at school, college, university and/or online played a role in these young people's decision to leave their families and communities.

Notwithstanding the previous discussion, we should never forget that COVID-19 provided opportunities to demonstrate how society and our communities can continue to come together through technology and continue to thrive. Social media platforms and gaming environments, mobile/cell phones and email/text messaging ensured that we stay connected with loved ones, colleagues, friends and those with whom we share interests. Online bullying and harassment are endemic, but it is not anonymous nor is it impersonal. All communications are traceable, and we all must remember that there is a human being behind every aggressive or demeaning text, post or image, and a recipient who can be hurt by them.

References

Athanases, S. Z., & Comar, T. A. (2008). The performance of homophobia in early adolescents' everyday speech. *Journal of LGBT Youth*, *5*(1), 9–32. https://doi.org/10.1080/19361650802092366.

Bacher-Hicks, A., Goodman, J., Greif Green, J., & Holt, M. K. (2021, July). The COVID-19 pandemic disrupted both school bullying and cyberbullying (EdWorkingPaper: 21–436). Annenberg Institute at Brown University. www.edworkingpapers.com/ai21-436.

Bhandal, J., & Horwood, M. (2021). The LGBTQ+ youth homelessness report. *AKT*. www.akt.org.uk/report.

Cénat, J. M., Blais, M., Hébert, M., Lavoie, F., & Guerrier, M. (2015). Correlates of bullying in Quebec high school students: The vulnerability of sexual-minority youth. *Journal of Affective Disorders*, *183*(September), 315–321. https://doi.org/10.1016/j.jad.2015.05.011.

Fish, J. N., McInroy, L. B., Paceley, M. S., Williams, N. D., Henderson, S., Levine, D. S., & Edsall, R. N. (2020). "Im kinda stuck at home with unsupportive parents right now": LGBTQ youths' experiences with COVID-19 and the importance of online support. *Journal of Adolescent Health*, *67*(3), 450–452. https://doi.org/10.1016/j.jadohealth.2020.06.002.

Hawke, L. D., Hayes, E., Darnay, K., & Henderson, J. (2021). Mental health among transgender and gender diverse youth: An exploration of effects during the COVID-19 pandemic. *Psychology of Sexual Orientation and Gender Diversity*, *8*(2), 180–187. https://doi.org/10.1037/sgd0000467.

Haztenbuehler, M. L. (2016). Structural stigma: Research evidence and implications for psychological science. *American Psychologist*, *71*(8), 742–751. https://doi.org/10.1037/amp0000068.

HESA (2022, March). What are students' progression rates and qualifications? *HESA*. www.hesa.ac.uk/data-and-analysis/students/outcomes.

Hinduja, S., & Patchin, J. W. (2008). Cyberbullying: An exploratory analysis of factors related to offending and victimization, *Deviant Behavior*, *29*(2), 129–156.https://doi.org/10.1080/01639620701457816.

Hinduja, S., & Patchin, J. W. (2020). Bullying, cyberbullying, and sexual orientation/gender identity. *Cyberbullying Research Center* (cyberbullying.org). https://cyberbullying.org/bullying-cyberbullying-lgbtq.

Howard, E., Khan, A., & Lockyer, C. (2021, July). Learning during the pandemic: Review of research from England. *Ofqual*. https://assets.publishing.service.gov.uk/government/uploads/system/uploads/attachment_data/file/998935/6803-4_Learning_during_the_pandemic-_review_of_research_from_England.pdf.

Jain, O., Gupta, M., Satam, S., & Panda, S. (2020). Has the COVID-19 pandemic affected the susceptibility to cyberbullying in India? *Computers in Human Behavior Reports*, 2(August–December), 100029. https://doi.org/10.1016/j.chbr.2020.100029

Mallet, R. K., Ford, T. E., & Woodzicka, J. A. (2016). What did he mean by that? Humor decreases attributions of sexism and confrontation of sexist jokes. *Sex Roles*, 75(5–6), 272–284. https://doi.org/10.1007/s11199-016-0605-2.

Moss, G., Bradbury, A., Duncan, S., Harmey, S., & Levy, R. (2020). Written evidence submitted by the International Literacy Centre, UCL Institute of Education to the Education Select Committee Inquiry into the impact of COVID-19 on education and children's services, July, 2020. *UCL Institute of Education*. https://discovery.ucl.ac.uk/id/eprint/10109023/. publications schools-and-coronavirus.pdf.

Ormisiton, C. K., & Williams, F. (2022). LGBTQ youth mental health during COVID-19: Unmet needs in public health and policy. *Lancet*, 399(10324), 501–503. https://doi.org/10.1016/S0140–6736(21)02872–5.

Pachankis, J. E., Haztenbuehler, M. L., & Starks, T. J. (2014). The influence of structural stigma and rejection sensitivity on young sexual minority men's daily tobacco and alcohol use. *Social Science & Medicine*, 103(February), 67–75. https://doi.org/10.1016/j.socscimed.2013.10.005.

Perren, S., Dooley, J., Shaw, T., & Cross, D. (2010). Bullying in schools and cyberspace: Associations with depressive symptoms in Swiss and Australian adolescents. *Child and Adolescent Psychiatry and Mental Health*, 4(1), 28. www.capmh.com/content/4/1/28.

Pettett, C. E. (2007). *Homophobia and harassment in school-age populations*. London: Routledge.

Rivers, I., & Noret, N. (2010). 'I h8 u': Findings form a five-year study of text and email bullying. *British Educational Research Journal*, 36(4), 643–671. https://doi.org/10.1080/01411920903071918.

Russell, S. T., & Fish, J. N. (2016). Mental health in lesbian, gay, bisexual and transgender (LGBT) youth. *Annual Review of Clinical Psychology*, 12(1), 465–487. https://doi.org/10.1146/annurev-clinpsy-021815–093153.

Salerno, J. P., Doan, L., Sayer, L. C., Drotning, K. J., Rinderknecht, R. G., & Fish, J. N. (2021). Changes in mental health and well-being are associated with living arrangements with parents during COVID-19 among sexual minority young persons in the U.S. *Psychology of Sexual Orientation and Gender Diversity*, published online Sept 13. https://doi.org/10.1037/sgd0000520.

Scottish Government (2020). Coronavirus (COVID-19): Mental health – transition and recovery plan. *Scottish Government*. www.gov.scot/publications/mental-health-scotlands-transition-recovery/

Time for Inclusive Education (2020). Online in lockdown: Wellbeing, bullying, prejudice. *Time for Inclusive Education*. www.tie.scot/s/TIE-ONLINE-IN-LOCKDOWN-REPORT.pdf

Timmins, N. (2021, August). Schools and coronavirus: The Government's handling of education during the pandemic. *Institute for Government*. https://www.instituteforgovernment.org.uk/sites/default/files/

Vaillanocurt, T., Brittain, H., Krygsman, A., Farrell, A. H., Landon, S., & Pepler, D. (2021). School bullying before and during COVID-19: Results from a population-based randomized design. *Aggressive Behavior*, 47(5), 557–569. https://doi.org/10.1002/ab.21986.

7 Cyberbullying and online hate speech in Thailand

Ruthaychonnee Sittichai and Ram Herkanaidu

Introduction

In Thailand, 84% of the nearly 70 million population are online and have a Facebook account (Internet World Stats, 2022). However, there are currently very few education programmes and initiatives and none at the national level (at the time of writing) that address issues surrounding online safety awareness. Online safety and digital well-being (as in other countries) are becoming increasingly important issues. A 2019 *Bangkok Post* article entitled 'Cries for help go unheard' (Mala & Wipatayotin, 2019) discusses the growing issue and awareness of suicides linked to depression in Thailand. It acknowledges that this is a very complicated area as the causes of depression are many and now include social media. Dr Varoth Chotpitayasunondh, a spokesperson for the Department of Mental Health, noted:

> I have found that people right now are very sensitive to negative interactions in relationships. That might be because of the influence of the online world. Suicide or self-destructive tendencies can reach a tipping point after something as seemingly trivial as a partner not replying to a Line message. They have less patience. Also, the comparative nature of social networks means people often compare their lives to those of their peers, leading to a loss of self-esteem if they don't feel like they match up. And, sadly, many also suffer from bullying which is all the more pernicious when mobile phones and social media leave them with the feeling that there are no longer any safe spaces to shelter from the storm.
>
> (Mala & Wipatayotin, 2019)

To address the issues this raises, it is important to determine their causes. However, it is generally accepted that when it comes to the digital well-being of young people, there is a research gap in most South-East Asian countries, including Thailand. Park and Tan (2015, 2016) produced two reports for the UNESCO Asia and Pacific Regional Bureau for Education in Bangkok. The first was entitled 'Fostering Digital Citizenship through Safe and Responsible Use of ICT' (Park & Tan, 2015) and then a follow-up on 'Building Digital

DOI:10.4324/9781003258605-9

Citizenship in Asia-Pacific through Safe, Effective and Responsible Use of ICT' (Park & Tan, 2016). In the first report, they highlight that

> experiences and practices of [Asia-Pacific] children remain under-researched, translating to the lack of policy responses to the issues . . . the lack of understanding is exacerbated in relation to the situation in developing and emerging countries in which ICT devices abruptly introduce totally different opportunities and risks to children.
>
> (Park & Tan, 2015, p. 3)

In Thailand's official cybersecurity policy 2017–2021, which can be found on the Office of the National Security Council's website www.nsc.go.th/, there are objectives that relate to raising awareness, especially strategy six.

Goals

- To have a mechanism that instils good awareness in the use of cyberspace in the right way and respects the basic rights and freedoms of others in the cyber world.
- To encourage the network of internet users to help supervise the use of cyberspace in an appropriate way.
- To promote learning especially among children and youth to be aware of the threats that affect cyberspace security.

Indicators

- Organising the 'Cyberspace Watch' project at many levels, such as projects for local communities and educational institutions.
- Training for internet users to both coordinate care and instil awareness in order to use cyberspace appropriately

Guidelines

- To promote the good values of the nation in the cyber world by promoting the use of information technology and public communications to maintain the nation, religion and the king.
- To promote a culture of using cyberspace responsibly and consciously for others and the society as a whole, to respect basic rights and freedom in the cyber world and not violate the law.

> (National Cybersecurity Strategy 2017–2021:
> www.nsc.go.th/?page_id=480)
> (Translated by Dr Tharabun Khuchinda)

However, while these are laudable goals, there are no national programmes (that the authors are aware of) that address them.

Cyberbullying

In Thai, there is no direct translation of the word 'bully' (Herkanaidu, 2020). Therefore, it is necessary to identify Thai words and phrases that encompass the meaning of the word. Sittichai and Smith (2013) provide the following:

> ***Nisai mai dee*** *means bad habit, generally bad behavior;* ***klang (klaĕng)*** *refers to more verbal behaviors, and* ***tum raai (thamrāi)*** *to more physical behaviors. Two other terms current nowadays are* ***rang kae (rangkaĕ)*** *which also means physical aggression and* ***raow*** *which means general aggression.*
>
> (pp. 34–35)

Other terms include **kan yok-lo**, which refers to teasing and **kan rangkae**, an academic term for bullying (Mahidol University, 2014).

Online hate speech

The phrase, online hate speech, sometimes referred to as cyberhate, is new in our lexicon. Institutions and countries have come up with various definitions. For instance, the Council of Europe (1997) defines hate speech as

> all forms of expression which spread, incite, promote or justify racial hatred, xenophobia, anti-Semitism or other forms of hatred based on intolerance, including intolerance expressed by aggressive nationalism and ethnocentrism, discrimination and hostility against minorities, migrants and people of immigrant origin.
>
> (Council of Europe, 1997)

In Thailand, the term for hate speech is, **ประทุษวาจา**) Pra-tud-sa-va-ja/) and on the government website, https://dmh.go.th it defines it as (using Google Translate):

> Hate speech or communication between groups of people in society. Expressions in 'words' or 'other means' that are intended to attack a group or individual. By focusing on the base of identity which may have been inherent, or it can happen later, such as race, religion, color, place of birth/ place of residence, political ideologies, occupations, or other characteristics that can be discriminated against the hateful act that appears to be disgraceful. Or reduce the value of humanity or incite and foster hatred as well as promoting violence.

Research studies

While acknowledging there is still a lack of research, there are a growing number of studies that deal with online safety issues, especially ones focusing on young people. Sittichai and Smith (2018) looked at the specific issue of bullying and cyberbullying in Thailand. They report on a study conducted in 2012 with 1,049 12–18-year-old students in the provinces of Pattani, Yala, and Narathiwat in South Thailand. They looked at the coping strategies employed by the victims of bullying and cyberbullying depending on age, gender and religion. Altogether 15.9% were traditional victims, and 15.1% were cyber victims. Boys were more often victims than girls for both traditional and cyber forms, but this was only significant for cybervictimisation. For traditional bullying, the most recommended strategy was telling someone (teacher/parent), followed by avoiding the bullies. Many also suggested asking them to stop or ignoring it. For cyberbullying, two-thirds mentioned blocking messages/identities, and nearly half mentioned changing their email address or phone number, followed by ignoring it.

Ojanen et al. (2014) conducted a study of online harassment and how it is linked to offline violence and in particular the role that gender and sexuality norms play. Their study comprised 1,234 participants. These were 15–24-year-olds and included those who were inside and outside of the education system. Around half the participants had experienced online harassment and a similar proportion to offline violence. A third had been victims of both while a third admitted to being the perpetrator. They found that males were more likely to be the perpetrator and the victim both online and offline. In terms of witnessing offline violence and online harassment, more than three-quarters had experienced this.

Herkanaidu (2020) carried out a study in the North-East of Thailand, an area commonly known as Isan. Surveys, in-person interviews and workshops were conducted in Nong Khai and Roi Et provinces. The online survey conducted was adapted from the research tools provided by the Global Kids Online project (http://globalkidsonline.net/). In doing so it allowed for cross-country comparisons. After the surveys were carried out in Nong Khai, they were compared to the EU Kids Online data (Herkanaidu et al., 2017). It was found that young people in Thailand were exposed to much more negative online content and interactions than their European peers. For example, 60% of young people in Nong Khai had been a victim of cyberbullying. The European figure for 2014 was 12% (Herkanaidu et al., 2017, p. 8). Figure 7.1 shows data once both the Nong Khai and Roi Et studies were completed. Overall, the study found that 69% (more than 2 out of 3) had been upset by an online interaction, and 55% felt they had been bullied. Interestingly, 41% admitted to being the perpetrator of bullying. Both Nong Khai and Roi Et are semi-rural areas, and a few of the schools catered for children from low socio-economic groups, yet around 9 out of 10 of the young people (12–18 years old) had smartphones. Facebook is the social network of choice, and Facebook Messenger the main chat app overtaking the Line Messenger app, which had been the top one previously. They were exposed to sites discussing disturbing issues such as committing suicide, self-harm, drugs, sexual content, promotion of eating disorders and hate messages aimed at particular groups and individuals. It was found that around one in five had sent a photo or video to someone that they

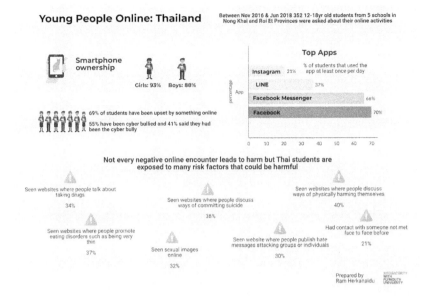

Figure 7.1 Young People's Online Survey Results

Source: (adapted from Herkanaidu et al., 2020)

had not already met offline, that is, strangers and potentially ones that are looking for victims to groom.

The surveys provided the statistical data and gave a broad picture of the situation, at least in Nong Khai and Roi Et provinces. The in-person interviews with the students provided valuable context. It was found that teasing and banter were common, and most had seen pictures and videos depicting violence on Facebook and YouTube and to a lesser extent sexual content. Some of the replies (translated by Thai teachers) were:

> Yes, his friends sent him some bad words, but it was just for fun
> She saw a video about a bad mother bullying her kids.
> Sometimes when he posts photos on Facebook his friends tell him he's ugly.
> She has watched videos about self-harm.
>
> *(Herkanaidu, 2020)*

One male student recounted an incident when someone wanted to pay him to meet. This was after two days of general chatting. He did not feel comfortable with this and blocked the person. A female student, when she was 12, recounted an unhappy incident when a stranger sent her a naked photo on Facebook. By chance, her father saw it and blamed her for it. Now if something like that happened, she says she would not dare tell him. In fact, most of the students only told close friends or no one about their negative online experiences. One possible reason is to do with the Thai concept known as 'kreng jai' explained later in the discussion section.

Kaewseenual (2018) looked at digital literacy in Thailand. It included workshops in public and private schools to determine what kind of teaching methods worked best for teaching issues around digital resilience and online safety. Although Thailand was supposed to have moved to a more student-centric education system, it was found that it was still teacher-centric reflecting the hierarchical nature of Thai culture. Students are supposed to be 'dek-dee' (a good child), that is, to behave well and follow what the teacher instructs.

> The teacher holds the central power of regulation and knowledge and the children are submissive to their authority. They are reinforced and measured as passive recipients, who are not able to think independently as autonomous persons. The children are constructed as obedient citizens, through traditional classroom teaching.
>
> (Kaewseenual, 2018, p. 179)

Kaewseenual argues that for children to become digitally literate and build resilience, they need to be freer to discover the digital world and be exposed to some risks in a safe educational space. To be effective it has to take account of the Thai cultural context, which is explored later in the discussion section.

Thinnukool et al. (2018) developed a research-based mobile application to investigate young Thais' perceived knowledge of cyberbullying, called the Cyberbullying Mobile Application (CBMA), the first research-based CBMA developed in Thailand. Two hundred and fifty-three participants were surveyed from high schools and universities in Chiang Mai province. The study found that users appreciated it and had confidence in the application. In some cases, users claimed they would consider continuing to use it.

Most of the respondents in this study were females, in high school and university between 20 and 26. The undergraduate student group had a higher percentage of perception than the high-school student group. However, neither sample group demonstrated good awareness of cyberbullying. After user testing, the app results showed that the CBMA could be more appropriate for high school students than for undergraduate students. Interestingly, the results show that both groups agree with the need to consult their family when they did encounter cyberbullying.

Wachs et al. (2021) looked at cyberhate victimisation among adolescents across eight countries. They report on a study conducted in 2021 with 6,829 adolescents between 12 and 18 years old from eight countries. The study sample included 221 Cypriot participants, 1,480 German participants, 670 Greek participants, 1,121 Indian participants, 756 South Korean participants 1,018 Spanish participants, 716 Thai participants and 847 American participants. In particular, they looked at cyberhate victimisation by considering adolescents' exposure to motivated offenders (witnessing cyberhate), capable guardianship (parental mediation strategies of internet use) and target suitability (adolescents' online disclosure of private information). This was achieved using a questionnaire in which participants were asked to rate their experience for each category. Frequency rates for ethnic-related cyberhate victimisation varied by form between 17.9% and 12.1% and for religious-related cyberhate victimisation between 18.4% and 10.7%. For adolescents who experienced cyberhate victimisation, it happened mostly very rarely (between 10.5% and 6.6%). For both, ethnic-related and religious-related cyberhate, the most common form of victimisation was someone making jokes about the victims because of their religious affiliation or their ethnic group (18.4% and 17.9%, respectively). They found that about half (49.1%) had encountered online hate. For being the perpetrator of online hate, 32.2% of Thais admitted this (Wachs et al., 2019). This is less than the Herkanaidu et al. study discussed earlier but it was the highest reported among the eight countries. The next highest was the United States reporting 24.5% and both contrasts with the 4.2% and 4.6% reported in South Korea and Cyprus, respectively. In terms of witnessing or as they put it, being a bystander of online hate, 65% of Thais had done so. This was second only to Spain, where 68% of young people reported they had witnessed online hate. The countries with the least prevalence were India (31.4%) and Cyprus (35.7%). As Herkanaidu et al. (2017) found, when it comes to international comparisons Thailand is unenviably at or near the top for cyberbullying and online hate.

Kaewseenual and Sittichai (2021) conducted a comparative study examining the forms and factors of self-adjustment and preparation to encounters with cyberbullying and online hate speech of elementary school students in Chiang Mai and Songkhla provinces. The investigation was conducted with grade 4 to 6 of the elementary schools in Chiang Mai and Songkhla provinces from December 2019 to December 2020. They used learning units on cyberbullying, online hate speech prevention, open-ended and close-ended questions, semi-structured interviews, group discussions with students, teachers and parents, participative observation and After-Action Review (AAR). It was found that primary school children in Chiang Mai had more experiences in cyberbullying than those in Songkhla. This is, in part, related to media accessibility. The Chiang Mai schools provide supportive factors that prepare students and help them to digitally adjust to negative encounters online like cyberbullying and online hate speech. In addition, there are good relationships between students, teachers and parents. This reflects the collectivist nature of Thai society, where the values of togetherness and collaboration are integrated with the student learning centre concept. These become positive factors for building digital resilience. This research can help the development of guidelines for students' preparation and adjustment to digital resilience for the benefit of their learning at a young age and their coping with cyberbullying and online hate speech.

The previous studies demonstrate that cyberbullying and, to a lesser extent, online hate speech are significant and worrisome issues in Thailand. To create effective strategies and initiatives to help alleviate the effects of the issues, it is important to understand the cultural context of those affected.

Cultural context

Thailand is known as the 'Land of Smiles'. What is less well known is that Thais tend to smile when they are happy, sad or angry (Browell, 2000). It is associated with the concept of 'losing face' or rather not losing face. Displaying negative emotions, for example, getting angry or frustrated will lead to losing face and be perceived to having lost control. In this scenario, it is best to smile and be accepting to avoid conflict and keep social harmony or, as Knutson et al. (2003) puts it, interpersonal harmony. This is closely associated with the concept of 'kreng jai' (Kainzbauer & Hunt, 2016). It has no direct translation into English, but it is where a person does not want to impose or cause inconvenience to others if they are older, especially parents and teachers. Very often when a person is faced with a problem, it is often ignored or at least hidden from others. In the North East Thailand study, when asked what they did if they had a negative experience online, the most common reply was that they would not tell their parents or teachers anything because it was not important enough (Herkanaidu, 2020). This fits in with Thailand's hierarchical and collectivistic nature, which has 'a preference of indirect and covert communication style, an obedient and conforming behaviour, a clear group identification, and a priority of group interest and harmony' (Knutson et al., 2003, p. 38). This cultural context needs to be taken into consideration when designing education policies and initiatives as well as mediation strategies, which are discussed in the next section.

Mediation

The most common coping strategies reported by those who had been victims of cyberhate in the Wachs et al. (2019) study were telling the perpetrator to stop doing it, blocking the person and ignoring it by spending time with friends to take their minds off it. The latter two behaviours are very much in line with the concept of kreng jai. The first, that is, telling the perpetrator to stop it, on the face of it, seems too direct but perhaps it is easier to do this online than in-person and risk losing face.

The three least-frequent coping strategies, all, in some way, involve retaliating against the perpetrator either acting alone or with friends via SMS, messaging or e-mail. Both males and females are affected by cyberhate. There were slight differences, in that males encountered cyberhate more often and were more likely to retaliate against the perpetrator. Overall, more than one in five of the participants admitted to taking such actions.

In the context of Thailand, this is not surprising as there are no national or local educational programmes (that the authors are aware of) that focus on online safety issues and offer coping strategies that can instil digital resilience. Herkanaidu (2020) designed a number of workshops to find out which types of learning methods worked best. Least effective were open discussions, question and answer sessions and presentations. This is because in a typical Thai classroom, the teacher is the authority figure and the source of knowledge (Kainzbauer & Hunt, 2016) and therefore expected to provide the answers. Active learning methods are being explored and Herkanaidu (2020) did find the use of videos, games and group work to be effective though more research and initiatives are needed.

Policies and regulations

There are general laws that cover the areas of cyberbullying and online hate speech, however, none (at the time of writing) that specifically addresses the issues. The official cybersecurity policy 2017–2021, mentioned earlier in the introduction section, generally advises Thais to be good digital citizens and to not do anything harmful. The 2003 Child Protection Act (Rahamathulla, 2021) has measures to protect children but nothing specifically cyber related. There is the Computer Crime Act 2007, but as Charoen (2012) notes, 'the crimes that this law addresses range from spreading viruses to posting inappropriate contents such as those considered harmful to national security or lèse majesté [against the crown]' (p. 520). There is also the Cybersecurity Act 2019, which 'was promulgated as an Act on 27 May 2019 in order to protect sovereignty in terms of national security, economic security, martial security, and public order in the country' (Gohwong, 2019, p. 13). There is nothing specific to cyberbullying or online hate speech in either piece of legislation. Ruiz (2019) points out that there have been limited campaigns around the subject of bullying, including the 'Doing Good Stop Bullying' program, but there was 'no literature found online that measures the efficacy of these strategies or whether schools are accountable for any oversight' (Ruiz, 2019, p. 1295).

Lastly, the Electronic Transactions Data Agency (www.etda.or.th/) does have information on online hate speech. However, as with the existing legislation, the emphasis is on prescribing being a good citizen and to refrain from doing harmful actions. An individual is to behave in a proper way, that is, not to post, like or share messages that insult others. If they receive insulting messages, they should not act in kind and if deemed serious enough, report it to the messaging platform and to the police.

Conclusion

Thailand is one of the most digitally connected countries in South-East Asia. Thais have adapted to the digital world and in particular social media, more so than in most countries. However, this rapid move to online has also had negative effects on people's mental health and well-being. One common theme from all the studies is that more research is needed. Basing policies and initiatives on evidence-based, systematic and pedagogically sound approaches will go a long way to help address online safety issues, like cyberbullying and online hate speech. As Herkanaidu (2020) argues,

> The goal is to deliver effective and meaningful programmes that build young people's resilience against negative online interactions while promoting the benefits and opportunities that the digital world can bring. For this to take place these programmes need to understand their target audience as well as the most appropriate and culturally relevant approaches in terms of both the material and teaching practice.
>
> (p. 189)

Having specific laws and policies on digital safety issues and not just focusing on cybercrime will provide a legal framework for initiatives and programmes. Appropriate interventions in schools, aimed at reducing cyberbullying and online hate speech, would (in the authors' view) go some way, help to protect and increase Thai students' digital resilience and make their online interactions more rewarding.

References

Browell, S. (2000). 'The land of smiles': People issues in Thailand. *Human Resource Development International, 3*(1), 109–119, https://doi.org/10.1080/136788600361975.

Charoen, D. (2012). The analysis of the computer crime act in Thailand. *International Journal of Information, 2*(6), 519–526, https://doi.org/10.1.1.301.7277.

Gohwong, S. G. (2019). The state of the art of cybersecurity law in ASEAN. *International Journal of Crime, Law and Social Issues, 6*(2), 12–23, https://dx.doi.org/10.2139/ssrn.3546333.

Herkanaidu, R. (2020). *Effective online safety awareness for young people in less developed countries* [PhD thesis], University of Plymouth, UK. https://pearl.plymouth.ac.uk/handle/10026.1/15813.

Herkanaidu, R., Furnell, S. M., & Papadaki, M. (2017). Online risk awareness and exposure of young people in Thailand. Presented at the 16th Annual Security Conference 2017, Information Institute Conferences, Las Vegas, NV, 18–20 April 2017. ISBN: 978-1-935160-18-2.

Herkanaidu, R., Furnell, S., & Papadaki, M. (2020). Towards a cross-cultural education framework for online safety awareness. In N. L. Clarke & S. M. Furnell (Eds.), *Human aspects of information security and assurance, HAISA 2020, IFIP advances in information and communication technology* (Vol. 593). Cham: Springer. https://doi.org/10.1007/978-3-030-57404-8_4.

Internet World Stats. (2022). Asia Internet use, population data and Facebook statistics – June 2021. Internet World Stats website. www.internetworldstats.com/stats3.htm#asia (Accessed 9 January 2022).

Kaewseenual, S. (2018). *Risky opportunities: Developing children's resilience through digital literacy in Thailand* [PhD thesis], University of Waikato, Hamilton, New Zealand. https://researchcommons.waikato.ac.nz/handle/10289/11712.

Kaewseenual, S., & Sittichai, R. (2021). Digital resilience of children towards cyberbullying and online hate speech. *Comparative Study of Educational Environment in Chiang Mai and Songkhla School, 39*(4) (October–December 2021), 20–45. https://doi.org/10.14456/jiskku.2021.20.

Kainzbauer, A., & Hunt, B. (2016). Meeting the challenges of teaching in a different cultural environment – evidence from graduate management schools in Thailand. *Asia-Pacific Journal of Education, 36*(Suppl. 1), 56–68. https://doi.org/10.1080/02188791.2014.934779.

Knutson, T. J., Komolsevin, R., Chatiketu, P., & Smith, V. R. (2003). A cross-cultural comparison of Thai and US American rhetorical sensitivity: Implications for intercultural communication effectiveness. *International Journal of Intercultural Relations, 27*, 63–78.

Mahidol University. (2014). Bullying targeting secondary school students who are or are perceived to be transgender or same-sex attracted: Types, prevalence, impact, motivation and preventive measures in 5 provinces of Thailand. Mahidol University. Plan International Thailand. UNESCO Bangkok Office. https://unesdoc.unesco.org/ark:/48223/pf0000227518.

Mala, D., & Wipatayotin, A. (2019). Cries for help go unheard. *Bangkok Post.* www.bangkokpost.com/thailand/special-reports/1641984/cries-for-help-go-unheard (Accessed 12 November 2020).

Ojanen, T. T., Boonmongkon, P., Samakkeekarom, R., Samoh, N., Cholratana, M., Payakkakom, A., & Guadamuz, T. E. (2014). Investigating online harassment and offline violence among young people in Thailand: Methodological approaches, lessons learned. *Culture Health and Sexuality, 16*(9), 1097–1112. https://doi.org/10.1080/13691058.2014.931464. Epub 2014 Jul 10. PMID: 25010363; PMCID: PMC4163092.

Park, J., & Tan, M. (2015). Fostering digital citizenship through safe and responsible use of ICT: A review of current status in Asia and the Pacific as of December 2014. APEID-ICT in Education, UNESCO Asia-Pacific Regional Bureau of Education. www.unescobkk.org/fileadmin/user_upload/ict/SRU-ICT/SRU-ICT_mapping_report_2014.pdf.

Park, J., & Tan, M. (2016). A policy review: Building digital citizenship in Asia-Pacific through safe, effective and responsible use of ICT. APEID-ICT in Education, UNESCO Asia-Pacific Regional Bureau of Education. http://unesdoc.unesco.org/images/0024/002468/246813E.pdf.

Rahamathulla, M. (2021). Cyber safety of children in the Association of Southeast Asian Nations (ASEAN) Region: A critical review of legal frameworks and policy implications. *International Journal on Child Maltreatment, 4*, 375–400. https://doi.org/10.1007/s42448-021-00087-5.

Ruiz, R. M. N. M. (2019). Curbing cyberbullying among students: A comparative analysis of existing laws among selected Asean countries. *PEOPLE: International Journal of Social Sciences, 4*(3), 1285–1305.

Sittichai, R., & Smith, P. K. (2013). Bullying and cyberbullying in Thailand: A review. *International Journal of Cyber Society and Education, 6*(1), 31–44. https://doi.org/10.7903/ijcse.1032.

Sittichai, R., & Smith, P. K. (2018). Bullying and cyberbullying in Thailand: Coping strategies and relation to age, gender, religion and victim status. *Journal of New Approaches in Educational Research, 7*, 24–30.https://doi.org/10.7821/naer.2018.1.254.

Thinnukool, O., Khuwuthyakorn, P., & Sittichai, R. (2018). The use of cyberbullying mobile application to increase perceived knowledge of cyberbullying among adolescents. *International Journal of Innovation and Technology Management, 15*(3), 1850029, 321–351. https://doi.org/10.1142/S0219877018500293.

Wachs, S., Costello, M., Wright, M. F., Flora, K., Daskalou, V., Maziridou, E., Kwon, Y., Na, E.-Y., Sittichai, R., Biswal, R., Singh, R., Almendros, C., Gámez-Guadix,

M., Görzig, A., & Hong, J. S. (2021). "DNT LET'EM H8 U!": Applying the routine activity framework to understand cyberhate victimization among adolescents across eight countries. *Computers and Education*, *160*, 1–13, https://doi.org/10.1016/j.compedu.2020.104026.

Wachs, S., Wright, M. F., Sittichai, R., Singh, R., Biswal, R., Kim, E.-M., Yang, S., Gámez-Guadix, M., Almendros, C., Flora, K., Daskalou, V., & Maziridou, E. (2019). Associations between witnessing and perpetrating online hate in eight countries: The buffering effects of problem-focused coping. *International Journal of Environmental Research and Public Health*, *16*(20), 3992. https://doi.org/10.3390/ijerph16203992.

8 Sexual harassment within the workplace after #MeToo and Time's Up

Francesca Stevens

Introduction

Sexual harassment can be defined as unwanted behaviour of a sexual nature, including making sexual remarks about someone's body, displaying or sharing sexual content, touching someone against their will and sexual assault, amongst others (ACAS, 2021). However, defining this concept has been one of the most constant and perturbing issues within relevant literature, to ensure it was precise enough to be of use in practice, yet extensive enough not to discount any of the myriad of experiences it can entail (Fitzgerald, 1990). The term 'sexual harassment' was pioneered by feminist academics in the 1970s; it became illegal once it was understood to be a form of sex discrimination (Gilmore, 2018).

The prevalence of sexual harassment is not a novel concern but one that recently became more prominent in public discourse. This can largely be attributed to the emergence of social movements like #MeToo, which aimed to tackle widespread sexual harassment and assault within institutions globally. On 24 October 2017, actress Alyssa Milano tweeted the hashtag #MeToo, asking people to reply if they had also experienced sexual violence. This was considering recent sexual assault claims against Hollywood producer Harvey Weinstein and the head of Amazon studios, Roy Price (Clair et al., 2019). Just hours after her initial tweet, Milano received 55,000 responses and #MeToo was the number 1 trend on Twitter, across 85 countries (Sayej, 2017). Further movements were then also born, including 'Time's Up', (Clair et al., 2019), started by 300 women who worked in the Hollywood entertainment business, to try and rectify the power imbalance in American workplaces (Buckley, 2018).

Sexual harassment has been a widespread problem for women since they began working in the marketplace, with narratives dating back to the colonial era (Fitzgerald, 1993). Farley (1978, pp. 14–15) specified that sexual harassment at work is 'unsolicited nonreciprocal male behaviour that asserts a woman's sex role over her function as worker'. Although men can certainly be victims too, evidence overwhelmingly shows that perpetrators are 'disproportionately' men, and women are 'significantly' more at risk of being victims of workplace sexual harassment (Parliament, HoC, 2018, p. 7). Despite it being illegal, there is not

DOI:10.4324/9781003258605-10

one clear overarching law in the UK that this offence falls under, so instead legislation including The Equality Act 2010 and Protection from Harassment Act 1997 are used to protect individuals. Although current laws are theoretically intended to protect people from sexual harassment, there is a disconnect from how they work in practice. It is presumed that when something becomes illegal, it no longer takes place, but this is not the case for such persistent manifestations of sexual violence like sexual harassment and rape, which are 'built into structural social hierarchies' MacKinnon (2018).

In this chapter, I present findings from in-depth semi-structured interviews conducted in London, in June and July 2019, with 18 female participants aged between 25 and 58 years, to explore their understanding of sexual harassment, experiences of being female in the workplace and opinions on the recent social movements such as #MeToo and Time's Up. At the time of my research, the UK government had yet to collect data on the pervasiveness of workplace sexual harassment (Parliament, HoC, 2018). However, consultancy firm ComRes (2017) had conducted a large-scale survey on behalf of the BBC, with a nationally representative sample consisting of 6,206 adults which explored their attitudes towards sexual harassment in the workplace, finding that 40% of women have been a victim of workplace sexual harassment.

Furthermore, a YouGov-commissioned poll, released in November 2018, found that only 38% of employees would be 'very likely' to report workplace sexual harassment, and regardless of movements like #MeToo and Time's Up, just 24% believe that media exposure has facilitated an advancement of a positive workplace culture (Cheng & Wakeling, 2018). Therefore, I wanted to consider, using a qualitative methodology, how (or not) these movements had helped to empower women to speak out if they were to experience sexual harassment at work. The context of the term 'speaking up' within my research was that of feeling empowered to share with their friends, family, colleagues or peers, details of sexual harassment incidents they experienced or witnessed, or may do in the future. Furthermore, I wished to analyse whether these social movements had a significant impact for 'everyday' women and not just celebrities, and whether they changed the conversation that exists around sexual harassment.

Additionally, I felt it was necessary to study the impact that these movements may have had regarding the public perception of victims, and whether there had been a change in the victim-blaming attitudes so commonly seen, as well as the stigma long associated with the 'victim' label. I posed the following research question: *How have attitudes towards female victims of sexual harassment changed since the recent #MeToo and Time's Up movements?*

Methodology

Sample The sampling method selected was purposive; I sought to interview women who ranged in age and worked within a variety of industries. The sample was narrowed down to working women in London, who had worked for a minimum of four years, meaning that by default they were all above 18 years. This condition was determined so that each participant would have worked for at least two years before the emergence of #MeToo and Time's Up, and nearly two years afterwards.

Prior to participant selection, ethical approval was obtained from the City, University of London Department of Sociology Research Ethics Committee. My sample was then found through a combination of Facebook and LinkedIn advertising, as well as snowball sampling. The 18 participants had worked in London ranging from 4 to 40 years and were aged between 25 and 58 years. These women worked in a variety of industries, including advertising, teaching, banking, property and third sector. It should be noted that I was not specifically interviewing women who had been a victim of sexual harassment or sexual assault. The aim of the research was to explore working women's opinions, and if they chose to share such an experience, it was their decision without any pressure or enquiring from myself. Furthermore, all participants were cooperative, open and eager to discuss the topics at hand. A few particularly mentioned their appreciation of the project for providing a space to reflect and talk about their experiences, which they had not necessarily been given before.

Data collection and analysis

Interviews were conducted in a range of locations, including co-working spaces, cafés and participants' homes, depending on where they felt most comfortable. Each participant was asked permission to record the interview via a recording device, which they all agreed to. I had pre-written an interview guide but felt it important not to be too rigid, so asked follow-up questions where necessary, depending upon the points raised by the women. I had considered providing a summary sheet defining the #MeToo and Time's Up movements, but after deliberation, decided against this. I did not want to risk leading any of the participant's answers. Ahead of beginning the interviews, I explicitly stated that participants could choose not to answer any question they did not wish to and were free to stop the interview at any point. Additionally, the anonymity of participants is ensured, with no names printed within the findings. Participants were asked at the end of their interview if they would like the telephone number for the Victim Support helpline, a precaution in case they needed support, or wished to speak to a professional regarding any topics that had been raised.

I selected Braun and Clark's (2006) six-phase thematic analysis method to analyse the data because I wanted to distinguish significant themes in the data with a bottom-up approach, without a pre-established coding frame. These phases were as follows: familiarising myself with my data, generating initial codes, searching for themes, reviewing themes, defining and naming themes, and finally, producing the report. The four themes that emerged were the prominence of and fear of victim-blaming, continued gender inequality within the workplace, the necessity for company support and procedures to be in place, and the unreliability and unsustainability of the #MeToo movement for working women.

Prominence of and fear of victim-blaming

The findings answered my research question, with my analysis demonstrating how female victims of sexual harassment are still frequently met with victim-blaming attitudes, which do not appear to have improved since the emergence of the #MeToo and Time's Up movements. All 18 participants expressed concern relating to negative outcomes that sexual harassment victims may face, or have faced, if they report or speak out about an incident. This included anxiety around potential loss of employment and reputational damage, not being believed and being seen as a liar, and fear that they would be blamed for having encouraged the behaviour in some way. The majority of participants did not reference any positive reaction or outcome being shown to or seen by victims after having found the courage to tell their story.

The media were cited by many as a significant part of society's victim-blaming culture, and the ways in which it often reports the victim negatively, painting a picture that they played a part in the crime committed against them or are not telling the whole truth. The press' treatment of two high-profile females was mentioned by several participants: Monica Lewinsky, who rose to fame due to involvement in a political sex scandal with US President Bill Clinton in the 1990s, and American Professor Christine Blasey Ford. Ford testified at the Senate in September 2018 that the then-Supreme Court nominee Brett Kavanagh had sexually assaulted her when she was just 15 years old; Kavanagh was then swiftly sworn in as a Supreme Court judge. The public backlash that Ford received was upsetting for some of the participants and did not make them feel as though they could speak out if in a similar situation. This underlined a need for society to carefully re-examine how the media is permitted to report, as this type of media reporting perpetuates negative attitudes and feeds into the subconscious and conversation, un-doing the work of movements like #MeToo.

Some participants expressed thoughts that they recognised to be of a victim-blaming mentality, and how this mind-frame has been encouraged by society's values they have grown up with due to it being ingrained within society. One explained that:

> Sometimes, and I hate myself for it, sometimes I'll catch myself thinking like "oh that's quite a short . . . (skirt)", but like, that's because you're so brainwashed to think it, and you're like "no, anyone can wear anything, no-one is inviting anything into it."

(Participant 18)

Many participants raised the notion of women lying about sexual harassment or abuse. Some proceeded to give examples of fabrication or exaggeration, and the effect this had on the potential perpetrator. One participant referred to a male family acquaintance who had been accused of rape, but it transpired that the girl's parents were very religious, so she did not want to admit she had had sex, but he went to prison. It was interesting that many participants referenced examples of women who have lied as they were not asked about this, but it became common sub-theme within the data. This is not to say that there are no instances where women have fabricated the truth, but these are the minority of cases.

Regarding the workplace, an inherent self-doubt was common amongst participants as well, with women who had experienced inappropriate behaviour at work, fearing that they somehow encouraged it, or that it was just 'banter' that they mis-interpreted, again placing the blame on themselves. Additionally, many felt that reporting sexual harassment would be difficult without 'proof' or 'evidence', otherwise they would likely be blamed or disbelieved. One participant explained how doing the following has become normalised behaviour:

> You question "am I being ridiculous?", like am I, I think it's such a classic female thing, to think like "maybe I'm in the wrong", like "maybe I led him on, maybe I'm over-reacting, maybe it wasn't that bad."
>
> (Participant 1)

Continued gender inequality in the workplace

Many participants described a range of examples of experiencing gender inequality in their workplaces; some had female CEOs, whilst others had male CEOs. A couple of participants spoke extremely positively of having a female CEO, feeling that it enabled gender equality to exist from the top-down. However, one participant who had a female manager felt she was worse than a man as she did so little for equality and the gender-pay gap, whilst another explained that her female CEO seemed like an inspiring woman but was out of touch with the realities of how the company was run day to day and the rife sexual harassment that existed below her. These findings demonstrate the importance of a company's culture, and the need for compulsory guidelines and procedures to be in place, instead of the presumption that a female leader will automatically ensure equality.

The gender inequality experienced included a variety of situations ranging from feeling and being treated as inferior, to having a profound constant awareness that they are 'different' from their male colleagues. One participant (2), a senior manager of a team consisting predominantly of men, commented that she thinks women 'always have to work a little bit harder to prove ourselves', and frequently at events with clients, people will assume that a more junior man in her team is more senior than her. The gender-pay gap was also a cause of concern for a number of the participants. One participant had previously been explicitly told that a male colleague who was both the same age and role as her was earning significantly more than she was. She explained that there is a huge gender-pay gap generally within the advertising industry. Other participants felt aware of such disparities in their industries and had suspicions that the companies they are employed by may be guilty of it too.

Gender stereotyping in the workplace was also commonly spoken about. One participant, who previously worked at Amazon, felt that the gender division she experienced there negatively affected her ability to network within the company. She also commented how she was always the team member expected to book lunch if they went out for a meal, or buy a colleague's birthday card and cake, how these administration tasks were always given to her as she was the only female on the team. These forms of stereotyping can be linked to the process of 'doing gender': we see often men 'doing dominance', whilst women do 'deference', which proved the case for several participants who felt their companies categorised them in roles that fit the typical expectations of how a woman should act, including menial tasks. Although such stereotypes may appear harmless on the surface, they are damaging and perpetuate attitudes that men should be treated one way, and women another.

Several participants expressed that there was a need for greater teaching in schools around topics including gender equality and stereotypes, as this early-stage education and awareness surrounding such issues could help to prevent sexual harassment later in life. One participant, a primary school teacher, spoke of how resource banks that teachers subscribe to are rife with gender stereotypes, and in nurseries, the role-play areas are designed like this too; toy cars for boys and dolls for girls. This highlights the need for educational institutions to tackle such stereotypes from a young age.

Necessity for company support and procedures

No participant had any detailed knowledge surrounding legislation related to sexual harassment in the UK. A few mentioned the Upskirting Bill, which had recently been made a criminal offence, and the admiration they had for Gina Martin, the activist behind it. Many participants expressed a desire for better guidelines, procedures and support in their workplaces in relation to sexual harassment.

The majority of participants did not feel that their Human Resources (HR) department provided adequate help or support, explaining that they did not know what processes were in place if they had a problem relating to sexual harassment or who they would even speak to. Participant 18 commented: 'I never know with HR, I always find, I'm always like in my head "is HR really for you? Or is it really for the company?"'.

Another participant spoke of a consultancy firm where she used to work, where one senior male sexually assaulted several women over many years, and, despite several of the victims reporting to HR numerous times, it was covered up because he was a shareholder. On reflection, she feels that a lack of processes in place, as well as the powerful position that the man held, contributed to this outcome. Common perceptions presume that when sexual harassment occurs, it is a manifestation of desire the perpetrator may feel for his victim. However, research links it instead to concepts concerning both power and dominance (Holland & Cortina, 2013). It is 'dominance eroticized'; it is not concerned with arousing the woman's (the victim's) sexual desire or indeed the male perpetrator but more about the reality that they can behave in this way if they choose to (MacKinnon, 1979, p. 162).

In contrast, a few participants shared stories of action that their company has taken to help tackle inappropriate behaviour in the workplace. For example, one participant mentioned her company has a whistle-blowing hotline, which created a safe and private place to report any untoward behaviour that may take place.

Unrelatability and unsustainability of the #MeToo movement

It was widely accepted by participants that the #MeToo movement is accountable for bringing the prevalence of sexual harassment in the workplace, and the issues surrounding it, into the public consciousness and conversation; #MeToo has given people a common language and a frame of reference to talk about their experiences within. It was also acknowledged that hashtags and social media are part of modern life and communication and are useful to aid spreading a message virally. However, some participants were quick to add that just because a hashtag is posted, it does not equate to action being taken. Most participants had little or no knowledge around the Time's Up movement, with most seeming unsure about its origins and what exactly it stood for. Interestingly, no participant knew that the original #MeToo movement has existed since 2006, whilst one stated that she thought it had been around since the 1980s.

Participants commonly felt that celebrities speaking out and playing such a pivotal role in #MeToo was a positive thing and liked that they were using their influence for good. One participant described her admiration, stating that she would never feel comfortable to criticise an individual for speaking out about their experiences. However, many participants did not feel that these celebrities' stories were relatable. Participant 4 explained she did not feel celebrities were able to 'sustain the message', and another participant (15) felt that celebrities speaking out was unrelatable because their world is so 'different and alien' from hers and did not think women were referring back to the #MeToo campaign if and when they speak to their managers about these issues if they arise.

Several participants described the need for women to speak out more about their sexual harassment experiences to improve things, but then admitted they were not sure that they would actually do so themselves. Many spoke of their fears of speaking up regarding incidents they have experienced of inappropriate behaviour at work, and although some explained that #MeToo had made them feel more confident, in practice – they did not think they would speak out about their story.

Furthermore, the identification of sexual harassment on a spectrum was mentioned by almost half of participants, with many understanding it as ranging from wolf-whistling or an inappropriate comment at one end, to rape at the other. This idea of a 'spectrum' is in line with Kelly's (1988, p. 97) 'continuum' of violence, ranging from everyday sexism to women who are murdered by men. Some participants expressed not feeling it appropriate to speak about incidents on the less severe end, as they were not as serious or violent as other abuses. This illustrates the need for society to better validate all experiences. On the other side, participant 9 explained that she has positive feelings about #MeToo because:

> it's a good thing in that it kind of draws that connection . . . between the minor, the casual comments, and the bad stuff . . . (it) creates a community, connection between women who have experienced it.

Conclusion

The four themes elicited from the data highlight the need for greater societal chance to improve both the circumstances for and the treatment of women. Until schools, workplaces, the government and the media act and implement the positive and necessary changes outlined earlier, victim-blaming and gender inequality will continue to exist. Policies and procedures must be put in place by all HR departments and employers to better protect employees. Action must be taken against perpetrators, so that victims are not left to suffer the consequences of the crimes committed against them. Furthermore, new sexual harassment legislation could help ensure these changes take place.

At the time I conducted my research, we were at a junction where there was a great awareness of sexual harassment, but a disconnect in the action being taken to prevent it. The Trade Union Congress' (TUC's) petition, *End sexual harassment at work*, called for employers to be required to have a 'legal duty' to prevent sexual harassment in their workplace (TUC, 2019). A government consultation ran from July to October 2019 regarding workplace sexual harassment, and in July 2021, the government confirmed their intent to establish a duty requiring employers to prevent sexual harassment, including by colleagues, clients or customers (TUC, 2021; GEO, 2021). Only time will tell exactly how this will develop.

Online sexual harassment

My research focused upon face-to-face sexual harassment; however, since the internet's existence, virtual forms have increasingly become a concerning issue within work environments. The rise of such behaviours is one of the most contemporary examples of the complexities of sexual harassment, and how the law has not developed accordingly (Franks, 2012). Cyber sexual harassment incorporates a myriad of behaviours, including cyberstalking, image-based sexual abuse and rape threats (Henry & Powell, 2016). As with 'traditional' sexual harassment, defining online forms has also proved to be complex, and it continues to develop as victims are experience novel behaviours.

Research demonstrates that adult victims of cyber abuse experience a multitude of negative outcomes, including depression, anxiety and suicidal ideation, illustrating how consequences of online victimisation are comparable to offline equivalents, and how harmful cyber abuse can be for adult victims as with younger populations (Stevens et al., 2021). Franks (2012, p. 682) described how targeted online sexual abuse not only creates the effects that 'real-life' harassment does but that it can be 'even more pernicious and long-lasting'.

COVID-19 pandemic

The onset of the COVID-19 pandemic resulted in countries across the world going into mandatory lockdowns, and in the UK alone, close to half of the working population were working remotely from home as of 23 March 2020 (Suzy Lamplugh Trust, 2020). Initial research illustrated that there has since been a surge in online sexual harassment whilst women work from home as it has become a '24/7 experience' (Strenio & Chowdhury, 2021), as perpetrators have 'taken advantage of online work platforms and social media' (Rights of Women, 2021).

Workplace sexual harassment is not chiefly attributed to 'physical access', but instead issues pertain to the 'workplace culture and power differentials' (Strenio & Chowdhury, 2021). Women's charity, Rights of Women (2021), conducted an online survey in November–December 2020, finding that of the 42% of women who reported experiencing sexual harassment at work have experienced some, to all, of it virtually. Furthermore, novel forms are being seen, such as 'zoombombing', which in this context refers to persistently harassing someone via video call on Zoom (Oppenheim, 2020).

Reflections

Research has shown that sexual harassment is an 'epidemic throughout global higher education systems' (Bondestam & Lundqvist, 2020, p. 397). Regardless of the perception that the #MeToo movement is responsible for many reporting harassment experienced within academia, research involving a sample of faculty and staff at American universities highlighted that the issue remains predominantly unreported (Kirkner et al., 2020).

In the UK, a University and College Union report (2021), *Eradicating Sexual Violence in Tertiary Education*, underpins pre-existing research regarding the disturbingly significant amounts of sexual violence in academia. It also high-lighted how staff and postgraduate researchers who are not in secure employ-ment; employees who are either disabled, trans and non-binary; and those whose sexual orientation is not heterosexual are at much greater risk of expe-riencing sexual violence.

Of particular interest is the experience of graduate students, who are in a 'unique' position as both employees and students, causing a 'complex power differential' (Lorenz et al., 2019, p. 205). Although an understudied area, Lorenz et al. (2019) found that of their sample (108 graduate students), 86% reported experiencing some form of harassment, including sexist gender harassment, sexual coercion and electronic harassment. Furthermore, the harassment was most commonly carried out by a faculty member (37%).

These findings demonstrate the need for action to be taken, so that universi-ties, as both a learning and work setting, are safer spaces. Furthermore, addi-tional research is needed as there is scant research regarding graduate students' experiences of online harassment (Lorenz et al., 2019), as well as the need to explore the increase in online sexual harassment and the new forms that are being experienced. We are only just beginning to understand the effect of the pandemic on all forms of cyber abuse.

References

ACAS (2021). Sexual harassment. *ACAS*. www.acas.org.uk/index.aspx?articleid=6078 (Accessed 10 November 2021).

Bondestam, F., & Lundqvist, M. (2020). Sexual harassment in higher education – a system-atic review. *European Journal of Higher Education, 10*(4), 397–419.

Braun, V., & Clarke, V. (2006). Using thematic analysis in psychology. *Qualitative Research in Psychology, 3*(2), 77–101.

Buckley, C. (2018). Powerful Hollywood women unveil anti-harassment action plan. *The New York Times*, 1 January 2018. www.nytimes.com/2018/01/01/movies/times-up-hol-lywood-women-sexual-harassment.html (Accessed 01 December 2021).

Clair, P. R., Brown, E. N., Dougherty, S. D., Delemeester, K. H., Geist-Martin, P., Gorden, I. W., Sorg, T., & Turner, K. P. (2019). #MeToo, sexual harassment: An article, a forum, and a dream for the future. *Journal of Applied Communication Research, 47*(2), 111–129.

ComRes (2017). BBC – Sexual harassment in the workplace 2017. *ComRes*, 11th December 2019. https://comresglobal.com/polls/bbc-sexual-harassment-in-the-work-place-2017/ (Accessed 25 November 2021).

Cheng, S., & Wakeling, A. (2018). Sexual harassment in the British workplace. We all know it's wrong, so why is it so difficult to stop? *Acas Workplace Policy*, November 2018. www.acas.org.uk/sexual-harassment-in-the-british-workplace-we-all-know-its-wrong-so-why-is-it-so-difficult-to-stop (Accessed 02 January 2022).

Farley, L. (1978). *Sexual shakedown: The sexual harassment of women on the job.* New York: Mc-Graw-Hill.

Fitzgerald, F. L. (1993). Sexual harassment: Violence against women in the workplace. *American Psychologist, 48(10)*, 1070–1076.

Fitzgerald, L. F. (1990). Sexual harassment: The definition and measurement of a construct. In M. A. Paludi (Ed.), *Ivory power: Sexual harassment on campus* (pp. 21–44). New York: State University of New York Press.

Franks, A. M. (2012). Sexual harassment 2.0. *Maryland Law Review, 71*(3), 655–704.

Gilmore, S. (2018). Sexual harassment in the workplace: Beyond the #MeToo campaign, *The Obstetrician & Gynaecologist, 20*(2), 85–86.

Government Equalities Office (2021). Consultation on sexual harassment in the workplace: Government response. *Government Equalities Office*, 21 July 2021. www.gov.uk/government/consultations/consultation-on-sexual-harassment-in-the-workplace/outcome/consultation-on-sexual-harassment-in-the-workplace-government-response (Accessed 14 December 2021).

Henry, N., & Powell, A. (2016). Technology-facilitated sexual violence: A literature review of empirical research. *Trauma, Violence, & Abuse, 19*(2), 195–208.

Holland, K. J., & Cortina, L. M. (2013). When sexism and feminism collide: The sexual harassment of feminist working women. *Psychology of Women Quarterly, 37(2)*, 192–208.

House of Commons Parliament. (2018). *Sexual harassment in the workplace: Fifth Report of Session 2017–19*. Women and Equalities Committee, 25 July 2018. https://publications.parliament.uk/pa/cm201719/cmselect/cmwomeq/725/725.pdf (Accessed 10 December 2021).

Kelly, L. (1988). *Surviving sexual violence*. Oxford: Polity Press.

Kirkner, A. C., Lorenz, K., & Mazar, L. (2020). Faculty and staff reporting & disclosure of sexual harassment in higher education. *Gender and Education, 34*(2), 199–215.

Lorenz, K., Kirkner, A. C., & Mazar, L. (2019). Graduate student experiences with sexual harassment and academic and social (dis)engagement in higher education. *Journal of Women and Gender in Higher Education, 12*(2), 205–223.

MacKinnon, A. C. (1979). *Sexual harassment of working women: A case of sex discrimination*. New Haven and London: Yale University Press.

MacKinnon, A. C. (2018). #MeToo has done what the law could not. *The New York Times*, 4 February 2018. https://archive.is/20180205122930/www.nytimes.com/2018/02/04/opinion/metoo-law-legal-system.html#selection-2291.0–2291.625 (Accessed 2 January 2022).

Oppenheim, M. (2020). Women subjected to new forms of online sexual harassment including 'zoombombing' during lockdown. *The Independent*, 3 June 2020. www.independent.co.uk/news/uk/home-news/lockdown-sexual-harassment-online-women-zoombombing-a9547371.html (Accessed 15 December 2021).

Rights of Women (2021). Rights of Women survey reveals online sexual harassment has increased, as women continue to suffer sexual harassment whilst working through the Covid-19 pandemic. *Rights of Women*. https://rightsofwomen.org.uk/news/rights-of-women-survey-reveals-online-sexual-harassment-has-increased-as-women-continue-to-suffer-sexual-harassment-whilst-working-through-the-covid-19-pandemic/) (Accessed 15 December 2021).

Sayej, N. (2017). Alyssa Milano on the #MeToo movement: "We're not going to stand for it anymore". *The Guardian*, 1 December 2017. www.theguardian.com/culture/2017/dec/01/alyssa-milano-mee-too-sexual-harassment-abuse (Accessed 20 December 2021).

Stevens, F., Nurse, J., & Arief, B (2021). Cyber stalking, cyber harassment and adult mental health: A systematic review. *Cyberpsychology, Behavior, and Social Networking, 24*(6), 367–376.

Strenio, J., & Chowdhury, J., R. (2021). Remote work during COVID-19: Challenges and opportunities for combatting workplace sexual harassment. *Feminist Perspectives, KCL*, 27 January 2021. www.kcl.ac.uk/remote-work-during-covid-19 (Accessed 5 December 2021).

Suzy Lamplugh Trust (2020). Cyber safety at work 10 November 2020 National Personal Safety Day. Suzy Lamplugh Trust. www.suzylamplugh.org/national-personal-safety-day-2020-cyber-safety-at-work (Accessed 8 October 2021).

Trades Union Congress (2019). Sexual harassment in the workplace – TUC response to GEO technical consultation. *TUC*, 30 September 2019. www.tuc.org.uk/research-analysis/reports/sexual-harassment-workplace-tuc-response-geo-technical-consultation (Accessed 10 December 2021).

Trades Union Congress (2021). Government policy change on sexual harassment is a victory for union campaigning. *TUC*, 21 July 2021. www.tuc.org.uk/news/government-policy-change-sexual-harassment-victory-union-campaigning (Accessed 10 December 2021).

9 Disablism, cyberbullying and online opportunities for engagement

Leah Burch

Introduction

Many disabled people experience hate and hostility on a regular basis. Indeed, research has suggested that disabled people are more likely than their non-disabled peers to be 'bullied' within their local communities (Beadle-Brown et al., 2014) within the ordinary spaces of their everyday lives. Notable hotspots include public transport (Olsen et al., 2017; Wilkin, 2020), pubs and clubs (Burch, 2021), local towns and streets (Hall, 2019), and within their own homes (McCarthy, 2017; Thomas, 2011). Building upon these findings, this chapter considers how the internet provides a particularly unique space for hate to be shared and directed towards disabled people, within the ordinary context of everyday life. Indeed, the internet hosts a range of online communication platforms that have changed the way in which most people access information, communicate with each other and build communities, including disabled people (Gelfgren et al., 2022). Notably, online platforms open up various avenues of communication, many of which offer users anonymity, privacy, immediacy and the ability to engage with a wide range of audiences (Nemes, 2002). Anonymity has been widely debated as a tool that enables a level of privacy that is not afforded within our offline worlds, while at the same time, a tool that can be manipulated to harm others (Sardá et al., 2019). Similarly, global outreach enables users to connect and form networks with others on an international scale. Hosting both opportunity and risk, the internet has fast become a part of everyday life for many parts of the world.

It is important to recognise how these boundaries have become increasingly blurred within the geographies of our everyday lives. Our digital worlds have fast become a part of, rather than something separate from, our offline lives. Many of us, particularly in the Global North, live our offline lives through technology; we post, share, like, tweet and scroll. It could also be argued that social media and social networking sites have taken on a new level of prevalence within our everyday lives. The COVID-19 pandemic has demonstrated the multiple, complex and layered faces of online communication. At its best, the internet enabled communication as a means of overcoming isolation and sharing hope during times of uncertainty. Indeed, research conducted by Pew

DOI:10.4324/9781003258605-11

Research Centre revealed the increasing use of social media technologies as a means of facilitating video calls with friends and families (McClain et al., 2021). Work by Wong et al. (2021) has similarly highlighted the use of social media within the healthcare sector, enabling healthcare professionals to communicate with members of the public when face-to-face interactions were not possible. At the same time, the internet has provided a site for the incitement of violence and scapegoating towards marginalised communities (Ka-Wei Lee & Li, 2020), and the sharing of fake news and conspiracy theories (Patwa et al., 2021). Within this context, it is not possible to understand online communication as entirely separate from the offline world but, instead, as inextricably interwoven with one another.

Due to the prevalence of the online world within our everyday lives, the digital world has fast become a site of research. For example, the uptake of social media has created what Williams and Burnap (2016) have termed a 'social sensor net' that can identify, monitor and trace social reactions to events both in real time and on reflection. In my own work, I have explored some of the possibilities and risks available to disabled people in the online world (Burch, 2017, 2018, 2020a, 2021). These research projects have engaged with text-based methods such as critical discourse analysis, and participatory methods to explore the topic of hate and hostility on a range of levels. In earlier work (Burch, 2017, 2018), I employed modes of textual analysis in order to critically engage with cultural representations of disability as presented upon various online platforms. Following this, I employed participatory methods in order to explore the ways in which disabled people experience, process and make sense of their experiences of hate within the context of their everyday lives (Burch, 2020a, 2021). Although methodologically different, these works have paid attention to the various ways that disabled people can utilise the facilities of online communication and social media as a tool for fostering relationships, self-empowerment and activism, as well as the ways that online disablism can permeate online spaces. In this chapter, I consider examples from these different works and explore some of the online opportunities for disabled people, in addition to the risks of cyberbullying and online disablism.

Online opportunities for disabled people

There are, as will be explored later in this chapter, a range of risks involved with all forms of online communication. Despite this, there are a variety of opportunities available to disabled people online that may not be as readily accessible in the offline world. Given the barriers present within the everyday lives of many disabled people, online communication presents an opportunity for new forms of citizenship to be harnessed (Cocq & Ljuslinder, 2020; Guo et al., 2005; Liddiard, 2014). In particular, social media and various forms of online communication can provide a 'second chance' for social interaction and the ability to distance oneself from social rejection in the offline world (Furr et al., 2016). One participant, Francis Emerson, discussed the value of online spaces created for specific groups of disabled people which can provide a site of mutual understanding and support. Similarly, members of a disabled person's organisation (DPO) supported the positive use of Facebook to share their work with other people in their local community, as well as DPOs nationally. In these ways, online technologies enable modes of self-empowerment and digital activism. Digital activism presents the opportunity for disabled people to create new forms of social movements that address concerns of disabled people and in ways that disrupt traditional conceptualisations of activism as tied to physical movement (Mann, 2018). Blogging in particular has made it possible for disabled people to call out inaccessible societies and their experiences of prejudice and discrimination (Cocq & Ljuslinder, 2020). In her interview, Ariel reflected upon blogging as a tool to share her experiences with her followers. In addition to sharing stories and raising awareness, blogging helped 'get it off your chest' and made her feel better knowing that someone else was reading about her story.

More broadly, online media and communication platforms offer new opportunities for traditionally marginalised communities to interact with a variety of campaigns and discussions (Trevisan, 2019) constituting what Trevisan (2013) has termed 'armchair armies'. Indeed, the accessibility of online communication methods for many (but not all) disabled people can enable greater participation in important conversations about disability that actively challenge traditional narratives. Importantly, such forms of communication allow for more creative and innovative ways for disabled people to present their own stories, rather than those that are storied by non–disabled people (Bitman, 2021). Used in this way, disabled people and activists can make use of online technologies as a platform to educate and raise awareness about disability.

There are some notable examples of 'armchair armies' that have emerged online in recent years. Following the first airing of Sally Phillips' BBC documentary *A World Without Down's Syndrome?*, an active online discussion arose between disabled people, parents and guardians, allies and professionals. Using the hashtags #worldwithoutdowns and #justaboutcoping on Twitter and Facebook, users collectively resisted an ableist imagination of a future without people with Down's syndrome and shared alternative, real and more positive stories of living with Down's syndrome (Burch, 2017). Disabled People Against Cuts (DPAC) was established in 2010 by disabled campaigners and academics in response to the Coalition Government's series of welfare cuts that disproportionately targeted disabled people (Ryan, 2020). Their online campaign was launched in 2013 and featured personal stories of disabled people affected by welfare changes. Due to their online following, DPAC were invited to parliamentary meetings to discuss some of the biggest changes to the welfare system (Pearson & Trevisan, 2015). In the United States, #CripTheVote sought to engage 'voters and politicians in a productive discussion about disability issues in the United States' as a means of ensuring that the needs and concerns of disabled people inform future political landscapes (Disability Visibility Project, 2016). Finally, the Disability Hate Crime Network (DHCN), established in

2007 by Robin Van De Hende, has subsequently secured an online presence as a Facebook group. The group is underpinned by the importance of providing an accessible forum for disabled people to share their ideas, observations and concerns relating to disability hate crime (Brookes, 2013) and, along with several others, I am very pleased to be one of the lead coordinators of this fantastic support network. The DHCN now has over 4,000 members and through close moderation by the coordinators is able to provide a safe and supportive online space for disabled people not only to share their experiences of hate crime but to stay informed of relevant news and events taking place across the country.

While online communication platforms can provide an avenue of opportunity for fostering relationships, developing a sense of community and means of digital activism, such facilities are not available to all disabled people. Indeed, online technologies grant 'conditional access' to disabled people, as many continue to be excluded from participation due to access barriers (Bitman, 2021; Cocq & Ljuslinder, 2020). Continued barriers to accessing online platforms is particularly troubling, given the opportunities that have been described. There is a clear tension then in moving towards greater online communication as a means of increasing accessibility against the risk of further marginalisation. This tension has been a particular problem for many disabled people's organisations and self-advocacy groups who have found new opportunities to reach members, raise awareness of projects and discussions and be visible in the wider community through their use of online platforms (Gelfgren et al., 2022). Indeed, to foster the opportunities that are available, greater attention needs to be paid to the widening of participation through finding ways to widen digital inclusion.

Online disablism

Some of the defining features of the internet that enable positive communication and identity formation simultaneously allow for the promotion of hate. According to Banks (2010), the internet has become the 'new frontier' for spreading hate and for bringing together hate-mongering communities. Indeed, while restrictions within the physical world might prevent similar-minded people from ever meeting, the potential for quick and easy global outreach online allows for greater communication and access to others (Duffy, 2003). And, since online platforms provide opportunities that are not always available to disabled people in their offline worlds, the presence of hate and hostility online can be detrimental.

Online disablism, as expressed through hate, hostility and various harmful narratives, contributes to several negative constructions of 'disability'. For example, in their analysis of disability-themed memes, Hadley (2016) identified three prevalent representations of disability: the 'charity case', the 'inspiration' and the 'cheat'. Memes are argued to make offensive or misleading messages more palatable through the use of humour (Elkhatib & Hill, 2021). Moreover, memes allow for the expression of instant social performance, an intertextual image that 'conveys a complex set of ideas, ideologies and discourses in a swiftly digestible package' (Hadley, 2016, p. 678). Memes that present disabled people as charity cases, inspirations and cheats are able to tap into culturally constituted narratives of disability under the veil of 'banter' (Levin, 2013). Indeed, these memes do not create new narratives of disability but present culturally constructed representations in more creative, innovative and, in turn, more implicit ways.

Work by Liddiard (2014) has shown how such simplistic representations of disability have similarly been used by non-disabled people and larger corporations as a means of commodification. In these cases, memes, images and narratives of disabled people (most notably disabled children) are shared for 'likes' and profits. Such practices, therefore, exploit disabled people while simultaneously replenishing harmful narratives that have been constructed by and for non-disabled people. Liddiard (2014) also noted the presence of such memes as perpetuating narratives of disabled people as scroungers and fraudsters in stark contrast to the superior, self-fulfilling, non-disabled person. My own research has exposed a wealth of disablist rhetoric present on the online bulletin board, Reddit, situated within the context of austerity. Upon this platform, disability was presented as an unfortunate and tragic prospect worse than death and, in turn, something that needed to be prevented. Indeed, my analysis of Reddit threads unearthed widespread support for forced sterilisation, mercy killing and euthanasia (Burch, 2020b). More closely connected to the context of austerity, disabled people were presented as a burden to society, a waste of resources and an infringement to the economic development of society (Burch, 2018). In these examples, online disablism serves a damaging purpose, regurgitating eugenic messages of eradication under the guise of economic and scientific justification (Burch, 2021; Quarmby, 2011). Narratives of austerity and disability are tied to the self-identification of non-disabled people to the independent, self-supporting 'hardworking taxpayer', who is the real victim of austerity (Hughes, 2015). Indeed, while such messages are innately hateful towards disabled people, they were presented as justifiable responses on behalf of 'hardworking taxpayers'.

It is important to highlight that online platforms do not create the harmful narratives described earlier but provide a means of sharing long-standing assumptions and stereotypes that continue to position disabled people as lesser and inferior to their non-disabled counterparts. Indeed, by tapping into long-standing assumptions, online disablism becomes more palatable and, in some contexts, a source of culturally accepted mockery and humour. Indeed, in an analysis of people's responses to memes of Harvey Price, Morris (2019) demonstrates how online disablism becomes an accepted part of memetic culture, rather than a contested presence. Thus, while examples of online disablism, such as those described earlier, do not directly target individual disabled people, their presence can have detrimental impacts on the everyday lives of disabled people, both online and offline. On a more personal level, misleading or offensive comments that appear on disabled people's feed or viral threads can harm the image of disabled users themselves (Bitman, 2021) and impede their sense of belonging. In addition to creating a space that is not for 'them', harmful narratives and images can be used directly against online disabled users and become part of a broader process of cyberbullying and online hate.

Cyberbullying

Despite there being an extensive history of literature exploring disabled people's experiences of hostility and harassment within their physical socio-cultural environments, less is known about how disabled people experience, perceive and react to cyber-harassment and cyberbullying (Alhaboby et al., 2016). This lack of knowledge does not, however, suggest that disabled people do not experience cyberbullying but that it exists largely hidden and unknown. Indeed, like for all victims, the internet provides another venue for bullying behaviour to take place. As Pritchard (2021) points out, the lack of regulation and promotion of Free Speech on various social media platforms presents an opportunity for the promotion of disablist hate speech against disabled people. Indeed, platforms such as Reddit allow their users to create 'throwaway' accounts as a means of enabling a greater sense of anonymity and freedom of expression (Burch, 2018). The facilities of the internet similarly provide access to a wider audience, who, without the facilities of the internet, would not have been in contact with. As a result, the internet not only enables communication between disabled people and perpetrators with little geographical boundaries but, as a part of our everyday life, can become an inescapable form of communication.

Although online geographies of hate were not extensively discussed in my own PhD research, it was reflected upon by some participants who had been directly targeted by hate online. Indeed, several participants shared experiences of being 'bullied' while using social media platforms such as Facebook and Snapchat. For example, Francis Emerson reflected upon being told to 'burn in hell' when engaging with online Christian communities due to his transgender identity. Particularly concerning, he also noted the number of people who would join online groups for autistic people in order to say 'horrible things to people'. In these instances, online spaces that have been created to provide a safe outlet for marginalised communities become a targeted site of hostility, a space that provides direct access to whole communities of disabled people. This includes such practices as hacking websites for epilepsy organisations through the use of flashing animations designed to trigger seizures among those with photosensitive epilepsy. Such expressions of hate are intentional and have clear direction and can therefore be considered as examples of cyberbullying.

In order to manage the presence of cyberbullying, Harry described some identity management techniques that he had engaged with, such as considering the images that are shared on his profile. He explained that posting photos of himself openly using his wheelchair would likely be used as 'ammo' against him and so would only share these photos with audiences he was familiar with. The management of identity, however, is not always possible. For example,

Pritchard (2021) noted the widespread posting of photographs taken of people with Dwarfism without their consent as a means of fuelling comments from other online users. Similarly, in my own research, several participants reflected upon this happening to them and their peers, particularly when using public transport. Some shared Incidents where images had been taken of them in public, and they had later been alerted to these images being shared on Facebook. Significantly, this form of cyberbullying relies upon the simplicity of a photograph as a means of eliciting hate as various derogatory language is attached to the photograph, shared and then reproduced by others. As discussed previously, the multimodal format of these images enables a quick and effective visual message, which in turn, can be more difficult to interpret by coding software than messages that are solely text-based.

Some participants explained that they did not use social media platforms due to the risks that this could entail, despite recognising some of the opportunities that could exist. For example, Shaz described the 'devastating' impact of hate crime via the internet in closing down his ability to socially engage with others and Francis Emerson explained limiting the types of online communities he was now associated with. As discussed earlier, such spaces offer a sense of community, identity formation and a platform to share experiences and voice opinions. Online spaces can, and in many cases do, present an opportunity to be present within a chosen community, which is vital for many disabled people. As such, greater regulation and prevention of cyberbullying and online disablism towards disabled people is vital.

Conclusion

In this chapter, I have explored various examples of the risks and opportunities for disabled people that are posed by online communication technologies. Drawing upon existing, albeit limited research, I have argued that online communication has become part of, and not detached from, our offline everyday lives. Given the immersion of online technologies within everyday life, it is important to raise awareness of the potential risks that this might entail. Indeed, I have explored the risks that all online communication can pose and how the very facilities that can offer possibilities for disabled people similarly provide the tools for the dissemination of hate. Forms of both online disablism and cyberbullying tap into culturally constructed narratives of disability that reinforce the exclusion and discrimination of disabled people more broadly. Such narratives contribute to the perception of disabled people as inherently inferior and lesser to non-disabled people (Burch, 2020b) and as an object of ridicule. As shown in the examples presented in this chapter, online disablism and cyberbullying are not always articulated in explicitly hateful terms but contribute to the normalisation of hate and so-called banter towards disabled people both online and offline.

Despite this, and in my determination to be optimistic, I would like to conclude this chapter with a focus upon the possibilities that online technologies can provide in order to challenge cyberbullying. Indeed, throughout this chapter, I have shown that online technologies can offer a myriad of opportunities for disabled people in terms of establishing communication networks, sharing knowledge and experience, and fostering a sense of collaborative resistance. While these opportunities should be located within the community, universities can, and do, similarly play an important role in supporting staff and students within their wider community. These opportunities can vary in focus, and, indeed, do not need to be specific to cyberbullying and disability but can touch upon broader issues relating to violence, harassment and hate crime. For example, in 2018 Leeds University Union and the University of Leeds ran a joint project entitled 'Draw the Line' where they introduced an online reporting system for staff and students to report incidents of hate crime, sexual assault and online harassment on the university campus. The Centre for Hate Studies at the University of Leicester have created a series of digital training modules to support better understanding and responses to hate and extremism, and the National Union of Students have worked on several campaigns to address sexual violence and harassment on campus. Finally, I am utilising my position within the university and actively working with disabled people to create an online and freely available disability hate crime toolkit. Such a resource will, when it is available, demonstrate the collaborative potential of working on campus, in partnership with communities.

While online, or digital activism, is not suggested to be the single means of ensuring the inclusion of disabled people within society, or the means to challenge hate and bullying in all facets of life, it does open up a number of opportunities. Thus, it is suggested that a hybrid model of online and offline communication strategies might enable a plurality of tactics and opportunities for disabled people to engage collaboratively and innovatively with activism (Pearson & Trevisan, 2015). So, if it is that online technologies are becoming an inescapable part of everyday life for many people, it seems helpful to focus our attention on supporting disabled people to use these platforms to their advantage. In doing so, it might be possible to work with disabled people and online platforms to tap into the ways that they are already engaging with online platforms to connect, collaborate and resist forms of disablism and bullying within their everyday lives, both online and offline.

References

Alhaboby, Z., al-Khateeb, H., Barnes, J., & Short, E. (2016). 'The language is disgusting and they refer to my disability': The cyber harassment of disabled people. *Disability & Society*, *31*(8), 1138–1143.

Beadle-Brown, J., Richardson, L., Guest, C., Malovic, A., Bradshaw, J., & Himmerich, J. (2014). *Living in fear: Better outcomes for people with learning disabilities and autism*. Main Research Report. Canterbury: Maidstone Community Care Housing Society.

Bitman, N. (2021). Which part of my group do I represent?: Disability activism and social media users with concealable communicative disabilities. *Information, Communication & Society*. https://doi.org/10.1080/1369118X.2021.1963463

Brookes, S. (2013). A case for engagement: The role of the UK disability hate crime network (DHCN). In A. Roulstone, & H. Mason-Bish (Eds.), *Disability, hate crime and violence* (pp. 126–134). London: Routledge.

Burch, L. (2017). A world without Down's syndrome? Online resistance on Twitter: #worldwithoutdowns and #justaboutcoping. *Disability & Society, 32*(7), 1085–1089.

Burch, L. (2018). 'You are a parasite on the productive classes': Online disablist hate speech in austere times. *Disability & Society, 33*(3), 392–415.

Burch, L. (2020a). Towards a conceptual and experiential understanding of disablist hate speech: Acceptance, harm, and resistance. In S. M. Olsen, T. Vedeler, J., & I. Eriksen (Eds.), *Disability hate speech: Social, cultural and political contexts* (pp. 67–87). Abingdon: Routledge.

Burch, L. (2020b). 'The stuff of nightmares': Representations of disability on the online bulletin board, Reddit. In J. Johanssen & D. Garrisi (Eds.), *Disability, media, and representations: Other bodies* (pp. 67–87). New York: Routledge.

Burch, L. (2021). *Understanding disability and everyday hate.* London: Palgrave Macmillan.

Cocq, C., & Ljuslinder, K. (2020). Self-representations on social media. Reproducing and challenging discourses on disability. *ALTER, European Journal of Disability Research, 14*, 71–84.

Disability Visibility Project (2016). Looking ahead: The future of #CripTheVote. https:// disabilityvisibilityproject.com/2016/11/17/looking-ahead-the-future-of-cripthevote/

Duffy, M. (2003). Web of hate: A fantasy theme analysis of the rhetorical vision of hate groups online. *Journal of Communication Inquiry, 27*(3), 291–312.

Elkhatib, Y., & Hill, K. (2021). Memes to an end: A look into what makes a meme offensive. In *Misinfo 2021 workshop on misinformation integrity in social networks*, 15 April 2021.

Furr, J. Carreiro, A., & McArthur, J. (2016). Strategic approaches to disability disclosure on social media. *Disability & Society, 31*(10), 1353–1368.

Gelfgren, S. Ineland, J., & Cocq, C. (2022). Social media and disability advocacy organizations: Caught between hopes and realities. *Disability & Society, 37*(7), 1085–1106, https:// doi.org/10.1080/09687599.2020.1867069

Guo, B. Bricout, J., & Hunag, J. (2005). A common open space or a digital divide? A social model perspective on the online disability community in China. *Disability & Society, 20*(1), 49–66.

Hadley, B. (2016). Cheats, charity cases and inspirations: Disrupting the circulation of disability-based memes online. *Disability & Society, 31*(5), 676–692.

Hall, E. (2019). A critical geography of disability hate crime. *Area, 51,* 249–256.

Hughes, B. (2015). Disabled people as counterfeit citizens: The politics of resentment past and present. *Disability & Society, 30*(7), 991–1004.

Levin, J. (2013). Disablist violence in the US: Unacknowledged hate crime. In A. Roulstone & H. Mason-Bish (Eds.), *Disability, hate crime and violence* (pp. 11–24). London: Routledge.

Liddiard, K. (2014). 'Liking for Like's Sake' – The commodification of disability on Facebook. *Journal on Developmental Disabilities, 20*(3), 94–101.

Mann, B. (2018). Rhetoric of online disability activism: #CripTheVote and civic participation. *Communication, Culture and Critique, 11*(4), 604–621.

McCarthy, M. (2017). 'What kind of abuse is him spitting in my food?': Reflections on the similarities between disability hate crime, so-called 'mate' crime and domestic violence against women with intellectual disabilities. *Disability & Society, 32*(4), 595–600.

McClain, C., Vogels, E., Perrin, A., Sechopoulos, S., & Rainie, L. (2021). The internet and the pandemic. *Pew Research Center.* www.pewresearch.org/internet/2021/09/01/the-internet-and-the-pandemic/ (Accessed 4 January 2022).

Morris, C. (2019). *'Come on, It's just a joke': Are persons with disabilities provided adequate protection from disablist speech online? A case study of Harvey Price Memes.* Undergraduate Dissertation, University of Leeds.

Nemes, I. (2002). Regulating hate speech in cyberspace: Issues of desirability and efficacy. *Information and Communications Technology Law, 11*(3), 193–220.

Olsen, A., Pepe, A., & Redfern, D. (2017). *A–Z of learning disability.* London: Palgrave.

Patwa, P., Sharma, S., Pykl, S., Gupta, V., Kumari, G., Akhtar, M., Ekbal, A., Das, A., & Chakraborty, T. (2021). Fighting an infodemic: COVID-19 fake news dataset. In T. Chakraborty, K. Shu, H. Bernard, H., Lui, & M. Akhtar (Eds.), *Combating online hostile posts in regional languages during emergency situation* (pp. 126–135). London: Springer.

Pearson, C., & Trevisan, F. (2015). Disability activism in the new media ecology: Campaigning strategies in the digital era. *Disability & Society, 30*(6), 924–940.

Pritchard, E. (2021). Using Facebook to recruit people with dwarfism: Pros and pitfalls for disabled participants and researchers. *Scandinavian Journal of Disability Research, 23*(1), 85–93.

Quarmby, K. (2011). *Scapegoat: Why we are failing disabled people.* London: Portobello Books.

Ryan, F. (2020). *Crippled: Austerity and the demonization of disabled people* (2nd ed.). London: Verso.

Sardá, T., Natale, S., Sotirakopoulos, N., & Monaghan, M. (2019). Understanding online anonymity. *Media, Culture & Society, 41*(4), 557–564.

Thomas, P. (2011). 'Mate crime': Ridicule, hostility and targeted attacks against disabled people. *Disability & Society, 26*(1), 107–111.

Trevisan, F. (2013). Disabled people, digital campaigns, and contentious politics: Upload successful or connection failed? In R. Scullion, D. Lilleker, D. Jackson, & R. Gerodimos (Eds.), *The media, political participation, and empowerment* (pp. 175–191). London: Routledge.

Trevisan, F. (2019). Using the Internet to mobilize marginalized groups: People with disabilities and digital campaign strategies in the 2016 U.S. Presidential Election. *International Journal of Communication, 13*, 1592–1611.

Wilkin, D. (2020). *Disability hate crime: Experiences of everyday hostility on public transport.* London: Palgrave Macmillan.

Williams, M., & Burnap, P. (2016). Us and them: Identifying cyber hate on Twitter across multiple protected characteristics. *EPJ Data Science, 5*(11), 1–15.

Wong, A., Ho, S., Olusanya, O., Antonini, M., & Lyness, D. (2021). The use of social media and online communications in times of pandemic COVID-19. *Journal of the Intensive Care Society, 22*(3), 255–260.

Theme 3

Legal perspectives

The boundaries of responsibility

10 Misogyny in the metaverse

Leveraging policy and education to address technology-facilitated violence

Shaheen Shariff, Christopher Dietzel, Kaelyn Macaulay and Sara Sanabria[1]

Over the past two decades, there have been growing concerns over the negative effects of social media on users' health and safety (e.g. Zheng & Lee, 2016). And yet, companies such as Meta (formerly Facebook) continue to prioritise 'growth and profits over combating hate speech, misinformation and other threats to the public' (Timberg, 2021). Some may support technological development and dismiss online violence as a phenomenon with no real-world consequences, but recent events such as live-streamed assault and rape have demonstrated how technology can facilitate violence and victimisation (Ampoloquoi, 2021; McPhate, 2016).

Technological advances in virtual reality (VR), which refers to computer-generated 3D spaces where users can interact with one another and their environment through head-mounted displays and handheld controls, have increased concerns about toxic online spaces. For example, Meta recently launched Horizon Worlds, a metaverse platform where users with VR hardware can see through the eyes of their avatar in an online world, and this technology is already allowing users to perpetrate new forms of violence (Petter, 2022; Eccles, 2022; Basu, 2021). Though often used in reference to Meta's new platform Horizon Worlds, the term 'metaverse' refers to any multiuser platform which allows seamless, real-time user communication and dynamic interactions with digital artefacts (Mystakidis, 2022).

VR has increased in popularity because users can create, design and customise their avatars, which supports their full body movement, rather than being controlled from behind a screen (Freeman & Maloney, 2021). It provides an immersive experience where people can meet, interact and socialise online (Freeman & Maloney, 2021). Thus, VR creates a range of new social experiences based in immersive, real-time interactions and grounded in a direct connection between the user and their online self. However, the widespread use of VR and the total immersion of its users raises concerns around how online violence will occur and how it will be tackled. Given how harm has manifested online in the past (Bugeja, 2010; Belamire, 2016), we are calling on Meta and other social media companies to implement more effective measures to make social media platforms and VR safe for all users. In this chapter, we argue that social media companies are responsible for their users' safety, and we consider

DOI:10.4324/9781003258605-13

the ways in which law, education, and other measures can be leveraged to address technology-facilitated violence in Canada.

Technology-facilitated violence

Researching the topic of harmful online phenomena is difficult due to a lack of standardisation in scope and methodology (Olweus & Limber, 2018). Terminology plays a key role in defining this topic, but unfortunately, it often fails to capture the wide range of harmful behaviours that occur via technology. The term 'cyberbullying', for example, places a disproportionate emphasis on victims who are children or teenagers (Vogels, 2021). The term 'online abuse' perpetuates the perception that virtual interactions are limited to digital platforms, where, in reality, these experiences span across online and offline spaces (Koole et al., 2021; Washington, 2015). We have therefore adopted 'technology-facilitated violence' (TFV) as an umbrella term that refers to sexual and non-sexual violence. TFV emphasises how technology enables harmful behaviours and recognises the impact that online interactions can have beyond digital spaces. As such, there are many forms of TFV, including but not limited to cyberbullying, doxing, harassment, and the non-consensual distribution of intimate images and personal information. These are a few types of TFV that we explore in this chapter.

Prevalence and impacts

TFV is a prominent problem in Canadian society. About one in five women and one in seven men report experiencing online harassment (Cotter & Savage, 2019). Notably, the prevalence of TFV is higher among young people and people with marginalised identities. In a study of the public-school population in Ontario, one in five students in grades 7 and 12 reported being victims of cyberbullying (Sampasa-Kanyinga & Hamilton, 2015). Other research similarly found that about one in five 15–29-year-olds experience TFV (Hango, 2016). About one in three Indigenous women and one in three queer women experience TFV (Cotter & Savage, 2019). Sexual minority men are about three times more likely to experience TFV than heterosexual men, and women and men with disabilities report higher rates of TFV than people without disabilities (Cotter & Savage, 2019).

Understanding the impacts of TFV can be challenging because of variations in studies' definitions, measurements and collection methodologies (Koole et al., 2021). Despite these obstacles, a recent systematic review revealed consistent associations between cyberbullying and negative mental health effects, such as depression, anxiety, hostility and suicidality (Kwan et al., 2020). Young Canadians such as Amanda Todd and Rehtaeh Parsons were lost to suicide after being the subjects of vicious online attacks (Shariff & Stonebanks, 2021).

It should be noted that online content can be easily downloaded and distributed, giving it a wider reach, a longer lifespan and a heightened sense of permanence (Koole et al., 2021). Offensive content can resurface and revictimise survivors of TFV, which can have long-term impacts on reputation and self-image (Shariff & Stonebanks, 2021). These facts are vital to dispelling the myth that online violence poses no real danger to victims.

Critics of TFV argue that victims should leave an online space to escape violence they experience in those spaces (Smith, 2013). Like the advice to ignore bullies on the playground, this argument shifts the responsibility to the victim, rather than to their perpetrator. This argument also ignores the responsibility of people in charge, such as administrators and policymakers, and how policies and practices enacted by social media companies can promote users' safety. In the following sections, we examine a few examples of TFV, reflect on Meta's responses to TFV and then consider legal avenues that victims of TFV can pursue in Canada.

Doxing and sexual harassment

Generations who grew up with access to the internet have been taught from an early age not to share their personal information online, lest predators use that information to track them down and commit physical violence (Valcke et al., 2011). The grim reality is that social media users have little control over their private information on the internet (Koole et al., 2021). For example, there are numerous websites where users can pay a nominal fee in exchange for accessing an individual's personal details, such as addresses, phone numbers, loan information, criminal record or anything else listed in public databases or the deep web (Otachi, 2020).

Some perpetrators of TFV engage in a practice known as doxing, where a person's private, identifying information is disseminated online with the intention to threaten or physically harm them in the real world (Douglas, 2016). Doxing was prominent in the so-called GamerGate of 2014, when a disgruntled ex-boyfriend falsely accused a female game developer, Zoe Quinn, of sexually engaging with an industry journalist (Jason, 2015). His public accusations included personal details such as the developer's name and location, and he incited an online hate mob to harass her, even after she obtained a restraining order (Jason, 2015). During the pandemic, doctors in British Columbia experienced doxing as patients aimed their frustrations with government mandates, issues with vaccinations and other problems at them (Daflos, 2021).

There is often an overlap between doxing and non-consensual intimate image sharing, especially in the context of abusive relationships. Perpetrators can post their victims' photos and contact information online, often as a form of punishment when their victim tries to leave the relationship (*R v AC*, 2017 ONCJ 317; *R v TD*, 2018 ABPC 232; *R v Lapointe*, 2019 QCCQ 4523). Victims have spoken out about the impacts of this violation, which include the perpetual fear that someone in their personal or professional life may have seen their intimate images (*R v Calpito*, 2017 ONCJ 129, para. 51).

Social media platforms encourage users to share personal content, and even extremely careful users might leave enough clues that a perpetrator could piece together. With individual users unable to protect their information, the prevention of doxing, sexual harassment and other forms of TFV rely on social media companies, which can moderate users' information and protect people from experiencing harm online and/or in person.

Virtual groping

Recently, there have been numerous news articles published about users' experiences in VR, with many of them indicating that there is a groping problem in VR spaces (Basu, 2021; Frenkel & Browning, 2021; Oppenheim, 2022). For example, in late 2021, a woman who was beta-testing Horizon Worlds reported that she was groped by a stranger (Basu, 2021). Following the incident, Meta updated Horizon Words with 'Personal Boundaries' that place a four-foot barrier between avatars to address concerns about groping and harassment (Iovine, 2022). Meta also now allows users to activate a 'Safe Zone', which stops anyone from touching them, talking to them or interacting with them in any way, thereby offering an additional level of security (Safer Schools, 2022). Reports of incidents such as this raise concerns regarding how adequate and effective measures like Personal Boundaries and Safe Zone are in protecting users and addressing the core problem of TFV.

It should also be noted that social media platforms like Facebook, Instagram and Horizon Worlds constitute a fertile ground for the recreation of pre-existing and deeply embedded social issues. An investigation into Reddit comments about cases of groping in VR indicates that most users believe that VP groping occurs in a 'playful context' (Sparrow et al., 2020). Research also found that most Reddit users' comments about VR groping are dismissive, misogynistic and abusive of the act (Sparrow et al., 2020). These responses to VR groping incidents demonstrate how TFV against women is condoned, excused, tolerated and normalised (Henry & Powell, 2014). As we have argued elsewhere (Shariff et al., 2022), jokes and 'playful contexts' that are offensive can result in even deeper harm to survivors when no one takes them seriously.

Meta's responses to TVF

In response to concerns about TFV, Meta has increased their effort to moderate content and address problematic online behaviour, including by revamping their Community Standards and establishing an 'Oversight Board' to review and make decisions about content shared on its platforms. Major improvements have been made to address a wide variety of issues, ranging from objectional content (e.g. hate speech, graphic content) to user safety (e.g. suicide, child exploitation, bullying) (Transparency Center, 2022). Looking at the main page of Meta's Transparency Center, there is now a 'remove, reduce, inform' strategy to manage and remove content that violates their Community Standards (Transparency Center, 2022).

Despite this, Meta has historically addressed TFV through an equality approach. Hate speech, which is one form of TFV, is defined as violent or dehumanising speech based on protected characteristics such as race, gender and sexuality (Dwoskin et al., 2020). Throughout the company's history, hate speech has been prone to false positives (Dwoskin et al., 2020), which refers to flagging non-problematic content as problematic and results in the improper removal of content. False positives can be caused by human error or the error of an algorithm.

Meta's equality approach also flags problematic posts based on their words, with limited consideration for context (Angwin et al., 2017). Therefore, a problematic comment about a cisgender white man was treated the same as a problematic comment about a transgender Black woman. *Prima facie*, this may not seem like an issue: everyone is treated equally, and the words are the only criterium for censorship or sanction. However, equal treatment does not lead to equal outcomes, nor does it address the more significant intersectional barriers and negative impacts on someone such as a transgender Black woman (Crenshaw, 1991).

Marginalised groups are more likely to be victims of TFV (Thomas et al., 2021). With the increased frequency of negative experiences, there is also an increased likelihood of sharing these experiences on social media. However, without proper consideration for context, posting about a negative lived experience became difficult under the equality approach. After complaints of unfair treatment (Dwoskin et al., 2020), an audit was launched by civil rights activists, like Color of Change, to evaluate Facebook's detection algorithms. The activists found that the company's 'race-blind' approach disproportionately censored and sanctioned users of historically marginalised communities (Dwoskin et al., 2020).

Since then, Meta has responded by overhauling its detection system to include a tiered system for hate speech. This initiative is known as the WoW Project, and it looks to address 'the worst of the worst' language on Facebook (Dwoskin et al., 2020). However, civil rights activists have continued to criticise Facebook's policy reforms for making decisions in favour of powerful individuals (Dwoskin & Zakrzewski, 2021). Thus, victims of TFV may turn away from social media companies like Meta and look elsewhere for help in addressing TFV and holding perpetrators accountable.

Legal responses to harmful online content

In Canada, depending on the nature and severity of TFV, victims may have options for legal recourse. A civil claim allows victims to summon their alleged abusers to court, where a judge rules on whether the offending party infringed on the victim's rights. If the judge rules in the victim's favour, the victim may be entitled to financial compensation or enforcement against the wrongful behaviour. The standard of proof for a civil claim is on the balance of probability, meaning that judges will rule according to whichever version of events they believe is more likely to have occurred. This standard accommodates conflicting facts between the parties, and judges are typically experienced in determining credibility, so civil claims may seem like an attractive option of redress for victims of TFV. However, the success of civil claims is limited to the protection of specific rights.

A defamation claim is another legal option for victims of TFV. This claim allows victims to pursue people who have wrongfully harmed their reputation. Since a defamatory statement only needs to be shared with a third-party, courts across Canada have accepted that claims on social media are subject to defamation claims (*Gagné v Fortin*, 2018 QCCQ 4470, para. 54; *Zhong v Wu*, 2019 ONSC 7088, para. 20; *Galloway v AB*, 2021 BCSC 2344, para. 319). Victims of defamatory claims can be awarded compensation for any financial harm so long as the victim proves that the harm directly resulted from the defamation. Punitive damages can also be awarded when the court deems the defamation to be particularly egregious. Furthermore, victims can name social media companies as defendants in their defamation cases, including when hosting defamatory content goes against the company's terms of service (*FE v TikTok Technology Canada Inc.*, 2021 QCCS 1520). In these circumstances, courts can order the companies to remove the abusive content.

Other options for victims of TFV are suits brought under copyright law or privacy law. Copyright laws such as the US *Digital Millennium Copyright Act* allow victims of non-consensual intimate image distribution to issue takedown requests because they are the original creator of the image (Chen, 2016). Privacy legislation such as the *Privacy Act* in British Columbia also prohibits sharing sensitive private information such as recorded conversations or emails, which could extend to intimate images (West Coast LEAF, 2014). There are categories of torts for breaching the right to privacy or intentionally inflicting mental suffering, but experts warn of the high threshold of severity that the offending behaviour must meet for these claims to be successful (West Coast LEAF, 2014).

These legal avenues are not without practical barriers that may prohibit justice for victims of TFV. Lawsuits require time and money, especially if a victim does not qualify for legal aid. The process of confronting an abuser in court can be (re)traumatising for a victim. Additionally, if a victim wishes to remain anonymous, this can draw out the length and cost of the file even more, with no guarantee of success (*Douville v St-Germain*, 2021 QCCS 3374; *AB v Bragg Communications* Inc., 2012 SCC 46). For these reasons, among others, victims may view the criminal justice system as another potential avenue for holding perpetrators of TFV accountable.

Canadian criminal law

Unfortunately, the recourses available under Canadian criminal law are even narrower than civil claims. First, the standard of proof is significantly higher.

To convict an individual of a crime, prosecutors must convince the judge or jury of their version of the events beyond a reasonable doubt. Second, the crime must be an act specifically prohibited in the *Criminal Code* at the time that the act took place. Criminal investigators face the same barriers as civil plaintiffs when it comes to tracking down perpetrators who act anonymously or from a different jurisdiction. On the one hand, victims of TFV may benefit from not having to pursue their abusers directly, because they do not need to draw on their own financial resources. On the other hand, victims may feel disempowered and displaced by the criminal justice system. Still, the *Criminal Code* addresses some of the most harmful content on social media, and the caselaw reflects that Canadian courts take expressions of violent behaviour very seriously, including when it occurs online.

Since the federal government implemented the *Protecting Canadians from Online Crime Act* in 2014, the *Criminal Code* (1985) has prohibited online distribution of 'an intimate image of a person knowing that the person depicted in the image did not give their consent to that conduct' (s. 162.1). Judges have noted the severity of this behaviour and adopted a broad interpretation of what constitutes a visual recording (*R v Walsh*, 2021 ONCA 43, para. 72). However, most cases have involved defendants who were previously in a relationship with their victims. This narrow application of a criminal provision may therefore fail to effectively discourage TFV for people not in an intimate relationship.

Criminal harassment applies to broader forms of TFV because it addresses any threatening conduct that causes victims 'reasonably, in all the circumstances, to fear for their safety or the safety of anyone known to them' (*Criminal Code*, 1985, s. 264(1)). In assessing a defendant's behaviour, judges will examine the individual circumstances that might impact a victim's sense of fear, even if the communication is exclusively online (*R v Weavers*, 2009 ONCJ 437, para. 72). Thus, any repeated, targeted communications – such as the ones directed at Anita Sarkeesian or Zoe Quinn, who were victims of doxing in the gaming community – could constitute criminal harassment, even if they do not include direct threats or intimate material (Jason, 2015; Jane, 2016). While Canadian courts have frequently upheld convictions of criminal harassment in digital spaces, community advocates have pointed out that the burden is still on victims to establish that the conduct was unwanted (West Coast LEAF, 2014). As a result, this may require victims to face their perpetrators, which few want to do. Unfortunately, legislative efforts to increase judicial powers in the fight against TFV have been difficult to implement.

Legislative movements against TFV

The first legislation against TFV in Canada was the *Cyber-Safety Act*, introduced in Nova Scotia in 2013 after the death of Rehtaeh Parsons (Bruce, 2020). The act sought to 'provide safer communities by creating administrative and court processes that can be used to address and prevent cyberbullying' (*Cyber-Safety Act*, 2013, s. 2). In practice, the act provided the courts with broad powers to grant and enforce protection orders against perpetrators of TFV. It also created a statutory tort of cyberbullying, which would allow victims to pursue damages and injunctions against defendants who had committed certain forms of TFV. Unfortunately, in 2015, a judge struck down the *Cyber-Safety Act* in its entirety after finding that its overly broad definition of cyberbullying violated sections 2(b) and 7 of the *Canadian Charter* (*Crouch v Snell*, 2015 NSSC 340, para. 221). While a latest version of the provincial legislation, the *Intimate Images and Cyber-protection Act* has been enacted in Nova Scotia, the history of the *Cyber-Safety Act* demonstrates the difficulty of implementing legislation that is powerful enough to meaningfully target perpetrators of TFV, which may explain some of the delays of this sort of legislation at the federal level.

In November 2020, the federal Liberal government introduced *An Act to amend the Broadcasting Act and to make related and consequential amendments to other Acts*, more commonly known as Bill C-10. As the title suggests, the act would have amended the *Broadcasting Act*, which mandates legal protections for Canadian content on traditional media broadcasters. Bill C-10 sought to update the legislation to bring the same values of cultural content protection into the internet age such that streaming platforms would no longer be able to skirt the rules. Specifically, Bill C-10 would have forced streaming services to offer specific amounts of Canadian content or to make Canadian content more 'discoverable' on their platforms and to financially contribute to Canadian cultural industries (Raman-Wilms & Curry, 2021). Critics took issue with an amendment that removed the bill's exception for user-generated content because they feared this could be used to regulate personal social media posts. The government defended this action saying it would not cover individual users' posts and that it was instead meant to ensure services like YouTube would be covered by the bill (Raman-Wilms & Curry, 2021). Bill C-10 was eventually tabled once Parliament was dissolved in the summer of 2021. It was reintroduced as Bill C-11 in February 2022 and amended to introduce clarified exclusions for social media users and for social media platforms. At the time of writing, Bill C-11 is being considered by the Canadian Senate.

In June 2021, the Trudeau government proposed Bill C-36, entitled *An Act to amend the Criminal Code and the Canadian Human Rights Act and to make related amendments to another Act (hate propaganda, hate crimes and hate speech)*. This bill would have amended the *Criminal Code*, the *Youth Justice Act*, and the *Canadian Human Rights Act* to better address the propagation of hate speech on the internet. The bill defined 'hatred' as 'the emotion that involves detestation or vilification and that is stronger than dislike or disdain' but created an exclusion for communications that solely 'discredits, humiliates, hurts or offends' (C-36, para 2). Additionally, the bill amended the *Canadian Human Rights Act* to make communicating hate speech over the internet in a way that foments detestation or vilification a discriminatory practice. However, the bill would have only applied to people posting hateful content and would therefore not address the specific platforms on which that content was posted (Woolf, 2021).

Meanwhile, Conservatives and other critics believed the bill would restrict freedom of expression while having a limited impact on hate speech itself (Stober, 2021). Like Bill C-10, Bill C-36 was tabled when Parliament was dissolved ahead of the September 2021 election. In February 2022, the government signalled it would reintroduce Bill C-36 shortly and that it may include extended measures such as the creation of a peace bond to prevent people from continuing to make hateful comments (Woolf, 2021). However, at the time of writing Bill C-36 has not been reintroduced to Parliament.

Conclusions and implications

The realities described earlier require urgent action, and as VR continues to reflect the issues that exist in our society, preemptive measures should be implemented to mitigate and address the potential for TFV. This means harsher consequences must be established and enacted measures should account for the uniqueness of VR (compared to other social media platforms). We also want to stress the importance of taking intersectional approaches that are grounded in empirical research, thereby paying attention to how identity factors into people's experiences. Next, we offer suggestions of how Meta and other social media companies can address TFV.

Online records

Since users rely heavily on the anonymity provided by their devices, new users of Horizon Worlds and other VR platforms should start their profile by sharing proof of ID, which would then appear on their profiles as a 'Verified User'. Thus, the system would be able to keep track of each user's records, for example, how many times they were reported and for what reasons. Such records would make it easier to hold people accountable if, or when, TFV is perpetrated in Horizon Worlds. It would also prevent blocked users from simply opening another account with different personal information. Additionally, each avatar should have a saved history of their social interactions. This can then be used to track the avatar's interactions so that if another user reports a potentially problematic behaviour, it can be reviewed and analysed in light of the user's history. This will allow moderators to evaluate in context whether the flagged behaviour is problematic or not, thereby addressing concerns about false positives. Of course, such moderation would require social media safety training, which we discuss next.

Educational interventions

No matter what safety features are implemented in social media and VR platforms, they are only helpful if users know how to effectively apply them. For example, one victim of virtual groping in Horizon Worlds was unaware of the safety bubble feature (Basu, 2021), which demonstrates a lack of awareness about the platform and its affordances. Thus, social media companies could implement mandatory training for all users to empower victims of TFV to prevent or interrupt harmful interactions. Such training modules could include, for example, an overview of available safety features, including how and when to use them; a workshop about what constitutes TFV, how to recognise it and how to prevent it; and active bystander training to help users report others who are perpetrating TFV.

Mandatory training would not only help victims identify and react to TFV, but it would also help educate potential perpetrators. Rather than putting the onus on victims to respond to and address their own victimisation, training modules offer a proactive approach to ensure that all users understand their responsibilities and how they can collectively contribute to the Community Standards of a digital space. Training everyone, not just potential victims, also recognises that one of the major contributing factors to TFV is the power differential that comes from abusers who have more technical expertise than their victims (Olweus & Limber, 2018). Training should also be provided to moderators who assess flagged content and to developers who create AI systems that auto-evaluate flagged content. Granted, it is unlikely that training will alone be enough to improve Meta's content moderation systems since, for example, Facebook moderators are only allowed about 30–60 seconds to review content and make decisions (Barrett, 2020), which is hardly enough time to make informed, contextual and consequential decisions about TFV. For this reason, educational interventions must be supplemented with systemic changes, such as policy improvements and legislative solutions.

Legislative solutions

Robust legislative solutions are needed to properly address TFV. Such changes should be made by various governing agencies, including social media companies like Meta as well as the Canadian federal government. Specifically, we urge the Canadian federal government to adopt Bill C-11 and to reintroduce and adopt Bill C-36. These bills would increase the Canadian judicial system's ability to hold perpetrators of TFV accountable, as well as the social media platforms that host such violence. We also urge jurisdictions around the world to enact similar legislation to better protect their citizens.

Additionally, the federal government should enact legislation in line with the technical paper produced by the Ministry of Heritage (2021), following consultations on the government's proposed approach to address harmful content online. Such an act would mandate that Online Communication Service Providers (OCSPs) take reasonable measures to identify harmful content and make that harmful content inaccessible to Canadians. It would also create a Digital Recourse Council of Canada that would be tasked with reviewing complaints submitted by affected Canadians related to content moderation decisions issued by OCSPs. Because the act would focus on five types of harmful content (i.e. child sexual exploitation, terrorist content, content that incites violence, hate speech and non-consensual sharing of intimate images), it would begin to address some, but not all, of the issues identified earlier.

Lastly, as VR becomes more common in society, it is imperative that governing agencies be adequately prepared to deal with the potential TFV that VR creates. Consequently, social media companies and governments should develop and allocate resources that support victims of TFV. Resources should also include financial support like research funding that would allow independent scholars to investigate issues related to VR, and TFV more generally. In closing, it is worth repeating that, regardless of government action, the responsibility of providing and maintaining user security rests with social media companies. Social media companies have a duty to ensure their users' safety, and they must not profit from technology-facilitated violence.

Note

1 Including Keighan Blackmore and Sarah Zreim as research contributors.

References

AB v Bragg Communications Inc. (2012). SCC 46.

Ampoloquoi, R. (2021, April 1). Twitch streamer caught assaulting his girlfriend live on stream. *Xfire*. www.xfire.com/twitch-streamer-caught-assaulting-girlfriend-live-stream/

Angwin, J., ProPublica, & Grassegger, H. (2017, June 28). Facebook's secret censorship rules protect white men from hate speech but not black children. *Pro*Publica. www.propublica.org/article/facebook-hate-speech-censorship-internal-documents-algorithms

Barrett, P. M. (2020). Who moderates the social media giants?: A call to end outsourcing. *Center for Business and Human Rights*. https://static1.squarespace.com/static/5b6df958f8370af3217d4178/t/5ed9854bf618c710cb55be98/1591313740497/NYU+Content+Moderation+Report_June+8+2020.pdf

Basu, T. (2021, December 16). The Metaverse has a groping problem already. *MIT Technology Review*. www.technologyreview.com/2021/12/16/1042516/the-metaverse-has-a-groping-problem/

Belamire, J. (2016, October 20). My first virtual reality groping. *Medium; Athena Talks*. https://medium.com/athena-talks/my-first-virtual-reality-sexual-assault-2330410b62ee

Bruce, S. (2020, June 10). Nova Scotia judge awards $85,000 in damages in cyberbullying case. Saltwire. www.saltwire.com/nova-scotia/news/nova-scotia-judge-awards-85000-in-damages-in-cyberbullying-case-460665/

Bugeja, M. (2010, February 25). Avatar rape. *Inside Higher Ed*. www.insidehighered.com/views/2010/02/25/avatar-rape

Chen, A. (2016, December 20). *Using copyright law to fight revenge porn?* Centre for Intellectual Property Policy. www.cippmcgill.ca/news/2016/12/20/using-copyright-law-to-fight-revenge-porn/

Cotter, A., & Savage, L. (2019). Gender-based violence and unwanted sexual behaviour in Canada, 2018: Initial findings from the survey of safety in public and private spaces. https://www150.statcan.gc.ca/n1/pub/85-002-x/2019001/article/00017-eng.htm

Crenshaw, K. (1991). Mapping the margins: Intersectionality, identity politics, and violence against women of color. *Stanford Law Review*, *43*(6), 1241–1299.

Criminal Code, R.S.C. (1985, c. C-46).

Crouch v Snell (2015 NSSC 340).

Cyber-safety Act, SNS (2013, c 2).

Daflos, P. (2021, May 28). 'We're just human beings': B.C. doctors face abuse, threats, doxing amid pandemic fatigue. *CTV News*. https://bc.ctvnews.ca/we-re-just-human-beings-b-c-doctors-face-abuse-threats-doxing-amid-pandemic-fatigue-1.5447899?cache=walqrkeg%3FclipId%3D89830%3FcontactForm%3Dtrue

Douglas, D. M. (2016). Doxing: A conceptual analysis. *Ethics and Information Technology, 18*, 199–210.

Douville v St-Germain, (2021 QCCS 3374).

Dwoskin, E., Nitasha, T., & Kelly, H. (2020, December 3). Facebook to start policing anti-Black hate speech more aggressively than anti-White comments, documents show. *The Washington Post*. www.washingtonpost.com/technology/2020/12/03/facebook-hate-speech/

Dwoskin, E., & Zakrzewski, C. (2021, October 27). Facebook's own civil rights auditors say its policy decisions are a 'tremendous setback.' *The Washington Post*. www.washingtonpost.com/technology/2020/07/08/facebook-civil-rights-audit/

Eccles, Louise. (2022, January 22). My journey into the metaverse – already a home to sex predators. *The Times*. www.thetimes.co.uk/article/my-journey-into-the-metaverse-already-a-home-to-sex-predators-sdkms5nd3

FE v TikTok Technology Canada Inc., (2021 QCCS 1520).

Freeman, G., & Maloney, D. (2021). Body, avatar, and me: The presentation and perception of self in social virtual reality. *Proceedings of the ACM on Human-Computer Interaction, 4*(CSCW3), 1–27.

Frenkel, S., & Browning, S. (2021, December 30). The metaverse's dark side: Here come harassment and assaults. *The New York Times*. www.nytimes.com/2021/12/30/technology/metaverse-harassment-assaults.html

Gagné v Fortin (2018 QCCQ 4470).

Galloway v AB (2021 BCSC 2344).

Hango, D. (2016). Cyberbullying and cyberstalking among Internet users aged 15 to 29 in Canada, Insights on Canadian Society. December. Statistics Canada Catalogue no. 75-006-X.

Henry, N., & Powell, A. (2014). The dark side of the virtual world: Towards a digital sexual ethics. In N. Henry & A. Powell (Eds.), *Preventing sexual violence: Interdisciplinary approaches to overcoming a rape culture*. Basingstoke: Palgrave Macmillan.

Iovine, A. (2022, February 5). Meta has a fix for virtual groping in its social VR space, Horizon Worlds. *Mashable*. https://mashable.com/article/meta-personal-boundary-horizon-worlds-facebook

Jane, E. A. (2016). Online misogyny and feminist digilantism. *Continuum, 30*(3), 284–297.

Jason, Z. (2015, April 28). Game of fear. *Boston Magazine*. www.bostonmagazine.com/news/2015/04/28/gamergate/

Koole, M., Clark, S., Hellsten-Bzovey, L.-A., McIntyre, L., & Hendry, B. (2021). Stalked by our own devices: Cyberbullying as a boundary crossing behavior. *Postdigital Science and Education, 3*, 1–27.

Kwan, I., Dickson, K., Richardson, M., MacDowall, W., Burchett, H., Stansfield, C., Brunton, G., Sutcliffe, K., & Thomas, J. (2020). Cyberbullying and children and young people's mental health: A systematic map of systematic reviews. *Cyberpsychology, Behavior and Social Networking, 23*(2), 72–82.

McPhate, M. (2016, April 18). Teenager is accused of live-streaming a friend's rape on Periscope. *The New York Times*. www.nytimes.com/2016/04/19/us/periscope-rape-case-columbus-ohio-video-livestreaming.html

Mystakidis, S. (2022). Metaverse. *Encyclopedia, 2*(1), 486–497.

Olweus, D., & Limber, S. P. (2018). Some problems with cyberbullying research. *Current Opinion in Psychology, 19,* 139–143.

Oppenheim, M. (2022, February 16). 'Repeated rape threats': Sexual violence and racist abuse in the metaverse. *Independent.* www.independent.co.uk/news/uk/home-news/metaverse-sexual-harasment-assault-racism-b2015741.html

Otachi, E. (2020, June 18). 10 search sites to find people online. *Online Tech Tips.* www.online-tech-tips.com/cool-websites/10-search-sites-to-find-people-online/

Petter, O. (2022, March 20). Why is no one taking sexual assault in the metaverse seriously? *Vogue.* www.vogue.co.uk/arts-and-lifestyle/article/sexual-assault-in-the-metaverse

Raman-Wilms, M., & Curry, B. (2021, June 4). What is bill C-10 and why are the Liberals planning to regulate the internet? *The Globe and Mail.* www.theglobeandmail.com/politics/article-what-is-bill-c-10-and-why-are-the-liberals-planning-to-regulate-the/

R v AC, (2017 ONCJ 317).

R v Calpito, (2017 ONCJ 129).

R v Lapointe, (2019 QCCQ 452)3.

R v TD, (2018 ABPC 232).

R v Walsh, (2021 ONCA 43).

R v Weavers, (2009 ONCJ 437).

Safer Schools (2022, June 10). A guide to Horizon Worlds. https://oursaferschools.co.uk/2022/06/10/horizon-worlds-metaverse/

Sampasa-Kanyinga, H., & Hamilton, H. A. (2015). Use of social networking sites and risk of cyberbullying victimization: A population-level study of adolescents. *Cyberpsychology, Behavior and Social Networking, 18*(12), 704–710.

Shariff, S., Macaulay, K., & Stonebanks, F. R. (2022). What is the cost of free speech for entertainment? A missed opportunity by the supreme court of Canada to reduce offensive speech and protect marginalized youth. *Education & Law Journal, 31*(1), 25–44.

Shariff, S., & Stonebanks, F. R. (2021). *Defining the lines with iMPACTS: A multi-sectored partnership policy model to rehumanize children's online communication ("iMPACTS Policy Model")* Kids & Technology Essay Series, Max Bell Institute of Public Policy, McGill University.

Smith, G. (2013, November 26). Cyberbullying is easy to stop, just log off. *The Churchill Observer.* www.thechurchillobserver.com/opinions/2013/11/26/cyberbullying-is-easy-to-stop-just-log-off/

Sparrow, L., Antonellos, M., Gibbs, M., & Arnold, M. (2020). From 'silly' to 'scumbag': Reddit discussion of a case of groping in a virtual reality game. *Proceedings of the 2020 DiGRA international conference: Play everywhere.* The Digital Games Research Association.

Stober, E. (2021, June 23). Liberals introduce bill to fight online hate with *Criminal Code* amendments. *Global News.* https://globalnews.ca/news/7976076/bill-c-36-online-hate-canada/

Thomas, K., Akhawe, D., Bailey, M., Boneh, D., Bursztein, E., Consolvo, S., . . . & Stringhini, G. (2021, May). Sok: Hate, harassment, and the changing landscape of online abuse. In *2021 IEEE symposium on security and privacy* (pp. 247–267).

Timberg, T. (2021, October 22). New whistleblower claims Facebook allowed hate, illegal activity to go unchecked. *The Washington Post.* www.washingtonpost.com/technology/2021/10/22/facebook-new-whistleblower-complaint/

Transparency Center (2022). At Meta, we're committed to giving people a voice and keeping them safe. *Meta.* https://transparency.fb.com/

Valcke, M., De Wever, B., Van Keer, H., & Schellens, T. (2011). Long-term study of safe internet use of young children. *Computers & Education, 57*(1), 1292–1305.

Vogels, E. A. (2021, January 13). The state of online harassment. *Pew Research Center.* www.pewresearch.org/internet/wp-content/uploads/sites/9/2021/01/PI_2021.01.13_Online-Harassment_FINAL-1.pdf

Washington, E. T. (2015). An overview of cyberbullying in higher education. *Adult Learning, 26*(1), 21–27.

West Coast LEAF. (2014). *#CyberMisogyny: Using and strengthening Canadian legal responses to gendered hate and harassment online.* www.westcoastleaf.org/wp-content/uploads/2014/10/2014-REPORT-CyberMisogyny.pdf

Woolf, M. (2021, November 21). 'Time to act': Advocates press feds to tackle online hate speech, raise wording concerns. *Global News.* https://globalnews.ca/news/8390694/online-hate-speech-bill-c-36/

Zheng, X., & Lee, M. (2016). Excessive use of mobile social networking sites: Negative consequences on individuals. *Computers in Human Behaviour, 65*, 65–76.

Zhong v Wu (2019 ONSC 7088).

11 Stalking in universities

Responding effectively as an
institution while prioritising the
safety of victims

Emma Short and James Barnes

Introduction

Young people between the ages of 21 and 25 years make up 66% of university students (Office for Students, 2022), and it is this group of people who are likely to be most at risk of sexual harassment and violent crime. The prevalence of stalking victimisation is also likely to be elevated. Indeed, a Freedom of Information (FOI) request made to universities by the Unfollow me campaign revealed that 381 students had made allegations of stalking or domestic abuse between 2015 and 2018. In 40% of those cases, the person who was accused of stalking and the person making the allegation studied at the same university (Vice, 2019).

The Statement of Expectations published by the Office for Students calls for the implementation of more effective systems, policies and processes to prevent and respond to incidents of harassment and sexual misconduct; stalking is included under this definition. Access to appropriate and effective support is a key principle in this statement. The necessity of adopting existing UUK guidelines to create a culture where such behaviours are highlighted as high risk and associated preventative education is also evident.

This chapter provides a context for the legislation and additionally examines academic institutions' legal duties in prevention, identification and responding effectively to online harassment and stalking and the barriers to enacting legislation.

The background: definitions and prevalence of stalking

Stalking remains a crime that is not widely understood and may include a pattern of events and experiences that can be both objectively neutral and frightening or violent. Victims themselves often find it hard to define. Generally stalking is recognised in academic literature to be a course of conduct that creates fear (Sheridan & Lyndon, 2012; Logan & Walker, 2021; Strand, 2020). Stalking does not have a legal definition but is identified under two offences as repeated persistent behaviours of harassment which involve a course of conduct that creates a fear of violence in an individual and amounts to stalking, or creates serious alarm and distress, but does not reach the threshold for fearing violence. The legislation specifically identifies that the effect of such behaviour is to curtail a

DOI:10.4324/9781003258605-14

victim's freedom, leaving them feeling that they constantly have to be careful (Crown Prosecution Service, 2018). This is highly problematic for anyone in the University community, where the expectation should be for students to succeed' and 'to feel safe, healthy and part of a tolerant, inclusive academic community.

The definition of a 'course of conduct' needs unpacking to communicate the disruption caused by persistent, repeated and unwanted intrusions. Therefore, an additional way of identifying stalking has been in terms of the frequency and prevalence of the behaviours. Cloonan-Thomas et al. (2022) suggest a combination of three elements when attempting to define stalking for the purposes of research which could helpfully be extended to identifying stalking in university settings. These elements are the frequency and duration of the unwanted intrusions as well as the target's experience of fear (McEwan et al., 2020). Purcell et al. (2004) suggested that unwanted behaviour from someone for a duration of longer than two weeks distinguishes persistent stalking from shorter patterns of harassment. During this two-week period, the repetition of behaviours is also considered, and it is generally agreed that the conduct includes five or more unwanted intrusions to amount to stalking behaviour. However, the number and nature of intrusions often go beyond this, with individual victims of stalking reporting up to 100 incidents before reporting them to the police (HMIC, HMCPSI, 2017). Beyond academic definitions, the difficulties with identifying stalking are just as challenging. In recognition of this, the College of Policing devised and now share a mnemonic to help identify stalking behaviour for those who are experiencing it and those who may be supporting them. If someone's behaviour is experienced as Fixated, Obsessive, Unwanted and Repeated (FOUR) and causes fear and distress, it should be identified as stalking.

Laws on stalking

Stalking is an offence under the Protection of Freedoms Act 2012, with two offences of stalking added to new sections 2A and 4A into the Protection from Harassment Act 1997. The Protection from Harassment Act 1997 states that stalking can be described as 'following another person, contacting or attempting to contact another person by any means, as well as publishing a statement or material relating to, suggesting relating to or originating from another person'. Under section 2A of the Act, it is an offence to pursue 'a course of conduct in breach of section 1(1), . . . [in which] the course of conduct amounts to stalking' (Crown Prosecution Service, 2018). The offence should be identified when a victim reports a course of conduct that occurs on at least two occasions, which causes alarm or distress to the victim. In addition, the perpetrator is required to understand that the course of conduct amounts to harassment to the victim. The general test in stalking cases is to ask whether a reasonable person with the same information would define the perpetrator's behaviour as harassment. The Act does not provide a definition of stalking but gives a list of behaviours and conduct that could be considered harassment. This has led to debate on the characterisation of behaviours around stalking and cyberstalking. Section 2A of the Act distinguishes cyberstalking as a subsection of the offence of stalking. A person guilty of the offence of stalking under section 2A can face a summary conviction to six months' imprisonment and/or a fine of up to £5,000.

Section 2B of the Act details police powers to enter and search premises in relation to the section 2A offence. Stalking which involves fear of violence or serious alarm or distress is recognised under Section 4A. Such offences must have occurred on at least two occasions; violence will be used against victim, or the course of conduct causes serious alarm or distress with a substantial adverse effect on his/her usual day-to-day activities. Consequently, section 4A encompasses aggravated forms of cyberstalking as well since it represents an aggravated form of section 2A. A person found guilty under section 4A can be sentenced to imprisonment for a term not exceeding ten years and/or a fine, and on summary conviction, to imprisonment not exceeding six months and/or a fine up to £5,000.

Under Scottish law, stalking offences are charged under section 39 of the Criminal Justice and Licensing (Scotland) Act 2010. According to section 39, a person commits the offence of stalking, when they engage in a course of conduct with the intention to cause the victim to experience fear or alarm which the perpetrator ought to know will likely cause the victim physical or psychological harm, or apprehension or fear for safety (UK Government, 2010a). Section 31 (6) of the Act classifies several types of conduct covered by section 39 including instances of cyberstalking. Again, as in the Protection from Harassment Act 1997, the list of examples given is non-exhaustive. It can be seen there is not a specific stalking law in the UK, but apart from the Protection from Harassment Act 1997 there are also several criminal laws that can apply to malicious communications, threatening violence and defamation (Table 11.1).

Table 11.1 A summary of the relevant legislation across the UK (the list is not exhaustive). (Tackling online harassment and promoting online welfare, UUK)

- Obscene Publications Act 1959 Public Order Act 1986
- Malicious Communications Act 1988
- Computer Misuse Act 1990
- Crime and Disorder Act 1998
- Protection from Abuse Act 2001 (Scotland)
- Communications Act 2003
- Sexual Offences Act 2003
- The Law of Defamation
- Sexual Offences (Scotland) Act 2009 Equality Act 2010
- Criminal Justice and Licensing (Scotland) Act 2010 (upskirting became a criminal offence under this Act)
- Criminal Justice and Courts Act 2015 (covers image-based sexual abuse in England and Wales)
- Abusive Behaviour and Sexual Harm Act 2016 (covers image-based sexual abuse in Scotland)
- Justice Act Northern Ireland 2016 (covers revenge)10 pornography
- Domestic Abuse (Scotland) Act 2018 (makes psychological and domestic abuse and controlling behaviour a crime)
- Voyeurism (Offences) Act 2019
- Draft Domestic Abuse Bill (England, 2019)

The UK government is clear on the principle of online safety. What is illegal offline is also illegal online, as introduced in the Digital Charter, which constitutes a rolling programme detailing the norms and rules of online behaviour and putting them into practice (UK Government, 2017, 2018). The Online Harms White Paper proposing a new regulatory framework to prevent online harms was also published in April 2019. Consultations on this closed in July 2019. In response to the process of consultation, the Bill was renamed the Online Safety Bill and introduced with the ambitious commitment to make 'the UK the safest place in the world to be online while defending free expression' (UK Government, 2022). This together with online literacy and citizenship skills for children and young adult online users may help address the emerging challenges ahead.

Stalking and technology

Technology has undoubtedly made it easy for everyone to gather information about other people and to communicate with them. The quantity of unwanted, e-communications, surveillance and unauthorised access to accounts and devices documented in cases of stalking is often reported as overwhelming. A wide variety of technology is being used in stalking (Woodlock, 2014).

It has been observed that being victim to cyberstalking is associated with a consequential distrust of technology (Stevens et al., 2021). Withdrawing from online spaces might seem to be a protective measure but can further isolate and disadvantage individuals, also presenting a particular difficulty to students who need university digital systems, networks and virtual learning environments to study and engage with the University community. A report based on two freedom of Information requests (Phippen & Bond, 2020) suggests that at the time of writing, many universities do not recognise the core role of digital technologies and social media in the lives of their students and have not effectively engaged with how they may come to harm in these environments or with online safeguarding. Evidence also suggests that the experience of regular online abuse is combined with low awareness of policy amongst students and staff about acceptable internet use or pathways to support (Short et al., 2016).

Impact of stalking

The impact of stalking is often profound and can result in tragic consequences for all those involved (HMICFRS, 2017). Serious harm can be experienced by the victims when they try to distance themselves from the offenders (Quinn-Evans et al., 2021), especially in cases where coercion and control have characterised the prior relationship. The fear is a realistic one as half of the stalkers carry out their threats (MacKenzie et al., 2009). Monckton Smith et al. (2017) found that stalking behaviours were found to be present preceding 94 per cent of 358 homicides reviewed. However, the impact of stalking should not only be estimated in terms of physical assault. In cases where physical violence does not occur, the experience of stalking is associated with psychological harm, along with financial, social and other enforced losses and alterations to living that affect well-being and functioning (McEwan et al., 2007; Short et al., 2014). Stalking also has serious health implications for victims, including the risk of developing psychological disorders such as post-traumatic stress disorder (PTSD), depression, panic disorders and anxiety (Dressing et al., 2005). The risk of increasing psychological and physical problems for individuals who have existing chronic psychological, psychiatric, developmental or physiological conditions and disabilities has also been documented in cases of cyber harassment (Alhaboby et al., 2016).

Stalking in the university population

While most university students have a positive experience academically and socially, evidence shows that a significant proportion of students are subject to sexual abuse, harassment and stalking. Universities are a microcosm of society, and the same damaging behaviours seen in wider society exist in these institutions. However, Fissel et al. (2020) found that the prevalence of stalking victimisation for college student samples seems to be greater than for nationally representative adult samples. Demographic characteristics and their association with the incidence of victimisation through stalking have been widely researched (Mullen et al., 2000; Chan & Sheridan, 2020). It is recognised that anyone can be a victim of stalking. However, more women are victimised than men and most offenders are male (Kuehner et al., 2012). Findings from the Crime Survey for England and Wales (CSEW) year ending 2019 indicate that about 1 in 10 men and more than 1 in 5 women between the ages of 16 and 74 have experienced stalking behaviour (ONS, 2019). Women also tend to report higher levels of fear during stalking when compared to men (Sheridan & Lyndon, 2012).

Government figures indicate that females aged 18–19 are the most likely group to be the target of harassment and sexual offences (8.2%) when compared to females in general (3%) and both genders (3%). Young people are more likely to experience interpersonal violence (Walby & Allen, 2004) and females in the age group of most students (16–24) are most vulnerable to sexual violence (Myhill & Allen, 2002). This makes the demographic profile of universities important when considering safeguarding and legislation. Figures show that the student body is made up of students across all ages. However, in 2020–2021, 37% of all students were under 21 (HESA, 2021) (57% were females), accounting for 2.7 million students in the UK, an increase of 9% from 2019/20. Men can also be the victims of harassment and stalking. Response to these acts must be effective irrespective of gender.

A study conducted by the British Freedom of Information laws explores the statistics of domestic and stalking abuse allegations in HE across Britain (Vice,

2019). Responses were received by 119 universities, out of a total of approximately 136 universities in the UK. 381 learners in higher institutions, especially public universities within the United Kingdom, reported domestic and stalking abuse between 2015 and 2018. The same study also reports that approximately 51% of the individuals accused of abuse remained at their respective institutions. In the last three years, it is estimated that universities encountered around 175 complaints on domestic and stalking abuse, with 46% of all cases taking place at Russell Group Universities.

Cardiff had the highest number of allegations. Between 2015 and 2018, Cardiff students reported 115 allegations of stalking or domestic abuse. However, this high number was attributed to the effective implementation of the university's disclosure reporting gateway. Here students are strongly encouraged to highlight any case of abuse and stalking. Acknowledging that some students may fall victim more than once, they also encourage students to report any historic abuse, prompting the rising number of reported cases. Although reporting systems for abuse such as this encourage victims and survivors to come forward and disclose incidents, as of 2019, only 13% of universities had anti-harassment and anti-bullying policies as part of the code of conduct among students. Cardiff's robust reporting practice is not the norm.

More recently, a Freedom of Information request submitted by Palatinate (2021) to Durham University identified that 96 claims of bullying and harassment were submitted in a 21-month period using the University's Report and Support tool up to June 2021. In cases where the gender of the reporting person was disclosed, three-quarters of bullying and harassment claims reported were submitted by women, identifying students and staff. This highlights the gendered nature of harassment. BAME staff and students were also disproportionately represented in these statistics as reports that disclosed the race of the reporting party showed that 30% of reports were made by BAME students or staff.

There are cases which highlight problematic responses to cases of stalking in universities. A recent report (BBC, 2021) detailed the experience of a 25-year-old female Oxford Brookes student who was stalked by a fellow student. He started messaging her; his conduct escalated to violent threats, use of multiple channels of communication and packages sent to her accommodation. The ordeal left her fearful, physically unwell and having to make changes to her daily activities. Four months after the incidence was reported, protective measures were put in place by the university. The report suggests that the University put these protective measures in place to protect the student only after the perpetrator committed the criminal offence of breaking a restraining order against him. Following this breach, he was suspended from the university and banned from the campus. The student was prosecuted and given a four-month suspended sentence and a restraining order of five years. This case highlights the lack of protective measures for victims of stalking when trying to force high-risk, criminal conduct issues of this kind into the existing practices of student misconduct. Statements from the university indicate the acknowledgement of the need for the improvement of policies where student behaviour or conduct may also constitute a criminal offence. This should be a priority across the sector.

Despite the prevalence of stalking and harassment among students, it has not led to significant legislation protecting these individuals within the university environment which presents a unique set of vulnerabilities. Increased autonomy, restricted movement in terms of regularly scheduled classes and other activities, communal working/living on or close to campus, and designated parking all contribute to students being consistently, predictably accessible and highly vulnerable to experiencing stalking risks compared to the general public (Fisher et al., 2002).

Universities are tasked with ensuring that the spaces where students study, work and live are safe. The interests of these students are guaranteed by acts such as the Equality Act of 2010, legislation, duty of care at common law and contract law, which put down legal obligations on universities to protect their students in various situations. Equality Act of 2010 (UK Government, 2010b) ensures that it is unlawful for a university to victimise, harass or discriminate against potential, current and former students. However, there is currently no legislation that legally requires universities to protect their students and thus far the reach of the university's obligations regarding the well-being of a student has not been tried out in the courts. So, a breach of this duty of care has not been tested.

The universities' obligation to the student is complicated, and it usually falls upon the academics within the university to collaborate and help the students with adverse situations. Consequently, many universities train their staff to ensure that they react appropriately to situations where a student is in a position of harm or difficulty.

Responses to stalking

How can we be sure that Universities offer effective support? Beyond universities, people who are being stalked sometimes approach healthcare professionals (HCPs) to help reduce the impact of stalking on their lives (Mullen et al., 2006). This often helps the victim to clarify their situation and adopt coping strategies, but the response and help given are reliant on the HCP's knowledge of the phenomenon (Kamphuis et al., 2005). In most cases, HCPs may underestimate the adverse effects of stalking on a victim's life. This underestimation can be common in cases where the boundaries in the situation do not fall within a still dominant stereotype of cases such as stranger stalking or gender of victim and perpetrator. The belief that stalking offenders are usually strangers is at odds with the experience of most victims (Weller et al., 2013). McEwan et al. (2007) found that being stalked by a former partner poses more threat and is sustained over a longer period (Eke et al., 2011). Stalking is also commonly seen as female victims at the hands of male perpetrators (Purcell et al., 2002). Thus, underestimation of stalking effects may occur in cases where such characteristics are not evident (Brooks et al., 2021). Practitioners may fail to understand the actual challenges facing male victims experiencing stalking by female perpetrators. At the same time, professionals fail to understand the complexity associated with stalking. As a result, this translates into the inability of individuals who are being stalked in accessing support health and social services needed to overcome their situation. This vacuum is recognised by the stalking sector in general, while there are specialist-trained practitioners known as ISACs (Independent Stalking Advocacy Caseworkers) who are usually based within stalking or domestic abuse charities. They offer both skilled support to victims and support for those working with victims of stalking. However, there are simply not enough. At the time of writing, the government is being petitioned to provide more funding for stalking advocates under 'Gracie's Law'. This is named after Gracie Spinks who was 23 and was stalked and murdered by a former colleague. In her memory, friends, family and agencies working in the stalking sector have come together to support this initiative. This lack of specialist services is likely to be mirrored in universities, with only 13% who responded to the FO1 request having specific policies on domestic abuse and stalking (Vice, 2019). The positive impact of providing more advocates is demonstrated by figures released by the Suzy Lamplugh trust (2022), who indicated that in stalking cases where a specialist advocate is involved victims are more likely to report to the police and have more success when pursuing legal action. As highlighted in the report, victims found that their stalking advocate was vital in supporting their overall well-being and mental health.

Universities UK (UUK) is the collective voice of 140 universities across the UK. It is the membership body of vice chancellors and university principals and aims towards continued improvement in HE. To support UK universities in tackling the rise of online abuse, UUK published guidance and practical recommendations designed to support universities in addressing online harassment, including stalking (UUK, 2019). The published report was based on evidence including academic articles, research reports from external experts and reference to practice in the international education sector. The report recommended seven principles in addressing online harassment and promoting online welfare. The first of these was for senior leadership within universities to take ownership and accountability for safeguarding of students and providing procedures of reporting, monitoring, and supporting student concerns. As stated in principle 2, this must be done through a strategic and university-wide approach and all stakeholders must be involved, including student unions, senior leaders and academics. Principle 3 states that students must be engaged in the creation and development of procedures and where possible survivor accounts should shape the future progress of such programmes. Principle 4 states that robust policies and procedures are effective in tackling the issues and that institutions should extend a zero-tolerance culture to matters of online harassment. Universities must also monitor and evaluate prevention and support activities. Accessibility is highlighted in principle 5, stating that universities must have a range of accessible mechanisms to make disclosures and report incidents. In addition, equality monitoring should be embedded into reporting systems and universities should consider peer-to-peer procedures to support students. Principles 6 and 7 are recommendations to promote online safety and welfare in collaboration with students and the student unions as well as considering adopting optional questions for the national student survey around online safety and well-being. Finally, the report recommends sharing good practices and research findings in tackling the issue.

Recommendations

The resulting recommendations are informed by the Office for Students (2022) and UUK (2019). There is a need to enact the principles outlined earlier to meet the expectations of university communities, and these will partly be shaped by training and resources. The response to stalking cases must improve, but so must the wider culture which tolerates harassing and stalking behaviours. Universities provide an environment where that can be challenged by integrating education on stalking to improve identification of stalking behaviours and to create a culture which rejects all forms of harassment.

The primary recommendation here is that university student services and staff who find themselves supporting members of the university community should undertake training in order to ensure that stalking behaviours can be identified, and the victims of stalking are supported by suitably informed staff who have knowledge of the correct referral routes for specialist services, support and access to justice. Disclosing the details of stalking can be very difficult, so the university systems and processes students and staff encounter need to be as supportive and as non-judgemental as possible. There are several national and regional organisations that form the National Stalking Consortium and who offer training in stalking awareness and the response to stalking. The Alice Ruggles Trust offers an Ofqual accredited qualification aimed at professionals who work with young people and has been attended by a variety of Student Services professionals. The Suzy Lamplugh Trust which chairs the consortium has an established history of education, campaigning and support for stalking and provides the National Stalking Helpline Service and offers both open-access stalking awareness courses and bespoke stalking awareness courses that can be tailored to the requirements of the team or organisation.

The second recommendation addresses the culture shift necessary to create a culture that prevents abuse like harassment and stalking. Cases studies that present positive movement towards this culture shift are included on the UUK webpage on tackling online harassment and feature a range of interventions.

In conclusion, the effectiveness of staff training and changing the culture on campus highlighted in the recommendations earlier will only be understood by a reduction in reported cases and an increased feeling of safety by individuals in the community. Universities have a role in providing information that might indicate that success. A baseline metric assessing university culture and feelings of safety might be a good place to start. We would also recommend that the National Student Survey adds to the core 27 questions by including a question about how safe students feel on campus and in their life at university.

This could also be included in staff surveys and would echo the expectation for students 'not only to succeed but to feel safe, healthy and part of a tolerant, inclusive academic community' (OfS, 2021).

Getting help or advice on stalking

National Stalking Helpline | The Suzy Lamplugh Trust: www.suzylamplugh.org/pages/category/national-stalking-helpline

Paladin: https://paladinservice.co.uk/

Alice Ruggles Trust https://alicerugglestrust.org/

The Cyber Helpline: www.thecyberhelpline.com/

Protection Against Stalking: www.protectionagainststalking.org/

Women's Aid: www.womensaid.org.uk/information-support/what-is-domestic-abuse/stalking/

Victim Support: www.victimsupport.org.uk/crime-info/types-crime/stalking-and-harassment/

Citizens Advice: www.citizensadvice.org.uk/family/gender-violence/domestic-violence-and-abuse-getting-help/

S

www.actionagainststa" cotland:

www.actionagainststal

www.mygov.scot/victim-support" king.org

www.mygov.scot/victim-support-stalking

Wales:

Safer Communities Wales: https://safercommunities.wales/vawdasv/stalking-and-harassment/

References

Alhaboby, Z. A., al-Khateeb, H. M., Barnes, J., & Short, E. (2016). The language is disgusting, and they refer to my disability': The cyberharassment of disabled people. *Disability & Society, 31*(8), 1138–1143.

BBC (2021). Student stalked at university calls for change. www.bbc.co.uk/news/education-59587275 (Accessed 12 July 2021)

Brooks, N., Petherick, W., Kannan, A., Stapleton, P., & Davidson, S. (2021). Understanding female-perpetrated stalking. *Journal of Threat Assessment and Management, 8*(3), 65–76. https://doi.org/10.1037/tam0000162

Chan, H. C. O., & Sheridan, L. L. (2020). *Psycho-criminological approaches to stalking behavior: An international perspective.* Chichester: John Wiley & Sons.

Cloonan-Thomas, S., Daff, E. S., & McEwan, T. E. (2022). Post-relationship stalking and intimate partner abuse in a sample of Australian adolescents. *Legal and Criminological Psychology, 27*(2), 194–215.

Crown Prosecution Service (2018). *Stalking and harassment*. www.cps.gov.uk/legal-guidance/stalking-and-harassment (Accessed August 2021).

Dressing, H., Kuehner, C., & Gass, P. (2005). Lifetime prevalence and impact of stalking in a European population: Epidemiological data from a middle-sized German city. *The British Journal of Psychiatry, 187*(2), 168–172.

Eke, A. W., Hilton, N. Z., Meloy, J. R., Mohandie, K., & Williams, J. (2011). Predictors of recidivism by stalkers: A nine-year follow-up of police contacts. *Behavioral Sciences & the Law, 29*(2), 271–283.

Fisher, B. S., Cullen, F. T., & Turner, M. G. (2002). Being pursued: Stalking victimization in a national study of college women. *Criminology & Public Policy, 1*(2), 257–308.

Fissel, E. R., Reyns, B. W., & Fisher, B. S. (2020). Stalking and cyberstalking victimization research: Taking stock of key conceptual, definitional, prevalence, and theoretical issues. In L. Sheridan, B. W. Reyns, & B. S. Fisher (Eds.), *Psycho-criminological approaches to stalking behavior: The international perspective* (pp. 11–36). Chichester: John Wiley & Sons.

HESA (2021). *Higher education student statistics: UK, 2020/21 – Student numbers and characteristics*. www.hesa.ac.uk/news/25-01-2022/sb262-higher-education-student-statistics/numbers (Accessed 12 July 2022).

HMIC, HMCPSI (2017). *Living in fear – the police and CPS response to harassment and stalking*. www.justiceinspectorates.gov.uk/hmicfrs/publications/living-in-fear-the-police-and-cps-response-to-harassment-and-stalking/ (Accessed 20 January 2022).

Kamphuis, J. H., Galeazzi, G. M., De Fazio, L., Emmelkamp, P. M., Farnham, F., Groenen, A., . . . & Vervaeke, G. (2005). Stalking – perceptions and attitudes amongst helping professions. An EU cross-national comparison. *Clinical Psychology & Psychotherapy: An International Journal of Theory & Practice, 12*(3), 215–225.

Kuehner, C., Gass, P., & Dressing, H. (2012). Mediating effects of stalking victimization on gender differences in mental health. *Journal of Interpersonal Violence, 27*(2), 199–221.

Logan, T. K., & Walker, R. (2021). The impact of stalking-related fear and gender on personal safety outcomes. *Journal of Interpersonal Violence, 36*(13–14), NP7465-NP7487.

MacKenzie, R., McEwan, T. E., Pathe, M., James, D. V., Ogloff, J. R., & Mullen, P. E. (2009). *Stalking risk profile: Guidelines for the assessment and management of stalkers* (1st ed.) Monash University.

McEwan, T. E., Harder, L., Brandt, C., & de Vogel, V. (2020). Risk factors for stalking recidivism in a Dutch community forensic mental health sample. *International Journal of Forensic Mental Health, 19*(2), 127–141.

McEwan, T. E., Mullen, P. E., & Purcell, R. (2007). Identifying risk factors in stalking: A review of current research. *International Journal of Law and Psychiatry, 30*(1), 1–9.

Monckton-Smith, J., Szymanska, K., & Haile, S. (2017). *Exploring the relationship between stalking and homicide*. Suzy Lamplugh Trust.

Mullen, P. E., Mackenzie, R., Ogloff, J. R., Pathé, M., McEwan, T., & Purcell, R. (2006). Assessing and managing the risks in the stalking situation. *Journal of the American Academy of Psychiatry and the Law Online, 34*(4), 439–450

Mullen, P. E., Pathé, M., Pathé, M., & Purcell, R. (2000). *Stalkers and their victims*. Cambridge: Cambridge University Press.

Myhill, A., & Allen, J. (2002). *Rape and sexual assault of women: The extent and nature of the problem* (pp. 48–50). London: Home Office.

Office for Students (2022). *Statement of expectations for preventing and addressing harassment and sexual misconduct affecting students in higher education*. www.officeforstudents.org.uk/media/d4ef58c0-db7c-4fc2-9fae-fcb94b38a7f3/ofs-statement-of-expectations-harassment-and-sexual-misconduct.pdf (Accessed 26 January 2022)

Office of National Statistics (2019). *Crime in England and Wales: Year ending March 2019*. www.ons.gov.uk/peoplepopulationandcommunity/crimeandjustice/bulletins/crimeinenglandandwales/yearendingmarch2019 (Accessed August 2021).

Palatinate (2021). *Three quarters of university harassment reports from women*. www.palatinate.org.uk/three-quarters-of-university-harassment-reports-from-women/ (Accessed 12 July 2022).

Phippen, A., & Bond, E. (2020). *Organisational responses to social media storms: An applied analysis of modern challenges*. London: Springer Nature.

Purcell, R., Pathé, M., & Mullen, P. E. (2002). The prevalence and nature of stalking in the Australian community. *Australian & New Zealand Journal of Psychiatry, 36*(1), 114–120.

Purcell, R., Pathé, M., & Mullen, P. E. (2004). When do repeated intrusions become stalking? *Journal of Forensic Psychiatry & Psychology, 15*(4), 571–583.

Quinn-Evans, L., Keatley, D. A., Arntfield, M., & Sheridan, L. (2021). A behavior sequence analysis of victims' accounts of stalking behaviors. *Journal of Interpersonal Violence, 36*(15–16), 6979–6997.

Sheridan, L., & Lyndon, A. E. (2012). The influence of prior relationship, gender, and fear on the consequences of stalking victimization. *Sex Roles, 66*(5), 340–350.

Short, E., Brown, A., Barnes, J., Conrad, M., Alhaboby, Z., Pitchford, M., Conradie, L., Stewart, G., & Dobocan, A. (2016). Cyberharassment and cyberbullying: Individual and institutional perspectives. *Annual Review of CyberTherapy and Telemedicine, 14*, 115–122.Short, E., Linford, S., Wheatcroft, J. M., & Maple, C. (2014). The impact of cyberstalking: The lived experience-a thematic analysis. *Studies in Health Technology and Informatics, 199*, 133–137.

Stevens, F, Nurse, J., & Arief, B. (2021). Cyber stalking, cyber harassment and adult mental health: A systematic review. *Cyberpsychology, Behavior, and Social Networking, 24*(6), 367–376.http://doi.org/10.1089/cyber.2020.0253

Strand, S. (2020). Risk assessment and management of stalking in Sweden: The importance of fear as a victim vulnerability factor. In L. Sheridan, B. W. Reyns, & B. S. Fisher (Eds.), *Psycho-criminological approaches to stalking behavior: The international perspective* (pp. 269–286). Chichester: John Wiley & Sons.

Suzy Lamplugh Trust (2022). *Bridging the gap*. www.suzylamplugh.org/Handlers/Download.ashx?IDMF=36e87aea-15ba-437a-97f6-d5966360878f (Accessed 6 July 2022)

UK Government (2010a). *Criminal Justice and Licensing (Scotland) Act 2010*. www.legislation.gov.uk/asp/2010/13/section/39 (Accessed 15 June 2022)

UK Government (2010b). *Equality Act 2010*. www.legislation.gov.uk/ukpga/2010/15/contents (Accessed 16 June 2022)

UK Government (2022). Online safety bill: Factsheet. www.gov.uk/government/publications/online-safety-bill-supporting-documents/online-safety-bill-factsheet (Accessed 15 June 2022).

Universities UK (2019). *Changing the culture: Tackling online harassment and promoting online welfare*. www.universitiesuk.ac.uk/sites/default/files/field/downloads/2021-07/tackling-online-harassment.pdf (Accessed 16 June 2022).

Vice (2019). *51 Percent of students accused of stalking or abuse allowed to stay at UK universities*. www.vice.com/en/article/qvy7yb/stalking-and-abuse-uk-university-campuses (Accessed 26 January 2022).

Walby, S., & Allen, J. (2004). *Domestic violence, sexual assault and stalking: Findings from the British crime survey*. London: Home Office.

Weller, M., Hope, L., & Sheridan, L. (2013). Police and public perceptions of stalking: The role of prior victim – offender relationship. *Journal of Interpersonal Violence, 28*(2), 320–339

Woodlock, D. (2014). *Technology-facilitated stalking: Findings and resources from the SmartSafe project*. Collingwood: Domestic Violence Resource Centre Victoria.

Theme 4

Coping

Strategies and interventions

12 Coping with cyberbullying (CB) and online harm

Fostering social connectedness across fluid sociotechnical ecosystems

Carmel M. Taddeo and Barbara A. Spears

Introduction

This chapter considers social connectedness (SC) within and across sociotechnical ecosystems (STEs) as a protective and coping mechanism for youth when experiencing online harm (OH), such as cyberbullying (CB) specifically (CB). Further, it explores how bidirectional SC across community and campus can be fostered, *as components of*, and *within*, STEs. By applying a strengths-based paradigm to understand *ways youth construct and enact SC*, the importance of the evolving and bidirectional nature of the sociotechnical spaces becomes evident and facilitates new understanding of how SC can be realised as a protective factor for youth health and well-being.

Coping is generally understood as being able to deal with difficult, often stressful, situations in healthy ways (Folkman, 1984). The importance of coping and supporting community and human connectedness has never been so front of mind as in the recent global climate, where the recent COVID-19 pandemic and Ukraine invasion crisis, in particular, have impacted and dominated social media.

Regarding OH, society has endeavoured to utilise existing/known and increasingly innovative avenues/interventions, including online tools, to improve coping responses and facilitate connection, with a view to supporting social and emotional safety and well-being of individuals and communities. With differential success in school settings (Gaffney et al., 2021), the approaches to addressing OH, including CB in evolving spaces, require reconsideration.

Initially, the off-on-line dichotomy of the early internet was construed as two distinct/separate domains, potentially requiring differential approaches. The 21st-century view, however, is that of a *fluidity* of off-on-line spaces and activities. In response to COVID-19, education settings/systems have had to embrace and enable *technological connectedness* for learning and social experiences.

The affordances of sociotechnical ecosystems

The coming together of social and technical spaces/systems, inclusive of social media platforms such as Facebook, Instagram [now META] and TikTok and

DOI:10.4324/9781003258605-16

comprising a significant part of the social and technical worlds of youth, can be referred to as *sociotechnical platforms*. Another term, *sociotechnical systems*, has a broader application and describes the complex interplay of interactions with, and between, humans, machines and the environment (Baxter et al., 2011). In this chapter, *sociotechnical ecosystem* (STE) defined as '*a dynamic community of competing and interdependent people, organizations, and computing systems operating in a complex, capricious environment*' (McConahy et al., 2012) will be used.

Sociotechnical comprises social, human and technical components and *ecosystem* communicates the complex, dynamic, inter-relatedness and interdependence of all elements within the ecosystem. Applying the STE lens, inclusive of infrastructures, platforms, and systems, *helps ensure the spaces, and ways in which young people exist, interact, engage, and immerse themselves are accurately captured.* An STE perspective further enables the simultaneous consideration of harmful challenges that surface in online spaces, such as CB, along with potential *protective* and *coping* mechanisms such *as SC*, facilitating a shift from an individual-centric and siloed-focused to more holistic, community and networked-focused solutions and supports.

Whilst OH such as CB can contribute to poor mental health and compromise life and well-being trajectories for those involved (Coelho & Marchante, 2018), there are many affordances of STEs for individual and collective experiences. One affordance of promise is that STEs, which include *existing* complex and dynamic broader social and organisational structures and systems [such as education, health, social media, and *future technological infrastructure* [e.g. metaverse], can be leveraged *to help build and sustain community, and facilitate connectedness*, potentially providing a protective buffer to support coping with OH and CB. It is important, however, for research to consider how initiatives that address C/B, that is both cyber and traditional bullying and/or promote SC *can be positioned within complex, dynamic sociotechnical ecosystems, to accurately mirror young people's interactions and engagement that occurs within, and across them.*

Definition of social connectedness

Belonging is proposed as a fundamental human need (Maslow, 2013) and a central tenet of SC (Van Bel et al., 2009). SC has been recognised as a construct of critical importance when examining health/well-being across various age groups and populations (Lee & Robbins, 1998; Nitschke et al., 2021; Nguyen et al., 2019; Rose et al., 2019). Whilst many studies have demonstrated significant relationships between connectedness and indicators of health/well-being (Barber & Schluterman, 2008; Leavell et al., 2019; Spears et al., 2016b), the field is yet to reach consensus regarding a SC definition and measure. This is despite calls for a more unified approach for SC measurements to enable universal comparisons.

Researchers have acknowledged the multidimensional nature of SC, which has seen the construct operationalised in different ways. These include *demonstrating or experiencing interpersonal bonds or general closeness to the social world, with* reference to terms 'enduring and 'ubiquitous' when describing closeness (Lee & Robbins, 1995, 1998). Others refer to *a sense of relatedness* (Rose et al., 2019); consider online *social network links/connections* (Leister et al., 2022) or draw attention to the role of self when connecting in a social context (Barber & Schluterman, 2008), along with the importance of quality interactions versus quantity (Barbosa et al., 2019).

Diverse contexts/settings also have been important considerations for investigations into SC. For example, researchers have examined connectedness and religion in migrant communities (Hashemi et al., 2020) and religious organisation membership and connectedness of college students (Turton et al., 2018). Bartoszek et al. (2020) found SC was a key determinant of resilience among Hispanic young adults, and Pittaway and Dantas (2021) examined connectedness through sport intervention programs for at-risk South Sudanese youth in Australia.

Additionally, sociotechnological settings and systems have been key focus areas for studies of connectedness. Vella et al. (2020) found differences in the way male and female players experience barriers to social connections in online video games. In studies of CB, Spears et al. (2016a) identified cyberbully-victims, and victims of CB were particularly vulnerable regarding their sense and experience of connectedness offline and online, with McLoughlin, Spears and Taddeo (2018) further revealing SC plays a significant role in how youth cope with CB.

In efforts to define SC then, there is much to consider. *What SC looks like in STEs could very well differ depending on the nature/type of online platform or offline context/space.* Similarly, *it also could differ for various cultural/religious groups, genders, and age groups.* The number of individual connections is also not always, nor necessarily ever, associated with, or a proxy for, connectedness. For example, large numbers of Facebook 'friends' or an extensive number of TikTok followers are not necessarily indicators of an individual's SC.

For the purposes of this chapter, *connectedness encompasses the role of self and the nature and quality of relationships, bonds and interactions with key others who co-exist in an individual's sociotechnical world, inclusive of off-on-line and hybrid spaces.* Hybrid spaces include education settings where students' learning and social activities can, and do, traverse both offline and online spaces.

SC as a protective and coping mechanism

SC has consistently been found to be core to an individual's well-being (Ceatha et al., 2019; Saeri et al., 2018). Social connection, or its absence, also has been recognised as a social determinant of health which can directly and indirectly influence health consequences/behaviours and risks (Holt-Lunstad et al., 2015; Leavell et al., 2019). There has been considerable past research which has focused on risk factors that contribute to mental ill-health in young people (Chung-Do et al., 2017). Yet, whilst it is important to understand risk factors to inform approaches to support youth mental health, a sole/primary focus on risk factors can contribute to a deficit approach to understanding the complexity/problem of youth mental ill-health. There is a concomitant need *to apply a strengths-based paradigm to the challenge of supporting youth health/wellbeing, to inform preventative and proactive approaches.* Whilst 'strengths-based' is a widely used term, the underlying assumption adapted from Maton et al. (2004) is that the challenge being addressed is not defined by its difficulty but instead improving a situation or addressing a challenge commences with identifying individual and collective strengths and then leveraging these strengths (Maton et al., 2004) to realise improvements/new solutions.

The relatively recent shift in focus to a strengths-based paradigm has seen an increase in research into protective factors that can support/foster positive health/well-being behaviours/practices (Chung-Do et al., 2017). Early research which investigated youth mental health from a strengths-based paradigm found SC provided an important protective factor for a young person's social well-being/development (Lee & Robbins, 1998). More recently, Saeri et al. (2018) explored the direction of the relationship between mental health and SC and found SC was a stronger predictor of mental health than the reverse.

The benefits of being socially connected also have been evident in research which has examined SC in education settings, with findings highlighting SC is linked to lower anxiety and stress of higher education students (Lee & Robbins, 1998; Nguyen et al., 2019). In other contexts, too, SC has been shown to provide a protective buffer against mental ill-health of homeless youth, serving as a mechanism for resilience (Dang, 2014), for LGBT communities (Ceatha et al., 2019) and for victims of CB (Mcloughlin et al., 2019; Spears et al., 2016a). More recently, Nitschke et al. (2021) found SC played an important role in mitigating distress during COVID-19.

There is widespread agreement that SC causally protects and promotes positive mental health (Saeri et al., 2018). Whilst conversely, the absence of SC has been found to lead, or be linked, to loneliness and to lack of purpose (Carroll et al., 2017), depression and poorer physical health (Cruwys et al., 2014) and increased risk of earlier mortality, than those who have strong SC (Holt-Lunstad et al., 2015). When considering the research collectively, social connection is a critical public health challenge (Leavell et al., 2019), highlighting the focus on SC within the complexity and dynamism of STEs as timely and necessary.

SC as a strategy to help youth cope with online harm

Technology as part of STEs has provided new ways of doing, learning, playing and working, along with new channels for communication and for connecting. Smartphones represent one technology which has seen massive uptake, particularly by youth (PEW, 2018). This access has corresponded with an increase in young people who report using the internet almost constantly (PEW, 2018). In a national Australian study of 20,207 youths aged 15 to 18 years, 77% reported spending more than five hours on screens/day (Tiller et al., 2021). However, whilst many young people engage across STEs, and enjoy positive experiences and benefits, 'within reach' opportunities for constant internet access also increase the prospect of coming across OH as a victim or bystander and increase opportunities where perpetrators can cause harm to others.

When reviewing CB statistics, one Australian study found just over one in five youths aged 15–19 reported experiencing bullying in the previous 12 months, and of those who had experienced bullying, eight in ten reported the bullying occurred at school/TAFE/university, while close to one in three indicated they had experienced bullying online/on social media (Carlisle et al., 2019). Another Australian study found just over four in ten teenagers had at least one negative online experience in the six-month study timeframe (eSafety Commissioner, 2021). Internationally, one in three young people in 30 countries reported being a victim of online bullying, and one in five reported they had skipped school due to CB and violence (UNICEF, 2019). Craig et al. (2020) with data from 180,914 young people aged 11 to 15 years across 42 countries found problematic social media use related to CB and cybervictimisation in most countries with effects strong enough to warrant public health interventions. When considering subgroups of youth populations, Tiller et al. (2021) also included data for gender-diverse youth and found specific challenges for this group, with almost one-third feeling extremely or very concerned about bullying/emotional abuse and their personal safety.

With CB widely recognised as a stressful OH event which can compromise well-being and SC critical for well-being, *understanding how SC can be leveraged as a coping mechanism is necessary, especially for youth who are vulnerable and disconnected.*

Whilst there are many contributing factors and predictors of mental health, research has shown higher levels of SC may provide a protective mechanism against mental ill-health associated with cybervictimisation (Spears & Taddeo, 2021) and further may play a role in predicting different coping strategies in response to cybervictimisation (McLoughlin et al., 2018). Yet, when examining SC in the context of CB, cyberbully-victims experienced lower levels of SC than those who had never been involved in cyberbullying as victim or bully (Spears et al., 2016b).

When investigating coping with CB, McLoughlin et al. (2018) found most young people *intended to cope 'actively'*. These 'active' strategies included working through solutions or seeking support/help-seeking. However, increased frequency of cybervictimisation was found to lead to an increased possibility of engaging in *emotion-focused coping: where a young person 'gives up' trying to cope with the CB.* Tendencies towards emotion-focused coping are of particular concern as this approach is linked to poorer mental health when compared to those who are more likely to cope actively. If, as studies suggest, SC provides a protective buffer against adverse mental health outcomes associated with frequent cybervictimisation (McLoughlin et al., 2019), and if youth who are socially connected are more likely to cope actively in response to cybervictimisation, and are more likely to seek help and have positive mental health as a consequence, *then helping young people to build and sustain social connections is critical for ensuring those experiencing CB have the capacity and supports for actively coping with cybervictimisation.*

Fostering bidirectional SC across community and campus

This next section considers strategies/approaches that may foster bidirectional connectedness across community and campus as components of complex and dynamic STEs.

Community and campus within STEs: understanding the space

The term 'bidirectional connectedness across community and campus' suggests some reciprocity/flow of connection between the two spaces/entities. If community and campus are further positioned within STEs, where interdependent individuals, communities and systems engage and operate in complex and dynamic environments, then any initiative/intervention that aims to foster bidirectional SC *needs to consider that SC can be experienced/enacted very differently across off-on-line and hybrid platforms/systems.* Consideration of how, and where, SC initiatives fit within existing affordances and constraints of STEs, along with consideration of the inter-related, interdependent and networked nature of STEs, is important to help improve ecosystems for those who exist and interact in the space, and particularly for those who are vulnerable and experience OH and CB.

Fostering young people's connectedness: the importance of offline connections

Young people's lives are fluid across/within STEs and can be contained within one element or spill across various components and actors within STEs. To better understand how youth connect offline and online, Spears et al. (2016b) employed the SC scale (Lee & Robbins, 1995) in a cross-sectional survey study (N = 1,106). Lee and Robbins' (1995) scale, originally developed before the advent of the digital environment, was modified with permission, to enable investigations into relationships between youth's perceptions of their off-online SC. Findings revealed for young people at that time: connecting online was related but not the same as connecting offline – particularly in relation to the active coping strategy of help-seeking (Spears et al., 2016b, p. 25). Additionally, the researchers found *'being online' was not necessarily a predictor of 'being socially connected'* (Spears et al., 2016b, p. 38), and instead could be an indicator of 'social disconnection'.

SC within STEs and role of education systems

It is possible there may be an overlap between social and school connectedness, with school connectedness often considered a multidimensional construct. It includes elements such as the nature of students' school involvement, their academic/learning motivation, their attitudes towards school and the quality of their relationships with teachers and peers (Chung-Do et al., 2017). There are numerous benefits for youth who experience school connectedness, for example, they are less likely to engage in interpersonal violence (Chung-Do et al., 2017). Additionally, a sense of connection with school has been shown to provide a protective mechanism for youth and a protective factor for their healthy development (Chung-Do et al., 2017). Given school connectedness can contribute to, and help deliver, many positive outcomes for youth and given findings which show a high number of young people experience bullying in education settings (Carlisle et al., 2019), *then education systems as a key component of STEs, have a critical duty to foster young people's SC as part of building their capacity to practice active coping, particularly when experiencing CB.* Further, education systems have a role in providing support structures/resources and in fostering social-emotional skills that may help ensure young people *have the social capital* along with support to establish and sustain respectful relationships and healthy connections.

Understanding how youth construct and enact SC

Relying on adult perceptions of phenomena that relate or involve youth is problematic, as assumptions can lead to ill- and misinformed understandings and responses to challenges like CB. Therefore, to better understand how young people perceive SC, youth (N = 1,106) who participated in a national Australian study, were asked what 'being socially connected' meant to them (Spears et al., 2016b). Responses indicated 'connection' for youth *traversed offline and online environments, and included technology-mediated connections, and face-to-face connections with family and friends.* Young people further highlighted that 'close' connections were important to them and for them (Spears et al., 2016b, p. 25). Connectedness also extended beyond relationships, with young people identifying the importance of local and global connections, including connection with information as part of global citizenship and being aware of the world in which they live (Spears et al., 2016b). Perhaps most evidently, *young people's responses highlighted the inter-relatedness and boundarylessness of SC.* Therefore, when considering initiatives to enhance SC across community and campus, the fluidity of young people's connectedness, the tools and systems that enable connectedness and informed global citizenship across STEs are important to address. Additionally, ensuring any efforts to foster SC are realised through active youth-driven initiatives is paramount so that solutions closely align with young people's lived experiences of SC and with the opportunities that are most likely to authentically enhance meaningful social connections for youth across STEs.

Strengths-based paradigm: targeting protective factors such as SC through creative approaches

A focus on protective factors such as SC can help ensure a strengths-based approach/paradigm is applied to address youth mental health challenges. SC was one of the core underpinnings of four online social marketing campaigns co-constructed with youths aged 12–17 years to promote and enable positive behaviours for help-seeking and well-being (Spears et al., 2016a). Social marketing involves active participation of the target audience/intended end-users across the design, development and delivery of related activities (Smith, 2006), and can provide an effective/creative approach to achieving social change. Online social marketing campaigns that extend across campus and communities, within and across complex and dynamic STEs, may provide an avenue for implementing strengths-based approaches that 'nudge' young people's uptake of protective strategies such as SC to support their mental health/well-being.

Targeted strategies: supporting youth who are socially isolated and have experienced online harm

Cyberbully-victims and victims of CB are consistently identified as vulnerable groups, particularly regarding their SC across offline and online settings (Spears et al., 2016b). The implications of being socially disconnected extend to many areas, and of particular concern is that those who are not socially connected are less likely to seek help (Spears et al., 2016b), further contributing to their vulnerability. Whilst there is a need for interventions to foster SC for these groups, *understanding the barriers to SC specific to this vulnerable group of youth may be required in the first instance.* Further, rather than addressing SC as a holistic endeavour, there may be a precursor: a need to help these young people build and strengthen their social capital, self-esteem and trusting relationships on a smaller scale so they can eventually and confidently draw on the skills to help them build and sustain social connections in other, sociotechnological contexts. Spears et al. (2016a) suggest the fundamental elements of trust, respect for self, and for others, should be key underpinnings of initiatives that aim to foster SC. Building SC needs to consider ways to support all youth to be able to recognise, experience and practise the fundamental building blocks of healthy relationships along with the skillsets that will enable them to connect with others for positive well-being. This is with a view to ultimately help shift social norms towards *normalising active coping and help-seeking, especially for those who experience OH such as CB.*

Final word: connectedness across fluid boundaries of community and campus

Maslow (2013) first identified belonging as a basic human need, and it has since been considered a core underpinning of SC (Van Bel et al., 2009). Research during the early years of the internet remained focused on SC from a predominately *offline* perspective (Lee & Robbins, 1995, 1998). In pre-COVID-19 years, research proceeded to explore SC in *both offline and online contexts,* acknowledging young people spent considerable time in both spaces, however, they were still considered predominately distinct spaces (Spears et al., 2016b). Now, as we move to the emerging post-COVID-19 era, society is experiencing continued *merging of off-on-line boundaries,* along with *increasing fluidity of engagement/interactions and growing hybrid opportunities particularly in education and health as part of the increasing inter-relatedness and interdependence of STEs.* As technological innovations and infrastructure such as the metaverse continue to expand and improve to support more seamless connections, research is needed to better understand how youth engage in these evolving fluid spaces, and what SC feels and looks like for young people in STEs, so initiatives that address OH and C/B are tailored to align with the needs and behaviours of youth whilst leveraging the interdependence and inter-relatedness of STEs and individual and collective strengths.

Fostering connectedness across campus and community, as components of STE, will require sustained and dedicated effort. Applying a strengths-based paradigm that provides dedicated strategies particularly to support young people who may be socially disconnected, and who may have experienced C/B, may help this vulnerable group of young people build their capacity to confidently connect with others. A strengths-based paradigm that also promotes SC as a protective factor by understanding how young people construct and enact SC in evolving STEs is necessary to ensure initiatives authentically align with the interactions/engagement of youth. Providing young people with opportunities to drive youth initiatives for STEs and that focus on building social capital, developing healthy respectful relationships and active coping strategies will help empower young people to experience and enact connectedness across fluid boundaries of campus, community and evolving STEs.

References

Barber, B. K., & Schluterman, J. M. (2008). Connectedness in the lives of children and adolescents: A call for greater conceptual clarity. *Journal of Adolescent Health, 43*(3), 209–216.

Barbosa Neves, B., Franz, R., Judges, R., Beermann, C., & Baecker, R. (2019). Can digital technology enhance SC among older adults? A feasibility study. *Journal of Applied Gerontology, 38*(1), 49–72.

Bartoszek, L. A., Jacobs, W., & Unger, J. B. (2020). Correlates of resilience in Hispanic young adults. *Family & Community Health, 43*(3), 229–237.

Baxter, G., & Sommerville, I. (2011). Socio-technical systems: From design methods to systems engineering. *Interacting with Computers, 23*(1), 4–17.

Carlisle, E., Fildes, J., Hall, S., Perrens, B., Perdriau, A., & Plummer, J. (2019). *Youth survey report 2019.* Sydney, NSW: Mission Australia.

Carroll, A., Bower, J. M., & Muspratt, S. (2017). The conceptualization and construction of the self in a social context – SC scale: A multidimensional scale for high school students. *International Journal of Educational Research, 81,* 97–107.

Ceatha, N., Mayock, P., Campbell, J., Noone, C., & Browne, K. (2019). The power of recognition: A qualitative study of SC and wellbeing through LGBT sporting, creative and social groups in Ireland. *International Journal of Environmental Research and Public Health, 16*(19), 3636.

Chung-Do, J. J., Goebert, D. A., Hamagani, F., Chang, J. Y., & Hishinuma, E. S. (2017). Understanding the role of school connectedness and its association with violent attitudes and behaviors among an ethnically diverse sample of youth. *Journal of Interpersonal Violence*, *32*(9), 1421–1446.

Coelho, V. A., & Marchante, M. (2018). Trajectories of social and emotional competencies according to cyberbullying roles: A longitudinal multilevel analysis. *Journal of Youth and Adolescence*, *47*(9), 1952–1965.

Craig, W., Boniel-Nissim, M., King, N., Walsh, S. D., Boer, M., Donnelly, P. D., Harel-Fisch, Y., Malinowska-Cieślik, M., de Matos, M. G., Cosma, A., & Van den Eijnden, R. (2020). Social media use and cyber-bullying: A cross-national analysis of young people in 42 countries. *Journal of Adolescent Health*, *66*(6), S100–S108.

Cruwys, T., Haslam, S. A., Dingle, G. A., Haslam, C., & Jetten, J. (2014). Depression and social identity: An integrative review. *Personality and Social Psychology Review*, *18*(3), 215–238.

Dang, M. T. (2014). Social connectedness and self-esteem: Predictors of resilience in mental health among maltreated homeless youth. *Issues in Mental Health Nursing*, *35*(3), 212–219.

eSafety Commissioner (2021). *The Digital Lives of Aussie Teens*. Canberra Australian Government.

Folkman, S. (1984). Personal control and stress and coping processes: A theoretical analysis. *Journal of Personality and Social Psychology*, *46*(4), 839.

Gaffney, H., Ttofi, M. M., & Farrington, D. P. (2021). What works in anti-bullying programs? Analysis of effective intervention components. *Journal of School Psychology*, *85*, 37–56.

Hashemi, N., Marzban, M., Sebar, B., & Harris, N. (2020). Religious identity and psychological well-being among middle-eastern migrants in Australia: The mediating role of perceived social support, SC, and perceived discrimination. *Psychology of Religion and Spirituality*, *12*(4), 475.

Holt-Lunstad, J., Smith, T. B., Baker, M., Harris, T., & Stephenson, D. (2015). Loneliness and social isolation as risk factors for mortality: A meta-analytic review. *Perspectives on Psychological Science*, *10*(2), 227–237.

Leavell, M. A., Leiferman, J. A., Gascon, M., Braddick, F., Gonzalez, J. C., & Litt, J. S. (2019). Nature-based social prescribing in urban settings to improve SC and mental well-being: A review. *Current Environmental Health Reports*, *6*(4), 297–308.

Lee, R. M., & Robbins, S. B. (1995). Measuring belongingness: The social connectedness and social assurance scales. *Journal of Counseling Psychology*, *42*(2), 232–241.

Lee, R. M., & Robbins, S. B. (1998). The relationship between social connectedness and anxiety, self-esteem, and social identity, *45*(3), 338–345.

Leister, C. M., Zenou, Y., & Zhou, J. (2022). SC and local contagion, *The Review of Economic Studies*, *89*(1), 372–410.

Maslow, A. H. (2013). *Toward a psychology of being*. London: Simon and Schuster.

Maton, K. I., Dogden, D. W., Leadbeater, B. J., & Sandler (2004). Strengths-based research and policy: An introduction. In K. I. Maton, C. J. Schellenbach, B. J. Leadbeater & A. I. Solarz (Eds.), *Investing in children, youth, families, and communities: Strengths-based research and policy* (pp. 3–12). Washington, DC: American Psychological Association.

McConahy, A., Eisenbraun, B., Howison, J., Herbsleb, J. D., & Sliz, P. (2012). Techniques for monitoring runtime architectures of socio-technical ecosystems. In *Workshop on data-intensive collaboration in science and engineering (CSCW 2012)*.

McLoughlin, L., Spears, B., & Taddeo, C. (2018). The importance of social connection for cybervictims: How connectedness and technology could promote mental health and wellbeing in young people. *International Journal of Emotional Education*, *10*(1), 5–24.

McLoughlin, L. T., Spears, B. A., Taddeo, C. M., & Hermens, D. F. (2019). Remaining connected in the face of cyberbullying: Why SC is important for mental health. *Psychology in the Schools*, *56*(6), 945–958.

Nguyen, M. H., Le, T. T., & Meirmanov, S. (2019). Depression, acculturative stress, and SC among international university students in Japan: A statistical investigation. *Sustainability, 11*(3), 878.

Nitschke, J. P., Forbes, P. A., Ali, N., Cutler, J., Apps, M. A., Lockwood, P. L., & Lamm, C. (2021). Resilience during uncertainty? Greater SC during COVID-19 lockdown is associated with reduced distress and fatigue. *British Journal of Health Psychology, 26*(2), 553–569.

Pew Research Centre (2018). *Teens, social media and technology.* Washington, DC: Pew Research Center.

Pittaway, T., & Dantas, J. A. (2021). The role of sport in coping and resilience amongst resettled South Sudanese youth in Australia. *Health Promotion International, 37*(2), 1–13.

Rose, T., McDonald, A., Von Mach, T., Witherspoon, D. P., & Lambert, S. (2019). Patterns of SC and psychosocial wellbeing among African American and Caribbean Black adolescents. *Journal of Youth and Adolescence, 48*(11), 2271–2291.

Saeri, A. K., Cruwys, T., Barlow, F. K., Stronge, S., & Sibley, C. G. (2018). SC improves public mental health: Investigating bidirectional relationships in the New Zealand attitudes and values survey. *Australian & New Zealand Journal of Psychiatry, 52*(4), 365–374.

Smith, W. A. (2006). Social marketing: An overview of approach and effects. *Injury Prevention, 12*(suppl 1), i38–i43.

Spears, B. A., & Taddeo, C. (2021). Coping with cyberbullying. In P. K. Smith & J. O'Higgins Norman (Eds.), *The Wiley Blackwell handbook of bullying: A comprehensive and international review of research and intervention* (Vol. 2, pp. 240–259). Chichester: Wiley.

Spears, B. A., Taddeo, C., Barnes, A., Collin, P., Swist, T., Webb-Williams, J., Kavanagh, P., Drennan, J., Razzell, M., & Borbone, V. (2016b). *Connect. Challenge. Do.: Design and evaluation of Goalzie: A goal-setting campaign to promote help-seeking for wellbeing.* www.semanticscholar.org/paper/Connect.-Challenge.-Do.:-Design-and-Evaluation-of-A-Spears-Taddeo/46f1d440bfad369f0ca3b22d223d0c0226bd121b

Spears, B. A., Taddeo, C., Collin, P., Swist, T., Razzell, M., Borbone, V., & Drennan, J. (2016a). *Safe and well online: Learnings from four social marketing campaigns for youth wellbeing.* www.uws.edu.au/__data/assets/pdf_file/0017/1101635/safe_and_well_online_report.pdf

Tiller, E., Greenland, N., Christie, R., Kos, A., Brennan, N., & Di Nicola, K. (2021). *Youth survey report 2021.* Sydney, NSW: Mission Australia.

Turton, G. M., Nauta, M. M., Wesselmann, E. D., McIntyre, M. M., & Graziano, W. G. (2018). The associations of Greek and religious organization participation with college students' social well-being and purpose. *The Journal of Psychology, 152*(4), 179–198.

UNICEF (2019). *U-Report highlights prevalence of cyberbullying and its impact on young people.* Geneva: UNICEF.

Van Bel, D. T., Smolders, K. C., IJsselsteijn, W. A., & De Kort, Y. A. W. (2009). SC: Concept and measurement. In *Proceedings of the 5th International Conference, Intelligent Environments, July 2009* (pp. 67–74). IOS Press.

Vella, K., Klarkowski, M., Turkay, S., & Johnson, D. (2020). Making friends in online games: Gender differences and designing for greater SC. *Behaviour & Information Technology, 39*(8), 917–934.

13 From bystanding to upstanding

Helen Cowie and Carrie-Anne Myers

Introduction

As Fenton et al. (2016) propose, over the years the field of violence prevention has shifted from a focus on victims and perpetrators to recognition that prevention must go beyond changing individuals to changing systems that include the whole college or university community. This is at the heart of bystander intervention. Sanderson (2020) proposes the urgent need for us all to speak out and intervene against injustice when we see it and argues convincingly that bystanders can 'learn to be brave'. Aggressive acts that are carried out systematically and repetitively by electronic means, such as texting by an individual or group, have been identified as cyberbullying (Royen et al., 2017). These acts are often witnessed and circulated by others, so the focus of this chapter is on the bystanders who are aware of online aggression towards a member of their peer group but who fail to take action to defend that person (Cowie & Myers, 2016).

The bystander role

The idea of the bystander has a long history. Latané and Darley (1970), in their classic studies of bystander apathy, proposed the Bystander Intervention Model, which states that the bystander typically experiences five phases in the decision-making process about whether to intervene or not when someone is being attacked by another person:

- Awareness of the event
- Interpretation of the incident as a problem
- Accepting responsibility to help
- Knowledge and belief in ability to intervene safely and effectively
- Taking action to perform the intervention

Their research also highlighted the critical importance of the social context in which the episode occurs, for example, the presence of other people, social cues about what other bystanders are doing and ambiguity about which person is responsible for defending the victim or challenging the aggressor.

DOI:10.4324/9781003258605-17

In-depth interviews with adolescents about how they would behave when they become aware of a cyberbullying episode (Patterson et al., 2016) confirmed the powerful impact of the social context. The researchers took young people's perceptions into account by inviting them non-judgmentally to explore a range of possible bystander responses and to estimate the extent of moral engagement or disengagement in different situations. This process would also involve challenging bullies' mechanisms for justifying moral disengagement (Zych & Llorent, 2018), such as euphemistic language ('it was only in fun'), distorting the consequences ('they'll soon get over it') or blaming the victim ('they have no right to be here so deserved it'). The participants reported that, in the absence of perceived physical danger to a cybervictim, they hesitated to intervene and in practice distanced themselves from online confrontations. Furthermore, young people often reported that they lacked the skill to challenge cyberaggression when they encountered it.

In a systematic literature review of factors that moderate the actions in cyberbullying of young bystanders under the age of 20 years, Domínguez-Hernández et al. (2018) identified two interacting factors that influenced bystander behaviour, namely the *social environment* and the relationship of *friendship*. Negative bystander behaviour is most strongly predicted by positive attitudes towards *passive* bystanding, which leads to an unwillingness to intervene. In line with Latané and Darley's (1970) model of *diffusion of responsibility*, the greater the number of passive bystanders, the less likely it is that an individual member of the peer group will step out of line to help the victim through fear of going against the norms of the group. Furthermore, where the social norms favour the bullies, the bystanders may even take pride in the actions of the aggressors or despise the victims for not defending themselves. Justifications related to moral disengagement within the peer group also act as a barrier to support for the victim (Zych & Lloren, 2018). Not surprisingly, high levels of moral commitment are linked to positive bystander behaviour. For example, the bond of friendship between bystander and victim facilitates the expectation of mutual help in times of trouble. In other words, a true friend will not let you down or betray you.

Not only is the concept of *individual* moral disengagement relevant. Gini et al. (2018) found that the response of the bystander was influenced by the students' perceptions of *collective* moral disengagement. Their study confirms the view that the response of the bystanders to a situation where someone needs help (as in the case of bullying) is strongly influenced by the social context in which the episode happens. If the expectation is that no one will intervene to help, the effect on the individual is to remain passive. Gini et al., (2018) identified a further influential factor in bystanding – the presence of perceived *collective* moral disengagement. Bystander apathy in the face of bullying, they argue, is more likely when students are personally inclined to moral disengagement and when they *also* believe that morally disengaged justifications are common in their peer group. This argument holds at all levels of the educational lifespan (Myers & Cowie, 2019). Their findings, of course, confirm the classic research on the unresponsive bystander by Latané and Darley (1970), who investigated the impact of bystander apathy in the face of a disturbing event and explained the phenomenon as being due to fear about stepping out of line when surrounded by a group of people who refrain from intervening to help. Conversely, there is a strong relationship between high levels of empathy with victim-support behaviours, whether they are close friends or not, and positive attitudes towards comforting or protecting someone in distress.

In answer to the question 'Which bystander behaviours are capable of spurring their friends and others to action to support the victim in cases of cyberbullying?', Domínguez-Hernández et al. (2018) concluded that it is crucially important to take account of both personal and social factors if interventions are to be effective. The findings from their systematic literature review indicated strongly that the capacity and willingness to intervene to defend a victim of cyberbullying depends not only on the levels of empathy for the victims on the part of bystanders but also on such social factors as perceived self-efficacy in the group, levels of popularity among peers and the extent of peer group moral engagement/disengagement. In other words, there is no one factor which will predict bystander behaviour but rather an interaction between contextual and personal factors which will have a moderating effect on whether bystanders intervene or not.

The evidence to date indicates the importance of actively helping young people to reflect on their values and to develop practical skills that will enable them to act rather than remain passive onlookers when online harms are perpetrated. Patterson et al. (2016, p. 64) concluded that if young people have learned how to challenge a cyberbully or to comfort a cybervictim, they are more likely to intervene when the bullying event occurs.

Participant roles in bullying/cyberbullying

Research into *participant roles* in bullying by Salmivalli and her colleagues (Salmivalli, 2014; Salmivalli et al., 1996) viewed bullying situations as *group* phenomena and identified a range of non-victim participant roles to include: *assistant* (who helps the bully carry out the aggressive act), *reinforcer* (who encourages the bully by laughing at the victim's distress or cheering on the bully), *outsider* (the passive bystander who ignores the bullying event or who appears to see no need to intervene) and *defender* (who protects or comforts the victim or goes to get adult help to stop the bullying episode). From this perspective, the outsiders appear to display passive indifference. If unchallenged, the outsiders are unlikely to develop a sense of empathy for the victim's plight; such moral disengagement perpetuates the view that there is no need to intervene to prevent bullying or support the victim. However, there is growing evidence that participant roles are not necessarily fixed and may vary according to the social context of the bullying episode (Gumpel et al., 2014). Since Salmivalli's research was first published, subsequent researchers have explored participant roles in detail with interesting results. Graeff (2014), for example, identified *upstanders*, a category of defender who was willing to uphold positive moral values in the face of the injustice of bullying a vulnerable peer.

Levy and Gumpel (2018) surveyed 1,520 Israeli students from middle school (13–14 years) and high school (15–18 years) and distinguished two types of defenders – the *opposers* (who challenged the bully) and the *help-recruiters* (who got help for the victim from friends, other bystanders or adults). The researchers noted that, while this kind of defender action did not necessarily stop the bullying, it at least provided emotional support for the victim. They also identified two outsider roles – the *passive bystander*, who was perceived by others as offering tacit approval for the bully, and the *disengaged outsider*, who indicated awareness of the bullying situation but refrained from taking prosocial action. In fact, they identified potential pathways from *disengaged onlooker* through to *upstander*. These researchers found a causal link between *outsiders* and *opposers*, suggesting that this category of disengaged bystander was potentially open to adopting a defender participant role, given the right circumstances (such as bystander training). A focus on the facilitation of upstanding lies at the heart of training interventions in UK universities as documented by Fenton et al. (2016).

Levy and Gumpel (2018) suggest that, instead of talking about participant roles, it is more helpful to have the concept of 'bullying circles'. Here, the followers of the bully actively engage in the bullying but do not initiate the attack. The supporters (passive bullies) encourage the bully. The passive supporters take the side of the aggressor but do not openly support him/her. The defender actively and openly assists the victim. This differs from the participant role approach in two ways: first, the bullying circle consists of two additional intervention styles: *passive supporters/possible aggressors* and *possible defenders*; second, the bullying circle approach portrays the participant roles as intervention *styles* situated on a continuum around the aggressor-victim dyad, rather than binary and independent individual traits. In other words, the intervention styles are fluid. The outsider participant role is portrayed by two separate constructs: *outsider* role (the original as portrayed by Salmivalli) and *neutral outsider*, who potentially might be a mediator or third party who helps to resolve the conflict. From this perspective, both outsiders and passive bystanders portray passive involvement, but they may differ in the extent of their pro-victim or pro-aggressor behavioural style. This is where bystander training has the potential to change intervention styles by focusing on the social context.

At the same time, there needs to be a strong recognition that many bystanders are reluctant to intervene for fear of retaliation or reprisals by the aggressors. For example, in the context of gender-based violence, Puigvert et al. (2021) identify the risk of Second Order of Sexual Harassment (SOSH). So, they argue, there is a need for the university at organisational level to protect not only direct support for victims but also for those who dare to help them. One solution, they argue, is the creation of an Upstander Social Network, a platform that disseminates testimonies (like the **#MeToo** movement), including survivors' accounts of their abuse, dialogues on effective legislation, as well as scientific evidence of the impact of bystander intervention in reducing gender-based violence.

Despite differences in the interpretation of the concept of participant role, there is widespread agreement that it is essential to recruit some of the bystanders to provide moral and emotional support for victims. Similarly, defenders need high-quality training to enhance their *individual* skills at responding effectively in a peer support team of upstanders.

Evidence of benefits of bystander training

Bystander training in the university context helps to change attitudes and behaviour *in general* as a means of facilitating prosocial behaviour on campus and consequently challenging discriminatory 'laddism' that promotes a social context where minority groups are targeted, bullied and socially excluded. Bystander prevention programmes need to be situated within a systemic whole-college/whole-university approach to the issue of cyberbullying and online harms (Gainsbury et al., 2020). For examples of such programmes, see Fenton et al. (2016), who review evidence of successful bystander intervention to prevent sexual and domestic violence on campus and who document the fact that as well as having an impact on the suffering of victims, participants in bystander training programmes typically develop enhanced critical, analytical, communication and leadership skills (Fenton & Mott, 2015). Fenton et al. (2016, p. 57) conclude that '. . . if implemented at scale, over time, bystander programming in university contexts can lead not only to positive attitudinal and behavioural change at the individual level but also to a reduction in perpetration and victimisation at the level of the whole community'. There are other benefits when this occurs. For example, McBeath et al. (2018) found that students' perceived sense of connectedness to their peer groups and to the university community, as well as access to high-quality bystander or peer support when needed, was significantly related to overall mental health and well-being, especially as they made the transition to work-placements and the employment market.

The evidence indicates the need at senior management level to change the culture on campus to foster a greater sense of inclusion among groups which are at particular risk of cyberbullying and online harms. McBeath et al. (2018) found that students' perceived sense of connectedness to their peer groups and to the university community, as well as access to high-quality bystander or peer support when needed, was significantly related to overall mental health and well-being, especially as they made the transition to work-placements and the employment market. When students feel that they belong to the university community, they are less vulnerable to bullying and sexual harassment (James et al., 2017; McLoughlin et al., 2018).

Graeff (2014), in the context of cyberbullying and moral reasoning, recommends that educators aim to model thinking processes and strategies that can lead to *upstanding* behaviour. He notes that the 'natural' response to an ethical dilemma, such as cyberbullying, is to look out for yourself or your friends. However, if the university takes a stance against online discrimination and social exclusion, and backs this up with relevant information as well as opportunities to draw parallels and prompt reflection on different outcomes, then these are the conditions in which upstanding is likely to flourish.

Typical bystander training involves role-play and scenarios which provide experiential opportunities to practise interventions and to reflect on the consequences. These situations build on students' capacity to take the perspective of another person and to develop further their empathy for peers in distress. The research by DeSmet et al. (2015) and others seems to confirm the need to create many opportunities for young people to develop empathy for the distress of others (e.g. through role play, storytelling, drama, active campaigning for groups experiencing discrimination, involvement in peer support activity). Educators who devise anti-bullying interventions should take account of the powerful impact of the immediate social context on young people's capacity for empathy and altruism, and the many opportunities to develop positive outcome expectations, social skills, empathic skills and the capacity for moral engagement in the social life of the university as a community. That way, the university culture can be changed to take account of the lifespan transitions from childhood, through adolescence into young adulthood into an increasingly diverse society. The literature continues to encourage many productive debates on such issues as the tensions between prosocial behaviour and moral disengagement, competing pressures on young people to be either passive bystanders or proactive upstanders, conditions that inhibit or promote resilience in individuals and groups, and social factors that facilitate inclusion or exclusion, xenophilia or xenophobia.

Mechanisms for dealing with reprisals against upstanders are also critical. Upstanders benefit from being members of a network, such as the Upstander Social Network platform, which provide information, legal advice, scientific evidence, as well as testimonies from survivors and those who supported them. Such a platform has the potential for 'building awareness among all social actors, communities and policymakers creating that point of social awareness which generates a social movement' (Puigvert et al., 2021, p. 10).

The experience of helping others in real-life situations further fosters their capacity to act prosocially through positive bystander intervention, even in the face of perceived *collective moral disengagement*, not only because their training and experience have heightened their sense of moral responsibility for the welfare of others, but also because they feel empowered *as a group* to challenge bullying/cyberbullying when they encounter it, knowing that their fellow upstanders will back them up.

Conclusion

How can we help students to shift from bystander to upstander roles? Evidence presented in this chapter indicates that bystander training offers practical and emotional guidance to those who would like to help victims of cyberbullying and other forms of online harm. But it will only be effective if it takes place at different levels of the system in a wider context of concern to protect vulnerable students. A range of different strategies is essential if universities are to be successful in the ongoing effort to create and sustain social and learning environments that are friendly and safe.

i) **Student action**: Build on existing initiatives developed by the National Students' Union. Strengthen the roles of student support roles, such as student ambassadors/floor wardens in halls of residence, foster relationships of friendship where possible in a range of contexts, such as in seminars, during group work, in halls of residence, in clubs and societies, in the Students' Unions. Think of bystander intervention as an extension of friendship and as one way of communicating the importance of intervention to prevent cyberbullying and online harm towards those who may hesitate to ask for help. Befriend students who may be potentially at risk. Be proactive in reaching out to fellow students. Think also about when and how to intervene. Encourage the cybervictim to ask for help from their friends.

ii) **Staff action**: Teaching staff can promote a positive social climate in lectures and seminars. Find opportunities to challenge online aggression and promote values of moral engagement. Proactively facilitate cooperative group work outside dominant friendship groups. Other staff (medical, counselling, nursing, librarians, security, catering) can alert colleagues to the fact that some students appear isolated, excluded and distressed.

iii) **Senior management action**: Create systems such as bystander training and peer support training. Create support roles. Celebrate and recognise staff who are exceptionally supportive of their students through their ability and dedication. Develop appropriate reporting and recording systems. Actively challenge negative behaviours, such as 'laddism', xenophobia, misogyny, racism and disablism. Take a strong stance on Equity, Diversity and Inclusion (EDI) issues (not as a tick-box exercise). Promote values that truly celebrate diversity and inclusion in as many ways as possible within the university community. Heighten awareness of the harm that can be done by cyberbullying and other forms of online harm.

References

Cowie, H., & Myers, C.-A. (Eds.) (2016). *Bullying among university students*. London: Routledge.

DeSmet, A., Bastiaensens, S., Van Cleemput, K., Poels, K., Vandebosch, H., Cardon, G., & De Bourdeaudhuij, I. (2015). Deciding whether or not to look after them, to like it, or leave it: A multidimensional analysis of predictors of positive and negative bystander behavior in cyberbullying among adolescents. *Computers in Human Behavior, 57*, 398–415.

Domínguez-Hernández, F., Bonell, L., & Martínez-González, A. (2018). A systematic literature review of factors that moderate bystanders' actions in cyberbullying. *Cyberpsychology: Journal of Psychosocial Research on Cyberspace*, *12*(4), Article 1. https://dx.doi.org/10.5817/CP2018-4-1 (Accessed 15 March 2022).

Fenton, R., & Mott, H. L. (2015). *The intervention initiative: Student feedback February 2015*. https://socialsciences.exeter.ac.uk/media/universityofexeter/collegeofsocialsciencesand-internationalstudies/research/interventioninitiative/resources/Student_Feedback_report.pdf (Accessed 15 March 2022)

Fenton, R., Mott, H. L., McCartan, K., & Rumney, P. N. S. (2016). *A review of the evidence for bystander intervention to prevent sexual and domestic violence in universities*. London: Public Health England.

Gainsbury, A. N., Fenton, R. A., & Jones, C. A. (2020). From campus to communities: Evaluation of the first UK-based bystander programme for the prevention of domestic violence and abuse in general communities. *BMC Public Health 20*, 674. https://doi.org/10.1186/s12889-020-08519-6

Gini, G., Thornberg, R., & Pozzoli, T. (2018). Individual moral disengagement and bystander behaviour in bullying: The role of moral distress and collective moral disengagement. *Psychology of Violence*, *8*(6), 1–10 http://dx.doi.org/10.1037/vio0000223

Graeff, E. (2014). Tweens, cyberbullying and moral reasoning: Separating the upstanders from the bystanders. In L. Robinson, S.R. Cotten & J. Schulz (Eds.), *Communication and information technologies annual (Studies in media and communications)* (Vol. 8, pp. 231–257). Melbourne: Emerald Group Publishing United.

Gumpel, T. P., Zioni-Koren, V., & Beckerman, Z. (2014). An ethnographic study of participant roles in school bullying. *Aggressive Behavior*, *40*(3), 214–228.

James, C., Davis, K., Charmaraman, S., Konrath, S., Slovak, P., & Weinstein, E. (2017). Digital life and youth well-being, social connectedness, empathy and narcissism, *Pediatrics*, *140*, 71–75.

Latané, B., & Darley, M. (1970). *The unresponsive bystander: Why doesn't he help?* New York: Appleton Century Crofts.

Levy, M., & Gumpel, T. P. (2018). The interplay between bystanders' intervention styles: An examination of the "bullying circle" approach. *Journal of School Violence*, *17*(3), 339–353.

McBeath, M. L., Drysdale, M., & Bohn, N. (2018). Work-integrated learning and the importance of peer support and sense of belonging. *Education and Training*, *60*(1), 39–53.

McLoughlin, L., Spears, B., & Taddeo, C. (2018). The importance of social connection for cybervictims: How connectedness and technology could promote mental health and wellbeing in young people. *International Journal of Emotional Education*, *10*(1), 5–24.

Myers, C.-A., & Cowie, H. (2019). Cyberbullying across the lifespan of education: Issues and interventions from school to university. *International Journal of Environmental Research and Public Health*, *16*(7), 1–17.

Patterson, L. J., Allan, A., & Cross, D. (2016). Adolescent bystanders' perspectives of aggression in the online versus school environments. *Journal of Adolescence*, *49*, 60–67.

Puigvert, L., Vidu, A., Melgar, P., & Salceda, M. (2021). BraveNet upstander social network against the Second Order of Sexual Harassment (SOHS). *Sustainability*, 13, 4135. https://doi.org?10.3390/su13084135

Royen, K. Van, Poels, K., Vandebosch, H., & Adam, P. (2017). "Thinking before posting?" Reducing cyberharassment on social network sites through a reflective message. *Computers in Human Behavior*, *66*, 345–352, https://doi.org/10.1016/j.chb.2016.09.040 (Accessed 17 March 2022).

Salmivalli, C. (2014). Participant roles in bullying: How can peer bystanders be utilized in interventions? *Theory into Practice, 53*, 286–292.

Salmivalli, C., Lagerspetz, K., Björkqvist, K., Österman, K., & Kaukiainen, A. (1996). Bullying as a group process: Participant roles and their relations to social status within the group. *Aggressive Behavior, 22*(1), 1–15.

Sanderson, C. A. (2020). *The bystander effect: The psychology of courage and inaction.* London: William Collins.

Zych, I., & Llorent, V. J. (2018). Affective empathy and moral disengagement related to late adolescent bullying perpetration. *Ethical Behavior, 29*(7), 547–556.

14 Rehabilitation and peer ecology

Johannes Nilsson Finne and Ida Risanger Sjursø

Introduction

Abusive bullying relationships are damaging for both the students who are victimised and the students who bully. On the surface, the students who bully appear to win through the abuse of their power over others. This provides rewards for continuing to engage in these kinds of behaviour, but in the longer term, the outcomes may be troublesome. Several studies have shown that, to a large extent, both the students who experienced victimisation and the students who have bullied have a history of these roles at earlier levels of education (Bauman & Newman, 2013), suggesting a continuity in these roles from childhood across the lifespan. Surprisingly, however, in a Norwegian meta-analysis, Breivik and colleagues (2017) found very little research addressing strategies that schools can use to support recovery post victimisation. The authors identified only 12 studies that examined recovery efforts, and all described victim-focused therapy. The school context was not considered.

A challenge regarding most anti-bullying interventions is that they tend to be too short. They are often superficial, and the dynamics of bullying are therefore likely to persist even if the bullying has been stopped. Hence, we argue that some form of rehabilitation needs to take place to change the quality of the 'peer ecology' in the classroom. For instance, the moral disengagement that occurs when bullying persists creates group norms that may continue even when the active forms of bullying have ceased because of a successful intervention. It is also important to note that what happens in the classroom is affected by what happens among the students online and vice versa, which might make the work of rehabilitation even more complex and necessary. Therefore, it is promising that the idea of rehabilitation is beginning to be discussed not only in relation to the school setting but also in the college and university sector, with a growing emphasis on changing the culture to one of tolerance and community (Myers & Cowie, 2019).

The interplay between traditional and cybervictimisation

Offline and online lives are interwoven, and authors agree that a large proportion of students experiencing cybervictimisation also experience being bullied

DOI:10.4324/9781003258605-18

in more traditional ways (Olweus & Limber, 2018). As the different kinds of bullying often involve the same students, what happens online affects the way the students interact with one another in the classroom within the same peer network and vice versa. Considering the overlap between cyber and traditional victimisation, it is however plausible to think that the actions of the teacher could also affect what happens between the students online. Recent research finds that cyberbullying is positively associated with non-intervention by teachers (Nappa et al., 2021). This confirms that what the teacher does or does not do in the classroom affects what takes place between the same students online. The relationship between the student who has been bullied and the students who bully is a difficult area to unpack when it comes to cyberbullying (Myers & Cowie, 2019). Our position is that very often the problems of cyberbullying are rooted in classroom relationships and therefore affect peer relations in the wider context of school or university.

Moral disengagement and relational practice

People do not always behave according to their own moral standards, and ICT media might contribute to this threshold being even lower. There is evidence that the students who bully can evaluate bullying as wrong (Gasser & Keller, 2009), but nevertheless they bully peers. To understand the possible gap between moral evaluations and actual behaviours, Bandura (1991) proposed his theory of moral disengagement. Moral disengagement refers to social-cognitive processes through which the person can commit actions that they evaluate to be wrong, by cognitively restructuring the events and, thus, selectively, avoiding moral censure and self-judgment. These mechanisms are used to reduce this uncomfortable inner state stemming from evaluating one's own behaviour as wrong. Moral disengagement has also been conceptualised as learnt socially from peers (Caravita et al., 2014). It first acts as an *a posteriori* mechanism, after the transgression has been perpetrated. Then, over time, moral disengagement can start to be used in the *while* or *before* perpetrating the transgressive action (a priori) (Caravita et al., 2021).

When a peer group adopts moral disengagement mechanisms, they can cause devastating harm and operate at the broader level of the class community (Pozzoli et al., 2012). For example, displacement and the diffusion of responsibility (Latané & Darley, 1968) are not just cognitive denial machinations; they are built into the very structure of social systems to obscure personal accountability. Research finds that a lack of moral values and remorse predicts both traditional and cyberbullying behaviour (Perren & Gutzwiller-Helfenfinger, 2012). The threshold may be even lower in cyberbullying, for instance when many peers share a picture. By removing communication of emotional content, the utilisation of ICT media may be necessarily structurally dehumanising (Runions & Bak, 2015).

These various psychosocial manoeuvres are not just 'techniques'. They are grounded in self-regulatory processes. Students who have been bullied or bullied others have been exposed to and learnt forms of interacting with others, and this internalisation of knowledge may leave a 'mark', in that past experiences could be used to mediate new encounters.

First, this might explain how and why someone's bullying experiences in one context (such as at school) can be reproduced in another setting. Second, this helps us to understand how and why the effects of bullying on psychological and behavioural processes are likely to persist under the surface even after a successful intervention stops the manifest behaviour and can be long lasting for an individual. Hence, in a school classroom, persisting group norms may hinder the student's recovery. Therefore, stopping bullying is vital but not enough. Some form of rehabilitation is necessary, and such rehabilitation should have a broad focus. The question, then, is how the peer ecology can be improved by more prosocial interactions and how this goal can guide classroom leadership strategies.

A model of rehabilitation in peer ecology

When students experience good proximal relationships in the classroom, this is productive not only for healing the negative effects of having experienced bullying, but it is also beneficial for students who have bullied and the rest of the peer group.

Situated focus

A group community develops through actions, common values and understandings, and shared cultural practices (Rogoff, 2003). Emotions, moral cognition and behaviour all interact as children develop, and patterns of behaviour are sustained and changed over time. This is a result of reciprocal interaction between individual and contextual factors (Bandura, 1986). Because of this reciprocity, we argue that rehabilitation should be situated, it should take place where the problems have occurred. Hence, we call it *situated rehabilitation* (Figure 14.1). Situated is a term Lave and Wenger (1991) introduced focusing on the process by which newcomers become a part of a community of practice. Relationships within communities are complex, and participants will each have different roles and responsibilities (Rogoff, 2003). Relations can be supportive, or conflictual, and may have agreed processes for resolving disagreements, within shared routines and attitudes about adaption and negotiation.

Participating in the community will involve learning the practices to facilitate and reinforce a sense of belonging. Therefore, bullying will be more common in peer groups where aggression, dominance and negative forms of interaction are normalised. Likewise, bullying will be less common in a peer group where prosocial actions are acknowledged and reinforced. Hence, rehabilitation should be focused on stimulating more prosocial components in the class community, re-creating the social structure and reducing the value of anti-social behaviour.

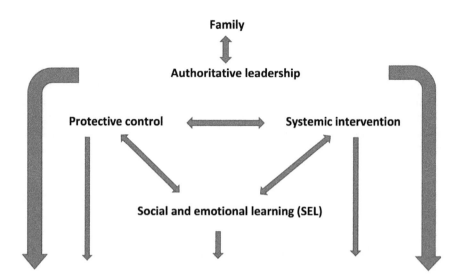

Figure 14.1 Model of situated rehabilitation

The authoritative leader

The authoritative parenting style promoted by Baumrind as the style being high on warmth and demandingness is associated with the best outcomes for children (Chan & Koo, 2011). Regarding the dimension of demandingness, there are two related components: monitoring and confrontive control, which refer to the claim parents make on their children to become integrated into and contribute to the family unit (Baumrind, 2013). The key to being an authoritative leader is to combine warmth with control. Initially, Baumrind's theory of the authoritative perspective was related to different types of parenting. It is today however also a perspective that is highly related to the role of the teacher. Demandingness in the classroom is often operationalised through structure and norms. With reference to the teaching context, these are important aspects when leading larger groups. The demands need to be based on an already established relationship between the teacher and the students. It is important that teachers support students' individuality and agency.

The observation that effective parents and teachers have many of the same techniques and characteristics is not new (Wentzel, 2002). Research shows that authoritative class leaders prevent bullying (Roland & Galloway, 2002), and an authoritative school climate is related to lower levels of bullying (Gerlinger & Wo, 2016).

Protective control

Ensuring that adequate measures are taken and that this information is given to students who have been bullied would contribute to these students' experience of a more predictable and safe school environment. Providing students with this predictability during the bullying intervention contributes to establishing safety, an important feeling for children who have experienced trauma (Bath, 2008). To provide this safety, the teacher needs to perform what can be referred to as *protective control* (Sjursø et al., 2019). In terms of stopping the bullying, protective control refers to whether the student who has experienced victimisation perceives the teacher as capable and/or willing to act to stop the ones who have bullied.

Although the concept of protective control is connected to the dimension of demandingness, it cannot be seen as independent of the dimension of warmth. To perform protective control, a good relation between the teacher and the student would have to be established. The dimension of warmth or responsiveness is important when performing protective control as the teacher needs to tune in to the student and be supportive of the student's individual needs. This combination of responsiveness and demandingness corresponds well with the authoritative leader described earlier.

Systemic intervention

Regardless of changing classroom dynamics, a group of students will continue to develop as a social system. For any social group, the concept of dominance and power is real in the everyday struggle of negotiating allegiances and jostling for social positions (Pörhölä, 2016). After terminating a bullying situation, the relational structure in the class may be in a vacuum for a certain period, and relationships may have different dynamics from those experienced during the period of bullying. Such a situation makes it possible to reconstruct the relationships and redistribute social influence on students who possess more prosocial attitudes and behaviours. The ideal opposite of the dysfunctional learning environment facilitating bullying is the *prosocial classroom*. However, the systemic perspective is not limited to peer relations in the class system. Classroom management should be understood as an integrated way of addressing both academic and social needs of individuals and the class system.

The teacher and class management

Teachers play a critical role as providers and approvers of language, behaviour, norms, and attitudes shown in the classroom. Teachers' efforts to intervene in bullying may affect classroom norms regarding bullying and related behaviours and, thus, they need a varied toolbox consisting of knowledge, language, strategies and positive reinforcement of prosocial behaviour. Caring, supportive and authoritative teachers establish positive relations with their students. Indirectly, such relations positively affect peer relations and norm development in the class (Pianta et al., 2012). Therefore, school classes that have more caring, warm and supportive teacher–student relationships tend to be characterised by similar peer relationships (Thornberg et al., 2018). The emotional safety that is a consequence of secure boundaries allows students to feel that there is a place for them in the class and that they belong.

Building alliances

Figure 14.2 illustrates a line between the teacher and students who have bullied, and this line is important for rehabilitation. Many students who bully are well integrated at their school, do not lack peer support (Farmer et al., 2010) and are often perceived as popular by their peers, especially in adolescence (e.g. Caravita et al., 2009).

However, it is not clear that students using bullying as a social strategy are happy with it. They may feel trapped in a role not representing who they want to be or what they want to do. However, high-status students, whose strategies have been most 'successful' in eliciting social rewards, appear to be the most resistant to efforts to reduce or replace abusive behaviour (Garandeau et al., 2014). These students may attempt to maintain the status quo because it is beneficial to sustaining their social power. However, as Hawley and Williford (2015) argue, one should not try to equalise the hierarchy. It is more effective to target the norms, perceptions, attitudes and efficacy beliefs to establish a climate and culture that promotes friendship and prosocial behaviour. The authoritative teacher may motivate and increase the value of prosocial behaviour that can lead students to reach social power. When students understand how they can become leaders and gain high levels of self-esteem by being

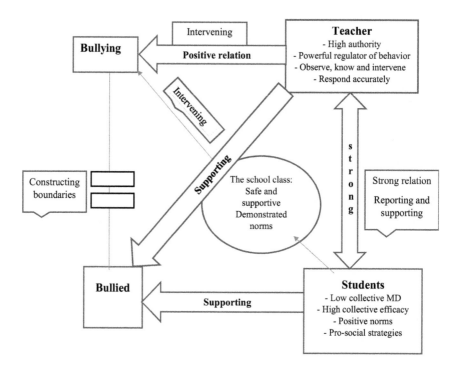

Figure 14.2 Systemic intervention

helpful, cooperative, friendly and sociable (De Bruyn & van den Boom, 2005), they may be more likely to develop prosocial strategies within their relationships. Because prosocial students have the welfare of their peers firmly in mind and place social relationships above their own instrumental goals, they may function as good role models for their peers (Hawley & Williford, 2015).

In addition, it allows for the important inclusion of bystanders, who should be utilised in such efforts because their behaviour might be easier to change than the behaviour of those most involved in the bullying. Consequently, the social rewards associated with bullying (and the motivation to bully in the first place) can be diminished (Salmivalli, 2010), and the goal of creating a supportive class community may be achieved more easily.

Promoting a supportive class community

Pörhölä (2016) suggests that supportive peer relationships may provide an arena in which negative beliefs about oneself, and others can be corrected, thereby reducing loneliness and enhancing self-esteem. When victimisation desists over time and victims can replace emotional-oriented coping styles with more adaptive coping styles, the impact of risk factors caused by bullying may be reduced (Garnefski & Kraaij, 2014). They may look less like stable victims and begin to exhibit the adjustment profile of those without a history of victimisation, demonstrating a pattern of positive adjustment (Rajabi et al., 2017). However, without access to social support, this change may be challenging.

Prosocial behaviour has a strong positive association with later peer acceptance (Caprara et al., 2000), and this relationship is likely to be bidirectional, as children who feel accepted are more likely to do things for others (Sandstrom & Cillessen, 2006). Another possible effect of a supportive community is a higher acceptance of deviance, and students may be more easily invited into common discussions about values, multiplicity, social inclusion, caring and tolerance. Regarding situated rehabilitation, the likelihood of peacefully reconstructing a prosocial class community increases when all students share mutual interest in repairing damage to their relationships and have access to relational-repair mechanisms (Cowie, 2011). These conditions may facilitate opportunities for all students, regardless of their former roles, to practise interaction skills and develop along with age-related expectations. Therefore, students should be provided with safe strategies to support vulnerable peers and behave in a prosocial manner.

Social and emotional learning (SEL)

Social and emotional learning (SEL) programmes commonly address a broad spectrum of knowledge, attitudes and skills that are required to behave in a prosocial manner. Although SEL programs usually are measured in relation to aggression and other externalising behaviours, they have demonstrated equally positive impacts for internalising problems (Durlak et al., 2011), but they have rarely specifically measured bullying. However, there are some exceptions. For instance, Rajabi and colleagues (2017) have shown that group-based SEL interventions, including elements from cognitive behavioural therapy (CBT), improve the use of constructive strategies and reduce the use of emotion-focused strategies for students being bullied. Further, meta-analyses examining school-based interventions that address traumatic stress demonstrate the beneficial support and effects that stem from CBT-based interventions (Jaycox et al., 2014).

Universal programmes are framed positively and provided independently of an individual's risk status, minimising their potential for stigmatising participants and making it easier to accept and adopt these programs in school classrooms (Domitrovich et al., 2010). This may prevent internalised problems that otherwise would go unnoticed and untreated and may help reduce the number of students who ultimately have higher levels of need. However, the core reason for arranging social and emotional learning (SEL) for the whole class is the need for changing relational practice in the peer community.

The content in SEL

Social concern and moral disengagement

Because a significant process in bullying is that those who bully construct a difference between 'us' and someone else, placing 'us' in the favoured position, like a moral asymmetry ('my welfare is important, but yours is not') (Arsenio & Lemerise, 2004), it is necessary to address the need for social knowledge about equalising the asymmetry by targeting moral disengagement and cognitive distortions. When learning and discussing these topics in a whole class setting, students may be able to recognise and adjust with one another. A SEL program was examined in a recent study of class-based Social Perception Training (SPT) (Finne & Svartdal, 2017), focusing on adjustments to the core mechanisms outlined earlier. This study showed that students' moral disengagement was significantly reduced, whereas the students' relationships with peers and teachers were positively influenced.

Prosocial actions

There are many ways to act on behalf of others. Typically, we apply the term 'prosocial' to any behaviour that is intended to benefit another, such as helping, sharing, and comforting (Carlo & Randall, 2002). By providing help and support to peers, students may indirectly benefit because of an increased probability of access to the same help and support when needed. Discussions and role-play may be used to clarify how different situations may be solved in the favour of all involved, and how these solutions can affect ourselves and others in social interaction. Using a variety of situations may lead to better understanding and generalisation and may gradually increase the ability to behave in a prosocial way.

Peer ecology

To change relational practice in the peer ecology, it is crucial to target the norm structure. Hidden and unspoken norms should be demonstrated and discussed. By making the norms explicit through discussions and role-play, students may experience that their own standards are shared with the majority. Language instruction and the introduction of useful terms provide an avenue for explaining problem-solving and a prosocial stance. Certain groups of words are applied to understandings of the antecedents and consequences of behaviour, such as 'prosocial', 'moral disengagement' or 'responsibility'.

This contributes to cue-interpretation skills through which students develop a vocabulary for interpreting the behaviour of others. Hypothetical and real-life scenarios in which characters resolve problems prosocially expose students to common alternatives for handling social situations without aggression, selfishness or unfairness. This should also include online situations.

Through interactions, the demonstrated standard may be reinforced by an authoritative teacher and supported by peers and parents. An encouraging outcome of student-based classroom interventions is the positive benefit for teachers' efficacy, beliefs and perceptions (Domitrovich et al., 2016). Consequently, student-based interventions may be an important contribution to the teacher's authority in the classroom. Such mutual synergies may favour the process of rehabilitating the peer ecology.

Family support

The family is a significant context regardless of age. Even though research on collaboration with parents in bullying cases is scarce, we can draw on related research. For instance, Epstein (2001) found that positive involvement of parents strengthened relationships with their children and their attitudes towards the teachers. Researchers have also found that the degree to which the student perceives the existence of commitment and mutual support between family members (Cohesion) acts as a protective factor against both cybervictimisation and cyber perpetration (Martínez-Monteagudo et al., 2019). The focus on family should receive more attention, including when the children become students at a university. The assumptions that students above the age of 18 are able to defend themselves needs to be challenged as positive relationships with the family emerge as a coping mechanism for involvement in cyberbullying, as they do for school students.

What can higher education learn from school?

To equip universities to deal with cyberbullying, the university sector should consider how and what they can learn from school. HE bullying seem to share features in common with school and workplace bullying (Harrison et al., 2022), and school-based understanding and interventions may therefore be feasible for the HE sector. The vulnerability of a young person does not necessarily decrease with age (Myers & Cowie, 2019). The need for an authoritative adult, peer support and support from one's family is of great importance. When being exposed to cyberbullying, lack of structure and support in HE and FE may increase the negative consequences. As in school, for students in HE the lack of rehabilitating efforts may be because many students don't tell, and if they do, staff do not believe them.

Perhaps what needs to be introduced for the university sector is why and how they can be involved in students' lives. The authoritative perspective may guide the understanding of the staff as significant others and for the leaders to acknowledge their responsibility to contribute with both personal warmth and constructive systems of support.

Conclusion

In this chapter, we argue that due to the reciprocal nature of traditional and cyberbullying, the social context at school is the better arena for rehabilitation involving peer ecology. We suggest that social support and prosocial interactions can buffer the negative effects of bullying and promote the development of social competence and constructive coping strategies along with age-related expectations. Because bullying is a relational attack, appropriate efforts to repair wounds should have an extensive focus on relational practices without losing the individual aspects. The costs and benefits of different strategies for gaining and maintaining status should be addressed in a way that makes aggression appear costlier than it is rewarding. Therefore, we propose that bullying should be stopped as soon as possible and situated rehabilitation in the peer ecology should be initiated. The current model of situated rehabilitation outlines three ways of working: (1) ensuring teacher authority to secure safe teacher–student relationship, (2) systemic intervention and (3) social and emotional learning (SEL).

It is necessary to point out that this initiative is not supposed to replace what is professional individual therapy or support. Some students may need both. Rather, we suggest that the situated approach may be more appropriate because this approach underlines both the responsibility and the solution, including the promotion of peer support and prosocial relationships, which is also of great importance in the student's digital lives.

References

Arsenio, W. F., & Lemerise, E. A. (2004). Aggression and moral development: Integrating social information processing and moral domain models. *Child Development, 75*(4), 987–1002. https://doi.org/10.1111/j.1467-8624.2004.00720.x

Bandura, A. (1986). *Social foundations of thought and action: A social cognitive theory.* Englewood Cliffs, NJ: Prentice-Hall.

Bandura, A. (1991). Social cognitive theory of moral thought and action. In W. M. Kurtines., & J. L. Gewirtz (Eds.), *Handbook of moral behavior and development* (Vol. 1, pp. 45–103). Hillsdale, NJ: Erlbaum.

Bath, H. (2008). The three pillars of trauma-informed care. *Reclaiming Children and Youth, 17*(3), 17–21

Bauman, S., & Newman, M. L. (2013). Testing assumptions about cyberbullying: Perceived distress associated with acts of conventional and cyber bullying. *Psychology of Violence, 3*(1), 27. https://doi.org/10.1037/a0029867

Baumrind, D. (2013). Authoritative parenting revisited. History and current status. In R. E.Larzelere, A. S. Morris, & A. W. Harrist (Eds.), *Authoritative parenting: Synthesizing nurturance and discipline for optimal child development* (pp. 11–34). Washington, DC: American Psychological Association. https://psycnet.apa.org/doin/10.1037/13948-002

Breivik, K., Bru, E., Hancock, C., Idsøe, E. C., Idsøe, T., & Solberg, M. E. (2017). *Å bli utsatt for mobbing. En kunnskapsoppsummering om konsekvenser og tiltak. [Being exposed to bullying. A systematic review of consequences and interventions.]* Stavanger: Læringsmiljøsenteret.

Caprara, G. V., Barbaranelli, C., Pastorelli, C., Bandura, A., & Zimbardo, P. G. (2000). Prosocial foundations of children's academic achievement. *Psychological Science, 11*(4), 302–306. https://doi.org/10.1111/1467-9280.00260.

Caravita, S. C. S., DiBlasio, P., & Salmivalli, C. (2009). Unique and interactive effects of empathy and social status on involvement in bullying. *Social Development, 18*, 140–163. https://doi.org/10.1111/j.1467-9507.2008.00465.

Caravita, S. C. S., Finne, J. N., & Fandrem, H. (2021). Two dimensions of moral cognition as correlates of different forms of participation in bullying. *Frontiers in Psychology, 12*. https://doi.org/10.3389/fpsyg.2021768503.

Caravita, S. C. S., Sijtsema, J. J., Rambaran, J. A., & Gini, G. (2014). Peer influences on moral disengagement in late childhood and early adolescence. *Journal of Youth and Adolescence, 43*(2), 193–207. https://doi.org/10.1007/s10964-013-9953-1

Carlo, G., & Randall, B. A. (2002). The development of a measure of prosocial behaviors for late adolescents. *Journal of Youth and Adolescence, 31*(1), 31–44. https://doi.org/10.1023/A:1014033032440.

Chan, T. W., & Koo, A. (2011). Parenting style and youth outcomes in the UK. *European Sociological Review, 27*(3), 385–399. https://doi.org/10.1093/esr/jcq013

Cowie, H. (2011). Peer support as an intervention to counteract school bullying: Listen to the children. *Children & Society, 25*(4), 287–292. https://doi.org/10.1111/j.1099-0860.2011.00375.x

De Bruyn, E. H., & Van Den Boom, D. C. (2005). Interpersonal behavior, peer popularity, and self-esteem in early adolescence. *Social Development, 14*(4), 555–573. https://doi.org/10.1111/j.1467-9507.2005.00317.x

Domitrovich, C. E., Bradshaw, C. P., Berg, J. K., Pas, E. T., Becker, K. D., Musci, R., . . . & Ialongo, N. (2016). How do school-based prevention programs impact teachers? Findings from a randomized trial of an integrated classroom management and social-emotional program. *Prevention Science, 17*(3), 325–337. https://doi.org/10.1007/s11121-015-0618-z

Domitrovich, C. E., Bradshaw, C. P., Greenberg, M. T., Embry, D., Poduska, J. M., & Ialongo, N. S. (2010). Integrated models of school-based prevention: Logic and theory. *Psychology in the Schools, 47*(1), 71–88. https://doi.org/10.1002/pits.20452.

Durlak, J. A., Weissberg, R. P., Dymnicki, A. B., Taylor, R. D., & Schellinger, K. B. (2011). The impact of enhancing students' social and emotional learning: A meta-analysis of school-based universal interventions. *Child Development, 82*(1), 405–432. https://doi.org/10.1111/j.1467-8624.2010.01564.x.

Epstein, Joyce L. (2001). *School, family, and community partnerships: Preparing educators and improving schools.* Boulder, CO: Westview Press.

Farmer, T. W., Petrin, R. A., Robertson, D. L., Fraser, M. W., Hall, C. M., Day, S. H., & Dadisman, K. (2010). Peer relations of bullies, bully-victims, and victims: Two social worlds of bullying in second grade classrooms. *The Elementary School Journal, 110*(3), 364–392. https://doi.org/10.1086/648983

Finne, J., & Svartdal, F. (2017). Outcome evaluation of Social Perception Training (SPT): Improving social competence by reducing cognitive distortions. *International Journal of Emotional Education, 9*(2), 44–58.

Garandeau, C. F., Lee, I. A., & Salmivalli, C. (2014). Inequality matters: Classroom status hierarchy and adolescents' bullying. *Journal of Youth and Adolescence, 43*(7), 1123–1133. https://doi.org/10.1007/s10964-013-0040-4.

Garnefski, N., & Kraaij, V. (2014). Bully victimization and emotional problems in adolescents: Moderation by specific cognitive coping strategies?. *Journal of Adolescence, 37*(7), 1153–1160. https://doi.org/10.1016/j.adolescence.2014.07.005.

Gasser, L., & Keller, M. (2009). Are the competent the morally good? Perspective taking and moral motivation of children involved in bullying. *Social Development, 18*(4), 798–816. https://doi.org/10.1111/j.1467–9507.2008.00516.x

Gerlinger, J., & Wo, J. C. (2016). Preventing school bullying: Should schools prioritize an authoritative school discipline approach over security measures? *Journal of School Violence, 15*(2), 133–661. https://doi.org/10.1080/15388220.2014.956321

Harrison, E. D., Hulme, J. A., & Fox, C. L. (2022). A thematic analysis of students' perceptions and experiences of bullying in UK higher education. *Europe's Journal of Psychology, 18*(1), 53. https://doi.org/10.5964/ejop.3669

Hawley, P. H., & Williford, A. (2015). Articulating the theory of bullying intervention programs: Views from social psychology, social work, and organizational science. *Journal of Applied Developmental Psychology, 37*, 3–15. https://doi.org/10.1177/0165025407074630.

Jaycox, L. H., Stein, B. D., & Wong, M. (2014). School intervention related to school and community violence. *Child and Adolescent Psychiatric Clinics, 23*(2), 281–293. https://doi.org/10.1016/j.chc.2013.12.005

Latané, B., & Darley, J. M. (1968). Group inhibition of bystander intervention in emergencies. *Journal of Personality and Social Psychology, 10*(3), 215. https://doi.org/10.1037/h0025589.

Lave, J., & Wenger, E. (1991). *Situated learning: Legitimate peripheral participation*. Cambridge: Cambridge University Press.

Martínez-Monteagudo, M. C., Delgado, B., Inglés, C. J., & García-Fernández, J. M. (2019). Cyberbullying in the university setting. Relationship with family environment and emotional intelligence. *Computers in Human Behavior, 91*, 220–225. https://doi.org/10.1016/j.chb.2018.10.002

Myers, C.-A., & Cowie, H. (2019). Cyberbullying across the lifespan of education: Issues and interventions from school to university. *International Journal of Environmental Research and Public Health, 16*(7), 1217. https://doi.org/10.3390/ijerph16071217

Nappa, M. R., Palladino, B. E., Nocentini, A., & Menesini, E. (2021). Do the face-to-face actions of adults have an online impact? The effects of parent and teacher responses on cyberbullying among students. *European Journal of Developmental Psychology, 18*(6), 798–813. https://doi.org/10.1080/17405629.2020.1860746

Olweus, D., & Limber, S. P. (2018). Some problems with cyberbullying research. *Current Opinion in Psychology, 19*, 139–143. https://doi.org/10.1016/j.copsyc.2017.04.012

Perren, S., & Gutzwiller-Helfenfinger, E. (2012). Cyberbullying and traditional bullying in adolescence: Differential roles of moral disengagement, moral emotions, and moral values. *European Journal of Developmental Psychology, 9*(2), 195–209. https://doi.org/10.1080/17405629.2011.643168

Pianta, R. C., Hamre, B. K., & Allen, J. P. (2012). Teacher-student relationships and engagement: Conceptualizing, measuring, and improving the capacity of classroom interactions. In S. L. Christensen (Ed.). *Handbook of research on student engagement* (pp. 365–386). Boston, MA: Springer.

Pörhölä, M. (2016). Do the roles of bully and victim remain stable from school to university?: Theoretical considerations. In H. Cowie & C.-A. Myers (Eds.), *Bullying among university students: Crossnational perspectives* (pp. 35–46). London: Routledge.

Pozzoli, T., Gini, G., & Vieno, A. (2012). The role of individual correlates and class norms in defending and passive bystanding behavior in bullying: A multilevel analysis. *Child Development, 83*(6), 1917–1931. https://doi.org/10.1002/ab.21442

Rajabi, M., Bakhshani, N. M., Saravani, M. R., Khanjani, S., & Javad Bagian, M. (2017). Effectiveness of cognitive-behavioral group therapy on coping strategies and in reducing anxiety, depression, and physical complaints in student victims of bullying. *International Journal of High Risk Behaviors and Addiction, 6*(2). https://doi.org/10.5812/ijhrba.41463.

Rogoff, B. (2003). *The cultural nature of human development.* Oxford: Oxford University Press.

Roland, E., & Galloway, D. (2002). Classroom influences on bullying. *Educational Research, 44*(3), 299–312. https://doi.org/10.1080/0013188022000031597

Runions, K. C., & Bak, M. (2015). Online moral disengagement, cyberbullying, and cyber-aggression. *Cyberpsychology, Behavior, and Social Networking, 18*(7), 400–405. https://doi.org/10.1089/cyber.2014.0670

Salmivalli, C. (2010). Bullying and the peer group: A review. *Aggression and Violent Behavior, 15*(2), 112–120. https://doi.org/10.1016/j.avb.2009.08.007.

Sandstrom, M. J., & Cillessen, A. H. (2006). Likeable versus popular: Distinct implications for adolescent adjustment. *International Journal of Behavioral Development, 30*(4), 305–314. https://doi.org/10.1177/0165025406072789

Sjursø, I. R., Fandrem, H., O'Higgins Norman, J., & Roland, E. (2019). Teacher authority in long-lasting cases of bullying: A qualitative study from Norway and Ireland. *International Journal Environmental Research and Public Health, 16*(7), 1163. https://doi.org/10.3390/ijerph16071163

Thornberg, R., Wänström, L., Pozzoli, T., & Gini, G. (2018). Victim prevalence in bullying and its association with teacher–student and student–student relationships and class moral disengagement: A class-level path analysis. *Research Papers in Education, 33*(3), 320–335. https://doi.org/10.1080/02671522.2017.1302499

Wentzel, K. R. (2002). Are effective teachers like good parents? Teaching styles and student adjustment in early adolescence. *Child Development, 73*(1), 287–301. https://doi.org/10.1111/1467-8624.00406.

15 Interventions to challenge cyberbullying and online harassment

The perspective from schools

Kathy Evans and Lynn Gazal

Introduction

Much research refers to the period prior to the coronavirus (COVID-19) pandemic and lockdown. During lockdown due to the Covid pandemic, most youngsters spent all day with their family or others who live in their household. They could only 'see' their peers through online platforms or by smartphone. With children's isolation at home and increased time spent on the internet, the split between in-person and online bullying is likely to have changed substantially during this period. Children's isolation at home and increased time spent on the internet are likely to have had a substantial impact on the split between real world and cyberbullying.

During the pandemic, it has been generally accepted and reported that experiences have become more challenging for many children and young people. The argument is that the 'new normal' way of life has in many instances been associated with less socialisation, an increase in family responsibilities, even a rise in child abuse. This may of course affect a child's emotional and mental well-being and therefore lead to greater vulnerability in relation to bullying and cyberbullying. However, it has also become evident that experiences have been reported as being easier for some; for example, young people who were already feeling anxious about school and other social mixing were content that much more was carried out from home where there were less demands on some types of socialisation. In Canada, Patchin and Hinduja (2021) discovered that students overwhelmingly said that they had been bullied less at school since the start of the pandemic. When it came to cyberbullying, most said they had been bullied online less or about the same as before, but about a quarter did report more cyberbullying during the pandemic. Similar findings were collected from perpetrators. Patchin and Hinduja draw attention to the reduced access that young people would have to counsellors, social workers and psychologists during lockdown.

Bullying, cyberbullying and mental health

There has been growing evidence of the negative health consequences arising from acts of bullying and cyberbullying, prior to the recent pandemic years (Al-Ghabban, 2018; Cowie & Myers, 2020). The negative results of bullying to both

DOI:10.4324/9781003258605-19

victims and sometimes perpetrators have been clearly outlined with an emphasis on frequent victims of bullying often going on to suffer long-term psychological problems. These include increased levels of anxiety, depressive symptoms, social isolation, loneliness and suicidal ideation. This is often explored in the fictional descriptions and the non-fiction narratives and documentaries in this area, again with a breadth of work that explores cyberbullying. Perhaps unsurprisingly perpetrators of bullying also risk experiencing psychological problems which would be currently labelled as anxiety, depression, conduct disorder as well as eating disorders and antisocial behaviour. Much has been written exploring the effect of the pandemic on the mental health of children and young people. However, there have been very important questions asked about the differences between what has been described as a resulting pandemic of severe mental health and a different perspective that argues that so-called mental health disorders only make sense in context.

This could reflect the long-term difference that has been noted between a professional asking *what is wrong* with a child, and *what is wrong with what has happened* to a child. This then also responds to differences in the assessment of, and response to, how children are coping with challenge. More specifically, this will lead to us visiting or revisiting the differences between children and young people being 'diagnosed and treated' in a more traditional way and assessed in a developing style that is often referred to as 'formulation'.

In a formulation approach, psychologists explore with children, families, friends and professionals the specificity and complexity of a child's experience and therefore offer perhaps different explanations and responses to challenging behaviour. This may make sense of the situation where for some children the pandemic experience has made life easier. For example, a young person may not avoid school simply because they have a mental health disorder such as anxiety. It may be simply because their emotional response and behaviour make sense if it is seen as related to something that has happened in the young person's life, and why it is therefore much more comfortable for the young person to stay away from a particular social situation or situations.

This can also explain the behaviour of perpetrators. A formulation approach would focus more on what has happened to the perpetrator that would explain why they engage in cyberbullying. The American Psychiatric Association suggests that some young people should not be diagnosed as having conduct disorder where young people are living in 'very threatening high-crime areas or war zones' (American Psychiatric Association, 2013, p. 474), and perhaps many of those who are seen primarily as being difficult and dangerous have had very challenging experiences themselves.

Overview of interventions

As our understanding of cyberbullying has increased, so has the range of responses to that. Although this is, in theory, the development of strategies that are useful for working with victims, perpetrators and observers, it is mostly presented in a dichotomous way, where the victims are being supported. Since cyberbullying was identified in the 1990s, responses to addressing cyberbullying are very diverse and are sometimes supported by experiential methods that focus on **who** are doing **what** and **where.** Consequently, sometimes the response to cyberbullying is individual or familial and not well-documented. Over time, many recorded responses have come from a wide range of collaborators, from which we would draw the following overview of practical responses.

> *Who?* This includes governmental bodies, charitable organisations and other institutions, many of which are grounded in health, welfare and education services. Schools, colleges and universities are key organisations here. We know that cyberbullying responses increasingly include collaboration with parents and carers, and more recently with children and young people. Importantly, this is an area that children and young people are introducing and leading in too. It is likely that young people's involvement progresses with time, partly of course explained by their knowledge and skills that relate to social technology.
>
> **What?** Strategies include familial support, peer support and professional support. Professional support includes therapeutic, creative, physical and cognitive responses working with individuals, working with groups and developing resources. Group work includes peer support, where young people are encouraged to support each other, and this is often used in response to cyberbullying in schools and universities. Professional and informal support also includes the use of media, particularly fiction and film, which we go on to discuss at the end of the next section.
>
> This area includes what is understood as providing social and emotional support to children, so there is a huge overlap here, with approaches taken to children and young people, who are perceived as having more significant social and emotional needs, and those often described as mental health needs.
>
> *Where?* Approaches to addressing cyberbullying are available online and offline, and as hybrid responses (hybrid in this instance referring to a combination of working online and offline). There are strategies that are available in situations that are felt to be very serious, though the difficulty here can be around adults being clear as to when a situation is dangerous. If it is felt that the danger is real then there is the option of calling the police, but there are also other sources of relatively rapid responses; in the United Kingdom examples would be the NSPCC Helpline or ChildLine. In these situations, those who are reporting cyberbullying will usefully have learnt more about how to evidence bullying, report it appropriately, understand the legality of social media and work with the social and emotional consequences of bullying.

A focus on interventions

First, we focus on internationally recommended ways to educate young people in internet safety and in how to respond to and evidence cyberbullying.

Next, we detail methods of reporting to trusted adults and social media providers, before exploring the emerging global legality of social media. Finally, we explore best practices when working with the social and emotional consequences of cyberbullying, such as providing appropriate support.

Internet safety and ways to respond to and evidence cyberbullying

It is important to create an environment where young people feel safe and where they know how to respond to cyberbullying and evidence it. This environment should emphasise the need for a zero-tolerance of cyberbullying and for incidents to be dealt with quickly and consistently. A positive and supportive atmosphere will be helpful, with fun activities, such as role-playing to open discussion about cyberbullying and how to handle it. Clear, age-appropriate guidance on display and leaflets to read and keep will give young people tools and help how to evidence bullying before any event occurs. These will also help them deal more confidently with it and perhaps take it less personally if it occurs.

Internet safety training for pupils should emphasise

- That the internet is not a private place
- That the internet isn't always safe
- Their rights and responsibilities online
- A positive use of technology, 'good netiquette'
- The importance of reporting cyberbullying when they see it
- Where to locate anti-bullying and cyberbullying policies

When young people are forearmed with actions to take, they will feel more prepared and more aware of possible steps to take, such as:

- Ignoring cyberbullying messages and not forwarding them
- Blocking cyberbully/ies
- Collecting evidence, with dates and times
- Saving and printing screenshots of emails and messages
- Reporting cyberbullying to the internet, social media and call providers
- Contacting the police or emergency services if there is immediate threat of danger

UNICEF reiterates the need to tell someone that you trust:

> If you think you're being bullied, the first step is to seek help from someone you trust such as your parents, a close family member or another trusted adult. In your school you can reach out to a counsellor, the sports coach, or your favourite teacher – either online or in person.
>
> (UNICEF, 2021, p. 2)

Reporting cyberbullying

To stop cyberbullying, it needs to be identified, so reporting is key. This also helps to reinforce to the bully that this type of behaviour is totally unacceptable. Trusted adults can assist with checking the terms and conditions of social media forums and can help young people understand which content type is reportable. They may also need to help the young person to feel more confident in reporting the cyberbullying to the relevant forum/s. Bullies will need to be blocked and settings may need to be made more secure.

UNICEF specialists and international cyberbullying/child protection experts teamed up with Facebook, Instagram, TikTok and Twitter, to answer some of the most common questions about online bullying and give advice on ways to deal with it:

Reporting to Facebook and Instagram

We also make it easy to report any bullying directly within Facebook or Instagram. You can always send our team an anonymous report from a post, comment, story or DM on Facebook or Instagram. We have a team who reviews these reports 24/7 around the world in 50+ languages, and we'll remove anything that's abusive or bullying. These reports are always anonymous.

Reporting to TikTok

We deploy both technology and thousands of safety professionals to help keep bullying off TikTok. We also encourage our community members to make use of the easy in-app reporting tools to alert us if they or someone they know has experienced bullying. You can report videos, comments, accounts and direct messages so that we can take appropriate action and help keep you safe. Reports are always confidential.

Reporting to Twitter

'We encourage people to report accounts to us that may break our rules. You can do this on our Help Centre or through the in-Tweet reporting mechanism by clicking on the "Report a Tweet" option'.

Understanding the legality of social media

Technically, social media companies are obliged to keep their users safe. However, there still is not an independent regulatory body set up to enforce this. Terms and conditions remain complicated and far from user friendly. However, there have been global calls for greater protective laws, such as UNESCO calling for advances in ethical standards and from the Children's Commissioner for England, who has rewritten social media terms and conditions into simpler, more accessible language for families and children.

Without a regulatory body, many countries have taken matters into their own hands, such as banning pornography on social media sites, opting for various types of censorship, or banning social media sites altogether. Mark Zuckerberg, founder and CEO of Facebook, has called for greater government regulation and global standards to help regulate social media. By updating the rules for the internet, he argues, we can preserve what's best about it – the freedom for people to express themselves and for entrepreneurs to build new things – while also protecting society from broader harms.

A series of high-profile abuse and bullying incidents, such as the racist abuse of Premier League footballers and the death of teenager Molly Russell, has led the UK government to try to be the first country to introduce 'world-leading' online safety laws and introduce 'The Online-Safety Bill' to the British Parliament to bring internet users a step closer to a safer online environment. The Online Safety Bill marks a milestone in the fight for a new digital age which is safer for users and holds tech giants to account. It will protect children from harmful content, such as pornography, and limit people's exposure to illegal content, while protecting freedom of speech. The Online Safety Bill aims to force social media forums to protect children, to tackle illegal activity and to uphold their terms and conditions. It will target paid-for scam adverts, pornography sites for age checks, anonymous trolls, cyber-flashing and more. The regulatory body, Ofcom, will have powers to fine companies up to ten per cent of their annual global turnover and block sites which are non-compliant. Companies that do not cooperate with their information requests could face prosecution or jail time within two months of the Bill becoming law.

In 2021, the UK has also introduced a new set of regulations aimed at protecting children, which is an amendment to the Data Protection Act of 2018. Those who break the new 'age-appropriate design code' risk being fined millions of dollars, which has led to a scramble of last-minute changes by some of the largest internet players. Rather than applying the changes to the UK alone, as they would be legally obligated to, TikTok, Instagram and YouTube have made the changes global.

Is cyberbullying illegal?

Yes and no. It is a criminal offence if cyberbullying is the cause of 'alarm or distress' to victims (under the Harassment Act 1997) or is 'grossly offensive' (Malicious Communications Act 1988 and the Communications Act 2003). It is the legal duty of schools to prevent all forms of bullying and they may implement actions such as detention, isolation or even exclusion.

Working with the social and emotional consequences of cyberbullying

Online violence including cyberbullying has a negative effect on academic achievement, mental health, and quality of life of students. Children who are frequently bullied are nearly three times as likely to feel left out at school as those who are not. They are also twice as likely to miss out on school and have a higher tendency to leave formal education after finishing secondary school.

(UNESCO, 2021, p. 3)

There are signs to look out for to identify cyberbullying in a young person, such as:

- Appearing upset or frightened after looking at a smartphone
- Showing anxiety when their phone beeps
- Being secretive about their digital life
- Losing interest in going out
- Isolating themselves generally
- Having disturbed sleep
- Eating less than before

Severe cases of cyberbullying may lead to anxiety and depression or even suicide. Cyberbullying is difficult to avoid and even harder to escape. Many young people use smartphones everywhere, so the bullying can feel invasive and inescapable. Falling prey to cyberbullying brings feelings of loss of control, feeling vulnerable and powerlessness. Often, young people will say things online that they wouldn't say in person. And to make this worse, cyberbullying also allows the message to be much more far-reaching. In just a few clicks, an embarrassing photo or nasty post can be shared all over a website for a whole school to see. Victims of cyberbullying often avoid telling parents or guardians, for fear of having their devices taken away. Bullies also may make threats, to put the victims off telling adults, such as uploading sensitive information about the victim to the internet, leading to feelings of shame and embarrassment.

Victims of cyberbullying often isolate themselves and avoid their friends and school. They lose out on precious friendships, important socialising and social development. If parents ask them to surrender their phones, this leads to further isolation.

Providing social and emotional support to children and young people

Family support

Showing empathy and support towards victims builds bridges and understanding, for example, when parents and guardians talk calmly, without judgment and gently ask about the whole story. This may prove difficult for some individuals, but showing support and solidarity helps victims to open up, which eases their burden. Telling them you are supporting them, whatever happens, helps to build their trust. Taking time to explain why we are taking certain actions gives the victims clarity. For example, it is best not to respond to a bully, and it is better to block them to prevent them from sending more unkind messages. Show them how to build records of evidence and explain why it is important to keep proof, to show teachers, the police or possibly the courts. Explain why all this is necessary. Try to be supportive and reassuring. If applicable, share personal experiences of bullying or that of others close to them. Explain how this was dealt with. They will benefit from realising that they are not the only ones facing these problems, they are not to blame, and a solution can always be found. Support your child to inform the school authorities and encourage them to seek counselling.

Media resources

Cyberbullying and online harassment have been explored using fiction, film and other media. We give some examples here but also think about the advantages and challenges of this approach. It is of course important here to think about the development of these ideas as there will be a mix of fiction and non-fiction and they, of course, are very differently useful.

Written resources

An extensive range of fiction explores bullying and a small number of texts explore cyberbullying such as *Chicken Clicking* (2014) and *Troll Stinks* (2017) by Jeanne Willis and Tony Ross. *Chicken Clicking* explores what can happen if a chicken borrows the farm computer to shop for everyone, scooters for the sheep and a car for the cow, and finally a camera for herself. She sets herself up on a site where she can meet friends, and sadly, her first friend is a large fox waiting for her under a tree! *Troll Stinks* explores the cyberbullying of a troll by two goats, a troll who turns out to be a tiny, frightened troll. A story that ends with the goats realising their mistake. For hundreds of years, dark topics have appeared in children's literature (Hans Christian Anderson, Lewis Carroll, Brothers Grimm, Sendak, Dahl and Rowling), where stories explore loss, death, fear and frustration.

For example, *Where the Wild Things Are* by Sendek and Schickele (1963) was banned in the 1960s in the United States as it was seen as upsetting and potentially damaging to young readers. There are also a variety of approaches to the management of children's books and in most countries, there is a system of book banding and banning of harmful books. It is difficult to censor texts according to age alone. Personal experience (KE) of working in a therapeutic community school where the students were mainly adolescents indicated that the television they watched regularly was nearly always children's television because given their childhood experiences, the effect of 'dark' texts or visual resources could be more challenging.

There are also several non-fiction cyberbullying texts, written for young people. Examples include *Cyber Bullying (Take a Stand Against Bullying)* Stuckey (2013) and *Staying Safe Online* (2016). *Staying Safe Online* covers social media, with a particular focus on storing personal information safely on your computer with strong passwords, updated software and a sense of the reliability of websites.

A cut too far?

Several fiction films focus on cyberbullying, for example, *Cyberbully* (2011), *Cyberbully* (2015), *The Duff* (2015) and *A Girl Like Her* (2015). There are also a number of 'horror films' that we do not reference here as their use remains controversial. *Cyberbully* (2011) led to discussion on the content of bullying films *Cyberbully* was rated PG-13, but this might not have been the best place to introduce younger children to the subject due to the subject matter, sexual references and strong language. This continues to be debated in relation to children's literature and films. *Cyberbullying* (2015), a Channel Four film, takes place entirely in the bedroom of a teenage girl in 'real-time'. As the content is sexual, it is a film only for older students. It is '(a) rare programme that felt authentic enough to persuade teens, while also engaging older viewers' Jones (2015). *The Duff* (2015) is described as 'a comedy teen film' which 'light-heartedly' explores the negatives of bullying. This assumes that some young people do not find their experience of cyberbullying particularly challenging, and whereas this might be true for some, it is often difficult to conclude how this kind of material is affecting a young audience. *A Girl Like Her* (2015) explores cyberbullying from both sides, a teenage girl responding to a fellow student who has been bullying her online,

There are also documentaries such as *Audrey and Daisy* (2016) and works by Childnet – which include *Let's Fight It Together* (2008) and *Gone Too Far* (2021). *Audrey and Daisy* explores the tragic story of two girls who were sexually assaulted at the ages of 15 and 14. After the assaults, the victims and their families were subjected to abuse and cyberbullying, and both girls went on to die by suicide. The film was nominated for several awards and given the Peabody Award of merit. *Staying Safe Online* was produced by Childnet for the Department for Children, Schools and Families (DCSF) and includes linked interviews with a number of children. *Gone Too Far* (2021) is also a well-received Childnet production which explores homophobic cyberbullying.

Conclusion

Finally, we consider what comes next, which includes encouraging the support of children and young people with the social changes that emerge post-pandemic. We emphasise the underlying mental health problems found in both the victims and the perpetrators of cyberbullying and the need for measured and unbiased responses from professionals. There is certain to be more literature regarding this in the future. We also propose a move away from adult-led research towards an approach that enables young people to choose the questions, the research style or methodology, better to reflect their realities on the ground.

Online resources

THE CYBERSMILE FOUNDATION is a global, award-winning non-profit organisation which is committed to digital well-being and has a help centre www.cybersmile

NSPCC is the UK's leading children's charity *www.nspcc.org.uk/* One of NSPCC's services is ChildLine. Childline is free to contact on 0800 1111. Childline counsellors are here to take calls 24 hours a day, 7 days a week from children and young people under 19. Childline counsellors are also available to speak to online through *1–2–1 chat* and via *email*

INHOPE supports and enables INHOPE hotlines in the rapid identification and removal of Child Sexual Abuse Material from the digital world. INHOPE is made up of hotlines around the world that operate in all EU member states, Russia, South Africa, North and South America, Asia, Australia and New Zealand. *www.inhope.org*

Childnet's mission is to work in partnership with others to help make the internet a great and safe place for children. Childnet works directly with children and young people from the ages of 3 to 18, as well as parents, carers, teachers and professionals, finding out about their real experiences online and the positive things they are doing. *www.childnet.com/*

References

Al-Ghabban, A. (2018). A compassion framework: The role of compassion in schools in promoting well-being and supporting the social and emotional development of children and young people. *Pastoral Care in Education, 36,* 176–188.

American Psychiatric Association. (2013). *Diagnostic and statistical manual of mental disorders* (5th ed., p. 474). American Psychiatric Association.

Cowie & Myers (2020). The impact of the COVID-19 pandemic on the mental health and emotional well-being of children and young people. *Children & Society, 35*(1), 62–74.

Patchin, J. W., & Hinduja, S. (2021). Cyberbullying among tweens in the United States: Prevalence, impact, and helping behaviors, *Journal of Early Adolescence, 42*(3), 1–10 https://doi.org/10.1177/02724316211036740 downloaded 14/09/2022.

UNESCO (2021). *International day against violence and bullying at school including cyberbullying 2021: Theme, importance, and safety* (p. 2). https://en.unesco.org/commemorations/daya-gainstschoolviolenceandbullying (Accessed 12 September 2022).

UNICEF (2021). *Cyberbullying: What is it and how to stop it.* www.unicef.org/laos/stories/cyberbullying-what-it-and-how-stop-it (Accessed 14 September 2022).

Theme 5

Effective policies to counteract cyberbullying and online harassment

16 Policies to address cyberbullying in schools and universities

Zoe Vaill and Marilyn Campbell

Cyberbullying is an important issue that negatively impacts students at both schools and universities. We know that cyberbullying victimisation in children and young people has serious consequences, such as anxiety and depression (Betts, 2016; Hinduja & Patchin, 2015), low self-esteem and suicidal ideation (Bonanno & Hymel, 2013), as well as substance abuse (Moore et al., 2017). However, research on the consequences of cyberbullying among university students is still scant. In fact, the prevalence of cyberbullying amongst university students has only been recently researched (Myers & Cowie, 2019) with about a third of American university students reporting being cyberbullied in the last two years (Byrne, 2021). The negative consequences of cyberbullying victimisation have been shown to be similar in university students to that of children, with anxiety, depression and dropping out of education (Larranaga et al., 2018).

Considering the similarities of the negative consequences of cyberbullying for students in both educational institutions, it would seem logical that prevention and intervention strategies would be similar. However, while there has been some research on the effectiveness of such strategies for schools, there seems to be none for universities. It has been shown that school-based measures in Australia have been shown to modestly reduce the problem of cyberbullying (Cross et al., 2019), but it still occurs, as it does internationally (Gaffney et al., 2019). Ttofi and Farrington (2011) conducted a systematic review and meta-analysis of the effectiveness of anti-bullying programs in schools and found that the programs reduced victimisation by 17–20%. Programmes which were intensive and long-lasting were more effective, as were programmes including parent meetings, firm disciplinary methods and improved playground supervision (Rudasill et al., 2018).

Although some schools have had success with whole anti-bullying programs, the most established and prolific strategy is the use of policies to prevent and intervene in cyberbullying (Campbell, 2018), although it has been shown that the effectiveness of these policies is quite low. Smith (2014), in an overview of international research, noted only a 'modest' relationship between strong school anti-bullying policies and lower rates of bullying. In an Australian context, Rigby and Johnson (2016) reviewed the effectiveness of anti-bullying school policies and found that while the many schools across all states and

DOI:10.4324/9781003258605-21

territories they surveyed reported they had a policy document, fewer than half the students in the schools surveyed knew about it. Similarly in universities, Vaill and colleagues (2021) found that of the students surveyed (from three major Australian universities), 60% did not know if their university had a policy relating to bullying and fewer than a quarter of students knew where they would find such a policy. It would seem that educational institutions favour the use of policies as an easier and certainly cheaper way than programs to show they are dealing with the problem of cyberbullying.

A policy is a document which details the governance of an institution, with six key areas of a policy being identified as necessary (Cismaru & Cismaru, 2018). Policies are implemented for several reasons including informing the educational community of what is and is not acceptable and if the process of misconduct is detected, minimising the educational institution's exposure to legal liability and ensuring they meet legal requirements (Butler et al., 2011). Not only do institutions use policies for cyberbullying prevention and intervention but university students also believe that these policies are useful (Faucher et al., 2015; Vaill et al., 2021). Policies should then act as drivers of practical actions: that is, the proactive and reactive responses of educational institutions to address cyberbullying (Nickerson & Rigby, 2017).

Although the use of policies is a standard way of presenting information and protocols, there are many differences and some similarities between anti-cyberbullying policies of schools and those of universities. The first and most important difference is that schools are required to have such a policy and universities do not. Second, there are differences in the content of the policies, with schools usually being provided with a template by the employing authority ensuring that there is adequate coverage of the content which research (such as Smith, 2014) has deemed necessary. On the other hand, universities often only comply with the legal requirement to provide staff anti-bullying policies and then add students in as an afterthought. This makes for a variety of content in different universities' anti-cyberbullying policies. Third, the language used in school and university policies is naturally different. In addition, there is a difference in expectation of the policies between schools and universities as well as differences in intent of the policies. Surprisingly, there are many similarities with problems of dissemination of the anti-cyberbullying policies in both educational institutions as well as similar difficulties in having top-down construction of the policies.

Differences in requirements for school and university anti-cyberbullying policies

Schools' requirements

Schools worldwide usually have a legislated, mandated requirement to have an anti-cyberbullying policy, while universities do not. This could be because of the focus of research initially on bullying among school students, with researchers not examining cyberbullying in university populations until recently. Another reason could be that society considers that school students are more vulnerable than university students and therefore adults in the school need guidance to prevent and intervene in cyberbullying while university students are usually adults themselves and might not need that guidance or protection.

In the United States and Australia, schools are legally regulated by the state government rather than the national government. Generally, policies must include definitions, reporting information and complaint processes, as well as plans for dissemination to students, staff and parents. Unlike in the United States and Australia, schools in the UK are not governed by state laws but rather have a national approach. Although managed differently, the requirements are the same as in the United States or Australia, with schools being legally required to have a policy outlining acceptable and unacceptable behaviour which includes bullying and cyberbullying (The Education and Inspections Act, 2006). The policies themselves in the UK are created by the individual schools but must be promoted to the whole school community, including staff, students and parents. Canada uses a combination of national and state approaches.

Universities' requirements

Like schools, universities are educational institutions, however, unlike schools there is no legislation for the prevention or intervention of bullying or cyberbullying, nor is there legislation that requires universities to have anti-bullying policies (Myers & Cowie, 2017, 2019). Although there are no legal requirements around cyberbullying within universities, some countries have brought in legal ramifications for various cyber-based abuse, which applies to the whole population and not just universities. These include various legislations and Acts, which vary slightly by country. For example, in Ireland it is prohibited to partake in cyber-based harassment or image-based abuse (Department of Justice, Ireland, 2021), England and Wales have multiple Acts which prohibit a variety of online harassment, abuse, stalking and sharing of unwanted images and information (The Cybersmile Foundation, 2021). Other countries such as Australia and Canada have state-based laws which prohibit cyber-stalking, online threats of physical harm, image-based abuse or online harassment (Youth Law Australia, 2021; Government of Canada, 2021).

The gap in legislation between what schools and what universities are required to provide for students is found in many countries around the world, including the UK, Australia, the United States, Japan, South Africa, France, and Sweden, requiring anti-bullying policies in schools and the workplace but not in universities (Henry Carus Associates, 2019). As there are no specific requirements for universities to have a policy, let alone what they need to provide in their policies, there are many differences between different universities. Some universities have policies which refer to a specific cyberbullying policy; there are those that include cyberbullying within their anti-bullying policies and those that do not mention it all (although cyberbullying does generally tend to be included in misuse of university technology policies

Differences in the content of schools' and universities' anti-cyberbullying policies

Content of schools' anti-bullying policies

Content of a policy is vital in determining how usable, impactful and informative the policy is to its intended audience. For schools, this involves providing information not only for students but also for staff and parents. There has been some research on school anti-bullying policies, which have identified key content that policies must have to be effective. These areas include clear definitions of all forms of bullying, including cyberbullying, proactive elements which communicate the importance of caring and respectful interaction, tolerance, guidance on what is and is not appropriate behaviour in cyberspace, a simple reporting process and an outline of consequences if the policy is breached (Butler et al., 2011).

Content of university anti-bullying policies

Due to the lack of legal requirements for universities to have an anti-bullying policy, it has been noted in multiple studies that many universities provide staff-only policies or have expanded the staff policy to include students (Vaill et al., 2020a). This is problematic as it means that information, language and 'what to do' content may not be relevant to students and may not use student-friendly language. The content of the policies varies widely between universities, as does the quality and accuracy of the information provided. It is difficult to get a concrete understanding of the presence of student cyberbullying-specific policies within universities and their content because there is a lack of research in this area, with most research having focused on schools. It is however possible to pull out cyberbullying-related information from student anti-bullying policies such as those analysed by Vaill and colleagues (2020b). This study found that of the 39 British universities investigated, 87% of universities mentioned cyberbullying using the internet (e.g. e-mail, social media, blogs), and 69% mentioned cyberbullying using a phone (e.g. text, phone calls, taking photos or videos). In comparison, of the 39 Australian universities included in the study only 69% mentioned cyberbullying using the internet, and 58% using a phone.

With the lack of government requirements and oversight, it is left up to universities themselves to determine not only whether they will have a policy related or specific to cyberbullying, or any form of bullying but also what information is included within that policy. This means that the information in these policies is not consistent in either accuracy or its presence (Vaill et al., 2021). The information provided by universities ranges from a mention of the use of internet/technology/social media when discussing bullying, including cyber-aspects in other policies such as appropriate use of university technology, use of library or lab equipment, sexual harassment or discrimination, right through to a cyberbullying specific policy for students.

This lack of consistency of where information is located, as well as the amount of specific information included, creates vague policies with a lack of clear direction, making it difficult for both students and the university to understand what is classified as cyberbullying, roles and responsibilities, and what the process is for making complaints and investigating incidents (Harrison et al., 2020). This problem is ongoing and global as can be seen by the spread of the studies which produced these findings. The lack of clear information and process not only is confusing for the university when action is required but also accounts for, in part, why students do not report cyberbullying to their university (Cismaru & Cismaru, 2018).

One area of a bullying or cyberbullying university policy which is more consistent is the inclusion of a definition. Across three countries (Australia, Canada and the UK) where the contents of university policies have been studied, the findings show a large proportion of universities met this criterion of defining bullying. In Canada, 45% of the 465 cyberbullying-related policies found across 74 universities included a definition of cyberbullying (Faucher et al., 2015). In Australia, between 58% and 69% of bullying policies included a cyberbullying definition (to some extent) (Vaill et al., 2020a). There have been two studies conducted on universities policy content in the UK, with one showing an average of 78%, of 39 universities (Vaill et al., 2020b) and the other finding 98% of 62 universities included some form of cyberbullying definition (Harrison et al., 2020). It has however been noted that some definitions provided are not accurate, too general or not student specific, and by providing guidelines to universities, similar to those geared towards schools, definitions and examples would be more consistent within and between universities regardless of where they are.

Overall, it has been found that universities provided information to students about who to report bullying to (although many did not provide specific contact information) and the general reporting process. Once again though, the detail of this information varied widely. Although many universities provided support service information (generally counselling), it was usually aimed at those who had experienced cyberbullying or bullying in general and support for the perpetrators was lacking from the majority of policies (Harrison et al., 2020; Vaill et al., 2020a, 2021). In this way, the policies act as an intervention strategy rather than as a preventative strategy, as instead of reducing likelihood of future perpetration (whether at the same or different university or workplace), the university merely punishes and moves on.

The last area of information within anti-bullying or cyberbullying policies which was identified by researchers as lacking in universities' policies was information on follow-up after resolution and implementation of perpetrator consequences, and the presence of peer support and a positive campus culture (Vaill et al., 2021). This was an area that has been identified in several studies as an important way to prevent cyberbullying and support vulnerable students (Cismaru & Cismaru, 2018).

Differences in language used in school and university anti-cyberbullying policies

School language

Language is an important element in communicating information, especially when that information may be complex or for a specific audience. In school anti-cyberbullying policies, the language is relevant in the titles of the policies, the terminology used in the policy, and whether the language is student-friendly and student-focused. It is more complicated in a school policy than perhaps it would be for policies in other contexts such as universities or the workplace because the policy needs to reach an audience of children, staff and parents who may have different levels of understanding as well as having different roles and responsibilities.

The titles of policies are important because it is what people look for when searching for cyberbullying information and therefore must indicate that cyberbullying is included within the policy. Unfortunately, most research on school policies has not included information on the titles of the policies. The terminology used in titles to help identify the behaviour governed by that policy varies so much because there is so much terminology used within this area. As there are so many related but separate behaviours, people reading the policies can become overwhelmed and confused by the differences. When we discuss bullying, it often becomes intertwined with harassment, abuse and discrimination or by one of its characteristics such as teasing or 'picking on' somebody. Cyberbullying, on the other hand, is one of many negative online behaviours which not only take on the in-person terms with the added cyber prefix (cyber-harassment, cyber-aggression, cyberbullying, cyber-abuse) but then also take on the variations of 'online' and 'technology-based' (online-abuse, online-harassment, technology-based-abuse, technology-based-bullying).

Language used in university anti-cyberbullying policies

The language used in universities for an anti-cyberbullying policy or the mention of cyberbullying in other policies varies depending on whether the policy is student or staff-focused and which policy the information is in. There are several terms found throughout research papers which study cyberbullying as well as language noted by the few researchers who have explored bullying- and cyberbullying-related policies. The term 'cyberbullying' is the most used term, similar to schools, but other terms used include 'cyber-abuse', 'cyber-exploitation', 'online-abuse', 'cyber-victimisation', 'online harassment' and 'cyber-civility' policies (O'Connor et al., 2018). There is differentiation for some of these terms as behaviours separate from cyberbullying, but that does not always mean these differentiations are used accurately, with the terms often used inaccurately interchangeably with cyberbullying.

If cyberbullying or bullying policies are not student-specific or are staff policies with students added, the language and terminology used are generally associated with workplace-specific behaviour. This means terms such as 'mobbing', 'workplace harassment' or 'bullying in the workplace' are used and the examples provided include behaviours specific to the workplace such as 'impeding another's career progression' or 'unreasonable work expectations'. The staff-focused policies are also often identified by their title with 'staff' appearing in the name of the policy, such as 'staff bullying prevention policy', whereas other staff-specific policies do not provide this clarity in their title 'bullying and harassment policy' (Vaill et al., 2020b). The same trend of variety in policy titles can be seen in the names of the various policies related to bullying and cyberbullying. Titles have been seen to vary, with some specifically including cyberbullying such as 'Bullying and Cyberbullying', others using more overarching and generic titles such as 'safety and respect' and 'Safer campus community', but with the majority using some variation of 'bullying and harassment policy'.

Difference of expectations of the policy from school and university students

Apart from the content of the policy, there is also a difference in expectations of students. It is understood that school students bully (whether in-person or via technology) each other, and although perhaps not approved of or deemed acceptable, it is accepted to a degree that it happens. When bullying does occur, school students are consistently taught to tell a teacher or a parent and report the incident. When those students reach university, however, there are different expectations. University students are seen as adults who should know better than to partake in such behaviours as bullying and therefore bullying in any form does not occur. On the occasions when it does occur, students believe that as adults they should be able to handle the situation and that it is shameful and often pointless to seek help from their university (Vaill et al., 2021). For this reason, university policies need to be clearer, provide plenty of support information, promote a positive campus culture and have better dissemination and the topic of cyberbullying needs to be discussed more.

Similarities in schools and universities' problems with dissemination of school anti-cyberbullying policies

Dissemination of school and university anti-cyberbullying policies

How universities promote their policies varies widely between universities but throughout all the research on why students do not or would not report bullying or cyberbullying to their university, each study reports that students lack knowledge of a policy, where the policy may be located, or the information which should be provided by a policy (Vaill et al., 2021). Having identified this, it is also important to note that some universities have been found to use multiple avenues to disseminate their policies to students. For example, in the UK, some universities utilise the Student Unions or Student Guilds associated with the university to help promote a safe environment, provide support to students, and disseminate relevant policies and information to students. Another example of universities promoting bullying and cyberbullying information to students comes from a Canadian study which noted universities' use of policies and information documents alongside educational sessions, symposiums, talks, workshops and training programs (Cismaru & Cismaru, 2018).

Problems of where the policies can be found

A school's anti-cyberbullying policy must be known and disseminated throughout the school community, including students, staff and parents. Some schools include their anti-bullying policy within their behaviour management policy, while others have a separate policy bullying prevention policy. Cyberbullying, as one form of bullying, is usually covered in the anti-bullying policy. However, there has been a movement lately to separate in-person bullying and cyberbullying in a school's policy. The proponents of such division argue that cyberbullying has more in common with internet safety than bullying (Siyam & Hussain, 2021).

One of the problems with both current school and university anti-cyberbullying policies is that the information is not always in one policy. This can be seen by the number of policies and other documents where cyberbullying information appears in. For schools, it has been found that relevant information is included in an average of five policies per school (Smith et al., 2012), and between two and five for cyberbullying-specific policies in one study (Butler et al., 2011). This tendency to have the information about cyberbullying in many different documents, increases for universities with one study findings an average of 6.3 cyberbullying-related policies (Faucher et al., 2015), and others finding results similar to schools, with universities averaging five anti-bullying policies in different documents (Vaill et al., 2020a). The number of policies is relevant and problematic because the more policies there are to find information in, the harder that information becomes to find. It also means there is a higher chance of their being inconsistent or contradictory information provided and that important information may get lost in the gaps between the policy scopes.

Universities also face a problem which doesn't affect schools, which is the number of clubs, societies, associations, collectives, teams and unions/guilds which have their own policies which may or may not include cyberbullying, and which may or may not follow the same governance outlines in the universities policies. This is another place where miss-information or inconsistent information may occur, as well as where certain behaviours are included or omitted from the policy reinforcing cyberbullying as a social norm (Myers & Cowie, 2017).

Problems with how the policy is constructed

It has been identified, however, that simply informing these populations of the existence of a policy does not go far enough to equate to a whole-school approach. The whole school or collaborative approach to the creation and dissemination of policy has been identified as the best way to build awareness and understanding throughout the school community (Campbell, 2018). Another inclusion of a collaborative approach involves training staff on identifying bullying and cyberbullying behaviour, and the policy. This training would also be extended to students, so they know what to look for, and what to do if they experience or witness these kinds of behaviours. It is also important that there is clear communication and promotion between staff, students and parents, of not just the policies but on information regarding bullying and cyberbullying as well as being made aware of incidents (Campbell, 2018). Researchers have also identified that policies need to be developed collaboratively with students, teachers and parents to have the most impactful policy (Campbell, 2015).

Under-reporting of cyberbullying in both schools and universities

Underreporting of cyberbullying incidents is also an issue, with the point that if students are not reporting the incident then the policy is not doing its job (Faucher et al., 2015). They also identified that to improve their policy, and therefore the likelihood of students reporting the incident, universities need to research and understand the underpinnings of why students are hesitant to report cyberbullying and to address these issues. Although these notions were identified in 2013, and although there has been research into why students do not report, there has been little progress in addressing these issues within universities' policies. The biggest reporting blocks which have been identified are a lack of knowledge of policy or how to get help, embarrassment, feeling they should be able to handle it on their own and not having confidence in the universities services or their ability to stop the problem behaviour. And yet many of these areas are still being identified by researchers who study these policies such as Vaill and colleagues (2020a, 2020b) and Harrison and colleagues (2020) and by students who are being surveyed such as those in Vaill and colleagues (2021). So the big question right now is why universities are not putting more into addressing these issues and supporting effected students.

Conclusion

Although at present there is scant research about the effectiveness of anti-cyberbullying policies in educational institutions, their use by schools and universities is prolific. More consistency in providing best practice guidelines for policies could be helpful with governments mandating their use, especially in universities. It is important that the policy be written for the audience it is intended for, with appropriate language and that the policy is disseminated and discussed with staff and students. However, without research on the effectiveness of policies, we are fumbling around in the dark. Hopefully, with well-constructed and disseminated policies together with educational programmes, we can do more to prevent cyberbullying.

References

Betts, L. R. (2016). *Cyberbullying: Approaches, consequences and interventions.* Palgrave Pivot. https://doi.org/10.1057/978-1-137-50009-0

Bonanno, R. A., & Hymel, S. (2013). Cyber bullying and internalizing difficulties: Above and beyond the impact of traditional forms of bullying. *Journal of Youth and Adolescence, 42*(5), 685–697. https://link.springer.com/content/pdf/10.1007/s10964-013-9937-1.pdf

Butler, D., Kift, S., Campbell, M., Slee, P., & Spears, B. (2011). School policy responses to cyberbullying: An Australian legal perspective. *International Journal of Law and Education, 16*(2), 7–28. https://eprints.qut.edu.au/49320/1/49320.pdf

Byrne, V. L. (2021). Blocking and self-silencing: Undergraduate students' cyberbullying victimization and coping strategies. *TechTrends, 65*(2), 164–173. https://link.springer.com/article/10.1007/s11528-020-00560-x

Campbell, M. (2015). Policies and procedures to address bullying at Australian universities. In H. Cowie & C.-A. Myers (Eds.), *Bullying among university students: Crossnational perspectives* (pp. 157–171). London: Routledge.

Campbell, M. (2018). Paper tiger or effective guidelines: The use of policies and procedures to address school bullying. In H. Cowie & C.-A. Myers (Eds.), *School bullying and mental health risks, intervention and prevention* (pp. 169–179). London: Routledge.

Cismaru, M., & Cismaru, R. (2018). Protecting university students from bullying and harassment: A review of the initiatives at Canadian universities. *Contemporary Issues in Education Research, 11*(4), 145–152. https://doi.org/10.19030/cier.v11i4.10208

Cross, D., Runions, K. C., Shaw, T., Wong, J. W., Campbell, M. A., Pearce, N., Burns, S. K., Lester, L., Barnes, A., & Resnicow, K. (2019). Friendly schools universal bullying prevention intervention: Effectiveness with secondary school students. *International Journal of Bullying Prevention, 1*, 45–57.

Department of Justice. (2021). *Cybercrime.* www.justice.ie/en/JELR/Pages/Cybercrime

Faucher, C., Jackson, M., & Cassidy, W. (2015). When online exchanges byte: An examination of the policy environment governing cyberbullying at the university level. *Canadian Journal of Higher Education, 45*, 102–121. https://files.eric.ed.gov/fulltext/EJ1061062.pdf

Gaffney, H., Farrington, D. P., Espelage, D. L., & Ttofi, M. M. (2019). Are cyberbullying intervention and prevention programs effective? A systematic and meta-analytical review. *Aggression and Violent Behavior, 45*, 134–153. https://doi.org/10.1016/j.avb.2018.07.002

Government of Canada. (2021). *Cyberbullying can be against the law.* www.canada.ca/en/public-safety-canada/campaigns/cyberbullying/cyberbullying-against-law.html

Harrison, E. D., Fox, C. L., & Hulme, j. A. (2020). Student anti-bullying and harassment policies and UK universities. *Journal of Higher Education Policy and Management, 42*(5), 1–16. https://doi.org/10.1080/1360080X.2020.1767353

Henry Carus Associates. (2019). *A guide to worldwide bullying laws.* www.hcalawyers.com.au/blog/bullying-laws-around-the-world/

Hinduja, S., & Patchin, J. W. (2015). *Bullying beyond the schoolyard: Preventing and responding to cyberbullying* (2nd edition). Thousand Oaks, CA: Sage Publications.

Larranaga, E., Yubero, S., Navarro, R., & Ovejero, A. (2018). From traditional bullying to cyberbullying. In W. Cassidy, C. Faucher, & M. Jackson (Eds.), *Cyberbullying at university in international contexts, volume 1* (pp. 99–110). London: Routledge.

Moore, S. E., Norman, R. E., Suetani, S., Thomas, H. J., Sly, P. D., & Scott, J. G. (2017). Consequences of bullying victimization in childhood and adolescence: A systematic review and meta-analysis. *World Journal of Psychiatry, 7*(1), 60. www.wjgnet.com/2220-3206/full/v7/i1/60.htm

Myers, C.-A., & Cowie, H. (2017). Bullying at university: The social and legal contexts of cyberbullying among university students. *Journal of Cross-Cultural Psychology*, *48*(8), 1172–1182. https://doi.org/10.1177/0022022116684208

Myers, C.-A., & Cowie, H. (2019). Cyberbullying across the lifespan of education: Issues and interventions from school to university. *International Journal of Environmental Research and Public Health*, *16*(7), 1217. https://doi.org/10.3390/ijerph16071217

Nickerson, A., & Rigby, K. (2017). Understanding and responding to bullying in the school setting. In M. Thielking & M. D. Terjesen (Eds.), *Handbook of Australian school psychology* (pp. 521–536). Cham: Springer.

O'Connor, K., Drouin, M., Davis, J., & Thompson, H. (2018). Cyberbullying, revenge porn and the mid-sized university: Victim characteristics, prevalence and students' knowledge of university policy and reporting procedures. *Higher Education Quarterly*, *72*(4), 344–359. https://doi-org.ezp01.library.qut.edu.au/10.1111/hequ.12171

Rigby, K., & Johnson, K. (2016). *The prevalence and effectiveness of anti-bullying strategies employed in Australian schools* (p. 204). Adelaide: University of South Australia.

Rudasill, K. M., Snyder, K. E., Levinson, H., & Adelson, J. L. (2018). Systems view of school climate: A theoretical framework for research. *Educational Psychology Review*, *30*(1), 35–60. https://link.springer.com/content/pdf/10.1007/s10648-017-9401-y.pdf

Siyam, N., & Hussain, M. (2021). Cyber-Safety policy elements in the era of online learning: A content analysis of policies in the UAE. *TechTrends*, *65*, 535–547. https://doi.org/10.1007/s11528-021-00595-8

Smith, P. K. (2014). *Understanding school bullying: Its nature & prevention strategies*. London: SAGE Publications Ltd.

Smith, P. K., Kupferberg, A., Mora-Merchan, J. A., Samara, M., Bosley, S., & Obsorn, R. (2012). A content analysis of school anti-bullying policies: A follow-up after six years. *Educational Psychology in Practice*, *28*(1), 47–70. https://doi.org/10.1080/02667363.2011.639344

Stopbullying.gov, www.stopbullying.gov/resources/laws

The Cybersmile Foundation. (2021). *Legal perspectives*. www.cybersmile.org/advice-help/category/cyberbullying-and-the-law

The Education and Inspections Act (2006). The Education (Independent School Standards) Regulations 2014. https://assets.publishing.service.gov.uk/government/uploads/system/uploads/attachment_data/file/623895/Preventing_and_tackling_bullying_advice.pdf

Ttofi, M. M., & Farrington, D. P. (2011). Effectiveness of school-based programs to reduce bullying: A systematic and meta-analytic review. *Journal of Experimental Criminology*, *7*(1), 27–56. https://link.springer.com/article/10.1007/s11292-010-91091

Vaill, Z., Campbell, M., & Whiteford, C. (2020a). Analysing the quality of Australian universities' student anti-bullying policies. *Higher Education Research and Development*, *39*(6), 1–14. https://doi.org/10.1080/07294360.2020.1721440

Vaill, Z., Campbell, M., & Whiteford, C. (2020b). An analysis of British university student anti-bullying policies: How British universities compare with Australian universities. *Policy Reviews in Higher Education*, *5*(1), 73–88.

Vaill, Z., Campbell, M., & Whiteford, C. (2021). University students' knowledge and views on their institutions' anti-bullying policy. *Higher Education Policy*, https://doi.org/10.1057/s41307-021-00244-y

Youth Law Australia. (2021). *Cyberbullying*. https://yla.org.au/nsw/topics/internet-phones-and-technology/cyber-bullying/

17 Cyberbullying of faculty

When worlds collide

Loraleigh Keashly

Bullying of faculty is workplace bullying.

Workplace cyberbullying is defined as

> a situation where over time, an individual is repeatedly subjected to perceived negative acts conducted through technology (e.g., phone, email, web sites, social media) which are **related to their work context**. In this situation, the target of workplace cyberbullying has difficulty defending him or herself against these actions.
>
> (Farley et al., 2016, p. 299)

Faculty work context is boundaryless. It is 'multiplatform and multimodal' (Hodson et al., 2021) – on campus and off campus; in person and virtual; involves a variety of media; and with multiple audiences, including students, fellow scholars (both within and outside the university), staff and administrators, and various publics (Cantwell et al., 2021). Thus, bullying (cyber or face to face) of faculty *is* workplace bullying.

Faculty are very exposed because of the nature and places of their work. With the increasing electronic nature of work, escalated by the pandemic, faculty exposure has increased and, as a result, to a much more varied set of audiences. While I would argue that the 'Ivory Tower' has never been insulated and isolated from spaces and audiences around it, it is less so now because of electronic visibility. Further, there are more stakeholders in positions to influence the context (universities and their funding) and the content of faculty work activity. Research on workplace bullying and cyberbullying, generally and academe, specifically, has tended to focus on what happens within the institutional community. Research appears not to have recognised that work occurs off-site and thus has not considered audiences of faculty work which are beyond institutional community boundaries (Hodson et al., 2021; Keashly, 2021). Not considering these other actors and their motives and intentions limits a university's understanding of the faculty experience of being targeted and thus, ways to respond and, indeed, prevent (Oksanen et al., 2021). There is, however, an active and growing parallel literature on the digital harassment of faculty and scholars,

DOI:10.4324/9781003258605-22

particularly by the public (e.g. Doerfler et al., 2021; Oksanen et al., 2021, Velet-sianos & Hodson, 2018), that will be drawn upon in this discussion. In addition, the availability and use of e-media create an opportunity for *mobbing* (multiple actors targeting a faculty member) at a scale and intensity that institutions and indeed the workplace bullying literature has not fully explored nor understood. Thus, considering faculty experiences as workplace, bullying means looking not only within organisational boundaries but beyond, broadening the consideration of who can be and are the actors, what are issues or triggers, and what precisely an institution can do in these circumstances (Hodson et al., 2021).

Faculty risk

Faculty are particularly vulnerable to cyberbullying because they are highly visible. Information about them, their teaching, scholarship and professional practice are widely available and accessible. This is due to several factors. First, many faculty teach online, which has increased exponentially during the pandemic, and is likely to remain high post-pandemic (Barlett et al., 2021). Communication in these courses is primarily electronic. Indeed, the initial research on cyberbullying of faculty by students focused on online education (see Snyder-Yuly et al., 2021, for a review). Even when faculty teach face to face, interaction with students beyond the classroom most often occurs through email and phone (voice and text), as well as through learning management systems such as Blackboard and Canvas. Second, communication regarding university business and thus with institutional members rely heavily on email, communication that can easily be shared beyond the original audience and beyond the institution. Third, faculty profiles are on university websites and frequently include the courses they teach, their research work and their contact information (phone, office address, email and social media handles). Fourth, faculty's unique role as public intellectuals and social critics requires their work and perspective to be shared and accessible to the public. Traditionally, this has been done through publication, conferences and symposia, and position papers. Electronic platforms have increased the venues through which this information can be shared. Social media such as Twitter, Facebook, Instagram, TikTok, websites and blogs are used by faculty to connect with and build their professional communities, share their research and creative activity, as well as their views on current social issues (Coleman et al., 2018; Doerfler et al., 2021). Even faculty who do not actively utilise social media may have their work or perspective publicised by others, including the university. In addition, universities are encouraging faculty to be more engaged electronically with their students and with the public (Bérubé, 2021; McKay et al., 2020). Even those faculty who may not have engaged electronically pre-2020 have been forced by the pandemic to move their teaching and their professional lives online (Oksanen et al., 2021). In essence, it is difficult if not impossible for faculty to avoid having a presence in the e-environment and, with this presence comes an increased risk for bullying and harassment (Smith & Duggan, 2018; Oksanen et al., 2021).

This visibility draws the attention of a more diverse range of people, often from outside the institution or specific scholarly community. At its best, this creates opportunity for enriched discussion, dialogue and debate and further honing of ideas, that is, a broadened form of peer review (Diamond, 2017). However, it also creates opportunity for conflict, hostility, bullying and mobbing as those who may not share the scholar's perspective engage with, and challenge, them. Further, not only the content may be in contention but also the rules of engagement for sharing one's evaluation or reaction (Veletsianos & Shaw, 2018). Thus, where scholars may be trained and expect lively and engaged debate and dialogue, that may not be the conduct they receive. Those outside of academe may not understand (nor care about) the nature of scholarly debate and critique and what the role of the public intellectual is. These audiences may also not be interested in honing their ideas but rather in silencing a perspective they find challenging, offensive or threatening (Cain et al., 2019; Doerfler et al., 2021; Thomas et al., 2021). Evidence suggests that faculty do not always appreciate nor understand that their work through these media will be viewed by multiple audiences who may have different ideas about what is appropriate content and rules of conduct (Veletsianos & Shaw, 2018).

While there are multiple means for electronic communication, social media appears to be a particularly rich and provocative environment for bullying and, particularly for mobbing. The Pew Research Center (Vogels, 2021) reported that social media was identified by the general public as the most frequent site for harassment. Social media platforms, due to their extensive use and reach, provide the opportunity and capacity for more actors to become involved, that is, cybermobbing becomes more likely in the form of public opportunistic harassment (random piling on) or the more egregious coordinated or networked harassment, organised by a third party such as CampusReform (Doerfler et al., 2021, McKay et al., 2020).

What we know about faculty experiences

Faculty at colleges and universities are sadly very familiar with bullying. In any 12-month period, approximately 25% of faculty will self-identify as being bullied by someone(s) associated with their university or more broadly, their work (Keashly, 2021). Faculty from marginalised groups, specifically, women, BIPOC, LGBTQA+, and those with disabilities, are more likely to be targeted regardless of who the actor is and regardless of where they are in the institutional hierarchy (Hollis, 2021; Keashly, 2021). Approximately 40% of faculty are aware of this happening to another faculty member (Keashly, 2021). The actors are myriad, including those internal to the institution such as students, faculty colleagues and administration (Keashly, 2021; Weiss, 2021) and those external to the institution such as fellow scholars (e.g. Noakes & Noakes, 2021), the public (e.g. Ferber, 2017; Hodson et al., 2021) and the state (Keashly, 2021). Further, the actor could be an individual or in the company, or with support, of others, that is, mobbing. The actor can also be the institution itself, that is, depersonalised bullying (D'Cruz, 2015).

The literature on cyberbullying of faculty is relatively nascent and has focused on cyberbullying by institutional insiders (students, colleagues, staff and administrators) (Weiss, 2021). In brief, students and faculty colleagues are the primary actors of cyberbullying. Cassidy et al. (2014) found 25% of faculty report being cyberbullied in the prior 12 months. The primary actors were students (15%) and faculty colleagues (12%). E-mail was the medium of choice for both types of actors (Snyder-Yuly et al., 2021; McKay et al., 2020). Increasingly, though, students have begun making use of social media platforms, such as anonymous rating sites like RateMyProfessor (McKay et al., 2020; Snyder-Yuly et al., 2021) and Yik Yak (Schmidt, 2015), as well as websites, Facebook, Twitter and organising petitions electronically (Acevedo, 2022).

The increase in electronic presence, particularly through social media, has invited 'new' external actors into faculty lives (Snyder-Yuly et al., 2021). In their study of university research and teaching faculty at five major universities in Finland, Oksanen et al. (2021) report that 30% of respondents experienced frequent e-hostility in the previous six months. While most hostility came from insiders, a notable proportion were from outside the institution. Social media presence was specifically identified as a risk factor for victimisation. Gosse et al.'s (2021) survey of scholars who had been cyberbullied reports that triggers for cyberbullying were social media posts (47%) and teaching activities (30%). Similarly, the American Association of University Professors Spring 2021 survey (Tiede et al., 2021) found that social media posts (78%), followed by teaching (9%) and research publications (8%), were identified by faculty as the triggers for attack. Attacks were carried out most frequently through email (89%), direct social media messages (57%) and phone calls (45%). In contrast to institutional actors, cyberbullying from the public occurs primarily on social media platforms. The specific e-medium used is an important consideration for universities as it shapes the manifestation, experience and impact on the targets. For example, email and text communication can be kept private unless they are shared (via cc, bcc or forwarding), thus limiting the 'size' of the incident. Social media posts and online blogs open the potential for more actors to become involved and for it to happen very quickly (Snyder-Yuly et al., 2021). Thus, the many faces and places of cyberbullying for faculty are important for universities to consider when assessing and ultimately responding to the situation.

When hostility comes from outside

Faculty experience of being bullied by the public challenges traditional assumptions of power and the bases of power. At first blush, external actors do not have access to the power sources of institutional hierarchy, structure and resources and certainly not to academic freedom and tenure. Further, the faculty (particularly tenured faculty) are presumably insulated, supported and protected by the institution. However, situating the institution within a larger political, social and economic context, certain publics have significant power. The public, particularly, donors, funders, alumni and politicians, can significantly impact the well-being and stability of the institution. Having good relationships with these publics is important to institutional thriving. Such power and, thus, imbalance of power are enhanced by the capacity of electronic communication particularly social media to quickly share information with almost infinite audiences (Doerfler et al., 2021). Thus, hostility and aggression from the public can be very powerful, placing faculty at risk and less able to defend themselves.

Faculty work and their comments on social issues are increasingly visible and accessible to the public. These views may be perceived as contrary and threatening to other perspectives, beliefs or ideologies and the response can be swift, stunning and overwhelming (e.g. Doerfler et al., 2021; McMurtie, 2017). Higher education trade publications such as *Inside Higher Education*, *The Chronicle of Higher Education* and the *Times Higher Education* as well as associations focused on academic life and academic freedom are replete with exemplars of faculty being targeted for specific tweets, blog posts, comments in classes, their orientation to, and observations about, a particular social or political issue or their social identity such as race and gender (e.g. Acevedo, 2022; Durrani, 2021; Flaherty, 2020). Kamenetz (2018) reported that over an 18-month period in 2017–2018, 250 professors had been targeted for aggression and harassment. In the four years since that publication, the availability and use of electronic communication and platforms has continued to increase and arguably US politics and ideology have become increasingly polarised. It is not a stretch to anticipate that professors who have become the focus of such hostility have also increased in number. In many of these incidents, attacks are accompanied by requests/demands that universities control or remove the offending faculty member as well as dire warnings to the institution for their viability. The situation becomes even more dire when institutions fail to respond or fail to support the faculty member and academic freedom. This can be experienced by faculty as betrayal (Pyke, 2018) and even as bullying itself (e.g. Acevedo, 2022). Thus, the institution's location in the space between faculty and the public makes the university a key guardian in this process and, thus, what they do (or don't do) to buffer, protect and prevent is critical.

The role of the university in addressing cyberbullying of faculty: what can universities do?

The unique requirements of academic work and faculty life make university experiences particularly relevant to our understanding of the ways to manage workplace bullying. Universities are required to support and defend the conditions for academic freedom and free inquiry, unlike what other organisations must do. This affects what universities can consider in responding and managing alleged cyberbullying of faculty. Unlike other organisations, universities cannot rely on 'corporate control' or top-down management of the speech and conduct of their employees, specifically faculty. This is a very challenging place for universities as they are working in, and navigating, the space defined by donors, the state, the public (as diverse as it is), staff, students and faculty. How they negotiate this space to permit co-existence of seemingly incompatible perspectives and processes while privileging one, that is, defending academic freedom and right to critique (Reichman, 2018), is the dynamic and evolving challenge. The question is how this connection can be facilitated in ways to permit constructive and vibrant engagement and critique, a cornerstone of a university education, while providing protection to faculty specifically and academic freedom and vibrant educational environments, generally.

A critical first step for universities is recognition and acknowledgement that faculty work (and thus attack) also occurs outside of institutional spaces, an understanding of the risks in these spaces and the responsibility of the institution to defend that work and the faculty no matter from where attack comes (Diamond, 2017; Hodson et al., 2021). Academic freedom applies in these workspaces and universities need to make explicit commitments and take visible action to defend and support faculty when targeted for their work and expertise (Hodson et al., 2021; Vepsä, 2021; Cain et al., 2019; Weiss, 2021; McKay et al., 2020). Universities often try to mitigate attacks or surveillance by minimising visibility (e.g. changing a course title to remove hot button words like critical race theory) and in some cases the accuracy of the event, that is, hiding rather than supporting explicitly (Marwick et al., 2016). The relief (if any) provided by such measures is temporary and may backfire, escalating the 'social media maelstrom', and the damage to the faculty and the institution. Another cost of not actively defending and supporting faculty expertise and academic freedom in these spaces is the risk of a 'digital spiral of silence' (Carter Olson & LaPoe, 2018; Cain et al., 2019), where faculty self-censor to protect themselves. Such silencing results in the removal of important voices and expertise, which at its least are missed opportunities for rich debate and critical thinking about pressing social challenges (at the heart of universities' educational mission) and at its worst can undermine an informed citizenry critical for democracy (e.g. Acevedo, 2022). Fortunately, universities are responding in creative and constructive ways.

Policies and protocols

Policies are a critical component of institutional operation and well-being. Policies focused on addressing mistreatment including workplace violence, sexual harassment, discrimination and harassment, human rights and codes of conduct are utilised to set the expectations and requirements as well as the consequences for institutional member conduct. Sadly, a recent review found that little, if any, attention, is paid to misconduct and mistreatment through electronic means in these conduct policies (Hodson et al., 2021). Institutional policies on the responsible use of Information Technology (IT) and social media policies do focus on electronic communication. IT policies focus on institutional members' use of university-controlled communication platforms with consequences for misuse, such as bullying and harassment, and include consequences such as denial of access. These policies do not explicitly recognise that faculty work and, thus, attack can occur outside of these university-controlled mechanisms.

On the other hand, social media policies do recognise that faculty work occurs outside university electronic spaces and university-managed technology. However, these policies focus on how faculty should present on these platforms with an emphasis on appropriateness of posts (content and tone), representation of the institution (distinguish when speaking for self and when speaking for the institution) and compliance with the law and other regulations (Kwestel & Milano, 2020; Pomerantz et al., 2015). There is little explicit recognition in these policies that social media can be venues for harassment and bullying (Ketcham, 2020).

It is critical, then, that universities explicitly recognise that social media and other electronic communication can be a venue for harassment, bullying and mobbing for, be spurred by, incidents that occur inside *and* outside the institution and understand the implications for ways to provide support to faculty as well as responding to external actors (Hodson et al., 2021).

The good news is that universities are responding to online harassment of faculty from those outside the institution. The University of Iowa (UI) has developed a faculty support and safety guidance document that has been influential in shaping the approach of other US institutions such as Penn State University, University of Illinois – Urbana-Champaign, and University of Massachusetts Amherst, to name a few. Here is an excerpt from the UI guide (emphasis added):

> This guide is designed to assist the **campus community in responding** to situations in which faculty members are targeted by individuals or groups **outside of the university** based on the **content of the faculty member's scholarship, teaching, clinical care, and/or service**.

Here, the university explicitly states its support for academic freedom and freedom of expression. Further, the guidance is 'content neutral', highlighting support for faculty who 'come under attack for their conclusions on social issues as well as faculty whose scientific methods are deemed controversial such as the use of stem cells and animal research'.

The approach emphasises:

- Unacceptability of targeting faculty, specifically labelling it as abuse and harassment versus a difference of opinion (Ferber, 2017).
- Responsibility, importance, and the role of the institution in responding to the incident and supporting faculty.
- Articulation of various institutional members' responsibilities.
- A variety and coordination of responses involving several units including public safety, public/media relations, IT services, Human Resources, health services and academic senate in a thoughtful and detailed way including measures to buffer and protect faculty, to show support both privately and publicly for faculty's work as well as support for faculty rights to express their work and public opinion (Doerfler et al., 2021; Vepsä, 2021).

- Importance of close collaboration with the faculty member (not leaving the faculty member to address the situation alone).
- Recognition that the victim net includes more than the faculty member. Others in the faculty member's environment may also be affected by that experience. For example, if the attack is directed at a specific research topic or the social identity of the actors, others who share those features may also feel threatened and worried. These vicarious victims need support.
- Recognition that with the speed of electronic communication, the institution and its members need to be prepared to respond rapidly and clearly when faculty are targeted, (Pomerantz & Sugimoto, 2015).

Further, the guide provides additional resources to facilitate institutional members' understanding of the risks of online harassment and ways to protect and buffer as an individual and as a community (see Appendix for exemplar resources).

Valuable sources of support and information for faculty and their institution also come from the sharing of experiences from those who have been targeted. Direct sharing of other universities' experiences and responses to specific incidents can be useful to institutions in developing their protocols. For example, Trinity College president Joanne Berger-Sweeney shared their experience in responding to the targeted harassment of a professor by myriad external actors, highlighting the importance of having an emergency management team with clear protocols (McMurtie, 2017). Sharing also occurs among faculty targets, through sponsored discussions with faculty targets sharing their experience, how they got through it and lessons moving forward (Gewin, 2018; Pen America, 2020). On an individual level, Isaac Kamola, a faculty member in political science at Trinity College, who experienced online abuse, contacts faculty who are currently being targeted letting them know what they can expect and suggestions on what they and their institutions can do, letting them know they are not alone.

What is missing from these guidelines, resources and indeed much of the discussion is how actors who are not institutional members will be held accountable for the cyberbullying (Weiss, 2021). This requires identification of the actors, which can be a challenge given the ability to mask identity. Once identified, what kinds of consequences are possible? (Weiss, 2021). When university IT and communication mechanisms are utilised, it is possible to identify IP addresses and, thus, the actors and consequences administered per misconduct and IT policies. Indeed, in their research on educating students about cyberbullying, detectability was a key driver in motivating changes in behaviour (Barlett et al., 2021). For external actors, using hardware and platforms beyond the university's control, this can be a very difficult task. It is not impossible as evidenced by cases of identification and arrests of actors (e.g. Dead Sea Scrolls case; Lederman, 2010) but requires substantial resources (personnel, time and money), wherewithal, and is more likely if a state or federal law has been violated, including substantiated threat to physical harm.

Prevention

Given that cyberbullying has immediate and long-lasting implications for faculty and their institutions, and it is challenging to identify and punish external actors, it is important to take actions to *prevent* the occurrence of these attacks. Telling faculty to minimise their social media presence (may be good in the moment but not in the long term), not use trigger words or encourage another line of research as general strategies are not appropriate nor useful (Cain et al., 2019; Quintana, 2017). They communicate that the faculty member is 'responsible' for the incident and that they or their work has created a burden for the institution (Snyder-Yuly et al., 2021; Veletsianos & Shaw, 2018). More broadly, such approaches undermine academic freedom and the important role of the public intellectual in facilitating the critical thinking and conversations required for a pluralistic democracy (Wright et al., 2022).

There is value in, and indeed a necessity to, build institutional members' awareness, knowledge, and skill to thoughtfully and agentically manage and control their digital presence and engagement with diverse audiences (Cain et al., 2019; Diamond, 2017; Doerfler et al., 2021). Education about, and support for, digital privacy and security practices, and more broadly, digital use and literacy (Joglekar et al., 2022) are critical in building digital competency and efficacy among faculty and indeed all institutional members, including the university itself. Of particular importance for faculty and their institutions is understanding the nature and structure of various platforms and their audiences to shape communication to be most impactful and productive for those audiences (Cain et al., 2019; Carter Olson & LaPoe, 2018; Diamond, 2017; Veletsianos & Shaw, 2018). The value and success of this education hinge on clearly defining what purpose is being served by posting (e.g. for professional connections, sharing scholarly research, engaging in debate and discussion or marketing) and what platform(s) best facilitate that purpose and what will undermine or distort the intention (e.g. UK Research and Innovation guide on social media use for researchers). In addition, unlike the traditional outlets for sharing faculty work, these platforms do not have the safeguard of rigorous peer review of tradition venues built into them (Diamond, 2017; Smith, 2019). Thus, faculty need to think carefully about what they are saying and the basis for it, given that other audiences may not view them as nascent or works-in-progress as a traditional venue would.

Taking the initiative – educating and engaging the public

Instead of waiting for what many see as inevitable (Quintana, 2017), universities need to embrace their educational mission and their position as bastions of critical thought and free inquiry by not only reactively re-setting but also proactively setting the tone and focus of the conversation and the engagement with faculty and higher education overall. Educating both their own institutional members and the public about what universities are, what faculty do and why they need to be allowed to do it provides critical context for understanding and evaluating speech and conduct. More specifically, educating about academic freedom, civil debate and dialogue, constructive dissent, and the enormous costs of public shaming, deplatforming and silencing to a vibrant democracy and societal well-being is important and useful (Doerfler et al., 2021; Letsas, 2022). In addition, universities, through the expertise of their faculty, can and should articulate the strengths and challenges of the nature, structure and use of the digital information environment, overall and specifically, social media, and actively work to change the engagement to facilitate constructive and vibrant conversation. This involves laying out the limitations of certain platforms that by their structure make this difficult (e.g. Blackwell et al., 2018; Wong-Lo & Bullock, 2014).

One final observation: A holistic institutional approach

Universities need to examine *all* manifestations of harassment (regardless of content, motive or medium) together to develop a clear and detailed picture of what is happening and the circumstances in which it happens (Oksanen et al., 2021). A deep and nuanced understanding of harassment and bullying can fuel the development of a holistic institutional approach. An interesting example of this approach is the University of Alberta School of Medicine and Dentistry (Smythe, 2021). Utilising a framework of psychological safety, the approach includes:

1   setting clear expectations of behaviour for all members (framed as professionalism and ethical behaviour); (Code and policy)
2   training leaders and members in expectations for behaviour, what is harassment in all its forms and consequences for violation; (Education – Raising awareness)
3   developing leader capacity to identify and engage with situations; for members to respond to harassment through ignoring, engaging (before or after) or by reporting; and guidelines for those to whom the target discloses the experience (bystanders/witnesses) and approaches to those who are harassing others; (Education – skills training) and
4   being aware of and addressing unique aspects of racial, sexual, and online harassment.

While the University of Alberta's approach is focused on institutional members, including students, the key facets are relevant for developing, in concert with institutional members and other relevant stakeholders, a comprehensive approach to preventing, addressing and mitigating online harassment, no matter from where it comes.

References

Acevedo, D. (2022). Tracking cancel culture in higher education. *National Association of Scholars*. www.nas.org/blogs/article/tracking-cancel-culture-in-higher-education
Barlett, C. P., Simmers, M. M., Roth, B., & Gentile, D. (2021). Comparing cyberbullying prevalence and process before and during the COVID-19 pandemic. *Journal of Social Psychology*, *161*, 408–418.

Bérubé, M. (2021). How to deal with the dark side of social media. *Chronicle of Higher Education*, September 8, 1–6.

Blackwell, L., Chen, T., Schoenebeck, S., & Lampe, C. (2018). When online Harassment is perceived as justified. In *Proceedings of the International AAAI Conference on Web and Social Media*, *12*(1). https://ojs.aaai.org/index.php/ICWSM/article/view/15036

Cain, J., Linos, E., & Chretien, K. C. (2019). Cyberbullying in academic medicine: A framework for managing social media attacks. *Academic Medicine*, *94*(5), 626–629.

Cantwell, D., Meehan, E., & Rubio, R. (2021). Dealing with the digital mob. *Duck of Minerva* August 2. www.duckofminerva.com/2021/08/dealing-with-the-digital-mob.html

Carter Olson, C., & LaPoe, V. (2018). Combating the digital spiral of silence: Academic activists versus social media trolls. In J. R. Vickery & T. Everbach (Eds.), *Mediating Misogyny* (pp. 271–291). Cham: Palgrave Macmillan.

Cassidy, W., Faucher, C., & Jackson, M. (2014). The dark side of the Ivory Tower: Cyberbullying of university faculty and teaching personnel. *Alberta Journal of Educational Research*, *60*(2), 279–299.

Coleman, B. C., Pettit, S. K., & Buning, M. M. (2018). Social media use in higher education: Do members of the academy recognize any advantages? *The Journal of Social Media in Society*, *7*(1), 420–442.

D'Cruz, P. (2015). *Depersonalized bullying at work: From evidence to conceptualization.* New Delhi: Springer India

Diamond, A. (2017). *Social media policies and academic freedom: Higher education faculty and administrator perceptions.* Unpublished dissertation, Concordia University – Portland.

Doerfler, P., Forte, A., De Cristofaro, E., Stringhini, G., Blackburn, J., & McCoy, D. (2021). "I'm a Professor, which isn't usually a dangerous job": Internet-facilitated harassment and its impact on researchers. arXiv preprint arXiv:2104.11145.

Durrani, M. (2021). Digital infrastructures of the internet outrage machine: An autoethnography of targeted faculty harassment. *American Anthropologist*, *123*(3), 698–702.

Farley, S., Coyne, I., Axtell, C., & Sprigg, C. (2016). Design, development and validation of a workplace cyberbullying measure, the WCM. *Work & Stress*, *30*(4), 293–317.

Ferber, A. L. (2017). Faculty under attack. *Humboldt Journal of Social Relations*, *39*, 37–42.

Flaherty, C. (2020). Saying the wrong thing. *Inside Higher Education*, June 4.

Gewin, V. (2018). Tackling harassment: Three real-life stories of online abuse and how scientists got through it. *Nature*, *562*, October 18.

Gosse, C., Veletsianos, G., Hodson, J., Houlden, S., Dousay, T. A., Lowenthal, P. R., & Hall, N. (2021). The hidden costs of connectivity: Nature and effects of scholars' online harassment. *Learning, Media and Technology*, *46*(3), 264–280.

Hodson, J, Gosse, C., & Veletsianos, G. (2021). Analog policies in a digital world: How workplace harassment policies need to adapt to an increasingly digital education environment. *Academic Matters*. May 19. https://academicmatters.ca/analog-policies-in-a-digital-world-how-workplace-harassment-policies-need-to-adapt-to-an-increasingly-digital-education-environment/

Hollis, L. (2021). High – Tech harassment: A chi-squared confirmation that workplace cyberbullying disproportionally affects People of Color and the LGBQ community in higher education. Available at SSRN 3885326.

Joglekar, Y., Purdy, D., Brock, S., Tandon, A., & Dong, A. (2022). Developing digital communication competency in the business classroom. *Business and Professional Communication Quarterly*, https://doi.org/10.1177/23294906221089887

Kamanetz, A. (2018). Professors are targets in online culture wars: Some fight back. *National Public Radio: All Things Considered*, April 4.

Keashly, L. (2021). Workplace bullying, mobbing, and harassment in academe: Faculty experience. In P. D'Cruz, E. Noronha, L. Keashly, & S. Tye-Williams (Eds.), *Handbook of workplace bullying, emotional abuse, and harassment. Volume 4. Special topics and industries & occupations* (pp. 221–297). Switzerland: Springer.

Ketcham, A. (2020). Report on the state of resources provided to support scholars against harassment, trolling, and doxxing while doing public media work and how university media relations offices/newsrooms can provide better support. https://publicscholar-shipandmediawork.blogspot.com

Kwestel, M., & Milano, E. F. (2020). Protecting academic freedom or managing reputation? An Evaluation of university social media policies. *Journal of Information Policy, 10*(1), 151–183

Lederman, D. (2010). New twist in dead sea scrolls case. *Inside Higher Education.* February 1.

Letsas, G. (2022). There is no free-speech right to a university platform. *Times Higher Education.* March 31

Marwick, A., Blackwell, L., & Lo, K. (2016). *Best practices for conducting risky research and protecting yourself from online harassment (Data & Society Guide).* New York: Data & Society Research Institute. https://datasociety.net/pubs/res/Best_Practices_for_Conduct-ing_Risky_Research-Oct-2016.pdf

McKay, R., Irwin, B., & Appel, R. (2020). When RateMyProfessor Meets the #MeToo movement: Bottom-up bullying in academia. *International Journal of Digital Society, 11*(2), 1591–1598.

McMurtie, B. (2017). What colleges can do when the internet outrage machine comes to campus. *Chronicle of Higher Education,* June 26

Noakes, T., & Noakes, T. (2021). Distinguishing online academic bullying: Identifying new forms of harassment in a dissenting Emeritus Professor's case. *Heliyon, 7*(2), e06326.

Oksanen, A., Celuch, M., Latikka, R. et al. (2021). Hate and harassment in academia: The rising concern of the online environment. *Higher Education,* https://doi.org/10.1007/s10734-021-00787-4

Pen America (2020, November 13). *Confronting threats and harassment against faculty.* www.youtube.com/watch?v=wCTYW96Hg_o

Pomerantz, J., Hank, C., & Sugimoto, C. R. (2015). The state of social media policies in higher education. *PLoS One, 10*(5), e0127485.

Pyke, K. D. (2018). Institutional betrayal: Inequity, discrimination, bullying, and retaliation in academia. *Sociological Perspectives, 61*(1), 5–13.

Quintana, C. (2017). If there's an organized outrage machine, we need an organized response. *The Chronicle of Higher Education,* July 18.

Reichman, H. (2018). Dealing with online harassment in collective bargaining environments. *Journal of Collective Bargaining in the Academy, 13,* Article 37.

Schmidt, P. (2015, January 29). A new faculty challenge: Fending off abuse on Yik Yak.

Smith, A., & Duggan, M. (2018). *Crossing the line: What counts as online harassment?* Pew Research Center.

Smith, J. E. H. (2019, May 13). How social media imperils scholarship. *The Chronicle of Higher Education.*

Smythe, P. (2021). An institutional approach to harassment. *CJC Open, 3,* S118–129.

Snyder-Yuly, J. L., Patton, T. O., & Gomez, S. L. (2021). Welcome to academia, expect cyberbullying: Contrapower and incivility in higher education. In *Handbook of research on cyberbullying and online harassment in the workplace* (pp. 242–265). IGI Global.

Thomas, K., Akhawe, D., Bailey, M., Boneh, D., Bursztein, E., Consolvo, S., . . . & Stringhini, G. (2021). Sok: Hate, harassment, and the changing landscape of online abuse.

Tiede, H., McCarthy, S., Kamola, I., & Spurgas, A. K. (2021). Data snapshot: Whom does Campus Reform target and what are the effects? *Academe*, Spring. www.aaup.org/article/data-snapshot-whom-does-campus-reform-target-and-what-are-effects#.Yr23oS-B2Mz

Veletsianos, G., & Hodson, J. (2018, May 29). Dealing with social media harassment. *Inside Higher Ed*.

Veletsianos, G., & Shaw, A. (2018). Scholars in an increasingly open and digital world: Imagined audiences and their impact on scholars' online participation. *Learning, Media, and Technology, 43*(1), 17–30.

Vepsä, S. (2021). Anticipating and managing the risks of online harassment. www.utupub.fi/bitstream/handle/10024/151948/Risks_of_Online_Harassment.pdf?sequence=1

Vogels, E (2021). The state of online harassment. *Pew Research Center*, January 13. www.pewresearch.org/internet/2021/01/13/the-state-of-online-harassment/

Weiss, A. (2021). Professor and victim: Cyberbullying targeting professors in the higher education workplace. In *Handbook of research on cyberbullying and online harassment in the workplace* (pp. 266–282). IGI Global.

Wong-Lo, M., & Bullock, L. M. (2014). Digital metamorphosis: Examination of the bystander culture in cyberbullying. *Aggression and violent behavior, 19*(4), 418–422.

Wright, J. M., Chun, W. H. K., Clarke, A., Herder, M., & Ramos, H. (2022). *Protecting expert advice for the public: Promoting safety and improved communications*. Royal Society of Canada. www.facetsjournal.com/doi/10.1139/facets-2021-0181

Appendix – resources on online harassment

American Association of University Professors. Toolkit for targeted harassment of faculty. www.aaup.org/issues/fighting-targeted-harassment-faculty

FeministFrequency (2018, July 5). Speak up and stay safer: A guide to protecting yourself from online harassment. https://onlinesafety.feministfrequency.com/en/

FemtechNet. Center for Solutions to Online Violence. www.femtechnet.org/csov/

Union of Concerned Scientists: Center for Science and Democracy (2020). Science in an age of scrutiny: How scientists can respond to criticism and personal attacks. www.ucsusa.org/sites/default/files/2020-09/science-in-an-age-of-scrutiny-2020.pdf

UK Innovation Research and Innovation (2022, January 27). How to use social media. www.ukri.org/councils/esrc/impact-toolkit-for-economic-and-social-sciences/how-to-use-social-media/

18 Accessible, inclusive and enabling contexts for university students from a refugee and migrant background

Carmel Cefai

Introduction

The 21st century has been marked by large migration flows in the Mediterranean, particularly from Africa and the Middle East towards Europe. Situated right in the middle of the Mediterranean Sea between North Africa and Southern Europe, Malta has been at the centre of this movement, serving as a transit to Europe. This has led to an increasing number of migrants in Malta over the past decades, with many settling down in Malta as a new home. In 2019, there were 3,406 sea arrivals from North Africa going down to 2,281 in 2020, most of them coming from the horn of Africa countries (UNHCR, 2021). In 2020, there were 2,419 applications and granting of protection status in Malta, going down from 4,090 submitted in 2019 (aida/ecre, 2021a). The number of refugees in 2020 was 9,208, a 3.37% increase from 2019 (Macrotrends, 2022). Other economic migrants from different parts of the world are also seeking employment in the country, with the number of non-Maltese living in Malta having more than doubled over the past decade, constituting more than 12% of the total population and over 12% of school children being non-Maltese (NSO, 2018, 2019).

Maltese society is thus becoming more diverse and multicultural and various efforts and projects have been dedicated to support the welfare and inclusion of migrants in Malta, especially those seeking protection status (aida/ecre, 2021b). Particular attention is being given to the education of school children, particularly challenges related to linguistic and cultural barriers, social inclusion and psychological well-being (Cefai et al., 2019). As migrant families settle down in Malta, more young people with a refugee or migrant background are faced with the opportunity for higher and tertiary education. Higher education plays an important role in the integration of migrants who would want to settle in the host country and contribute to its society and economy (TanDEM, 2019; Ramsay and Baker, 2019). As a result of their education, refugee graduates can make a better contribution to the labour force and economy, lead a good quality of life as empowered citizens and serve as leaders and positive role models to help foster the aspirations of future generations to university education (UNHCR, 2016, 2018). Their participation in the academic and social

DOI:10.4324/9781003258605-23

activities of higher education organisations can also have a positive impact on the local student population, promoting a more positive perception of migrants and refugees and consequently fostering inclusion in Maltese society (TandEM, 2019, Cefai et al., 2020).

Challenges

The pathway to higher education for students with a refugee or migrant background (RMB), however, is not an easy one. Despite their potential, they face numerous challenges, in both accessing higher education and completing their studies successfully, over and above the challenges faced by university students in general. Lambrecht (2020) called them 'the super-disadvantaged'. They remain an 'underrepresented equity group' in higher education (Naidoo et al., 2015), with only 1% of refugees accessing higher education (UNHCR, 2016). Their participation and completion of studies are behind those of domestic students (European Commission/EACEA/Eurydice, 2018). In their study on the experiences of university students from a refugee background themselves, Naidoo et al. (2015) reported that whilst young people with a refugee background have high aspirations and motivation to enter higher education, they face various challenges in getting access and participation, especially the lack of targeted academic, linguistic and pastoral support they require.

Accessibility

One of the major challenges of getting access to higher education for students from a migrant background, particularly those with a refugee status, is the interrupted education and exposure to different educational systems, which do not always recognise and complement each other (Cefai et al., 2020; UNHCR, 2019). Language issues and language requirements such as language skills to follow the programme of studies and entry requirement for proficiency in the language/s of the host country are another major hurdle to get into university life (Ramsay & Baker, 2019). These academic and language issues may be aggravated by inflexible entry requirements, which do not always make allowance for prior learning experiences and lost opportunities due to forced displacement and other similar experiences. Another obstacle is lack of resources, particularly in families from low socio-economic status with no previous exposure to higher education and low educational and professional aspirations, particularly in view of poor family income.

In a study on tertiary education for students with RMB in Southern Europe, including Malta, various challenges were identified, such as lack of concrete higher education measures included in the top-level policy documents, relatively high tuition fees for those without official humanitarian protection, some programmes are restricted to local and European students only, lack of adequate preparation for admissions to address academic skills mismatch or having to repeat programmes such as foundation years, and bureaucratic procedures such as visa and work permits. The following issues were identified by students ((TandEM, 2019).

> It would be helpful if there was a specific department . . . to give us com-
> prehensive and correct information, advise on the necessary steps to take,
> including for the visa . . . also removing, or at least reducing, the [fees] gap
> between domestic and E.U. citizens and TCN students.
>
> I believe the mindset should change. Rather than looking at us accord-
> ing to our legal status in the country, they should look into the education
> we already have, if we have some sort of diploma or other relevant qualifi-
> cations. This is essential to guarantee equality.

Since then, some of the issues have been addressed as will be discussed in this chapter. The University of Malta is one of the few Universities in Europe where on average, migrants are more likely to have higher education than locals (OECD, 2018). However, the share of non-European Higher Education Area international students in 2007 was just 2% (TandEm, 2019).

Completing studies successfully

Another challenge is to complete the programme of studies successfully, with higher rates of attrition among RMB than other students. Issues include lack of tailored academic and social services, such as mentoring programmes, academic support and programme differentiation according to the diverse and multicul-tural needs of the learners (Ernest et al., 2010; Ratković et al., 2020). Financial and accommodation issues are another difficulty, as even though students may not be charged registration fees, they would still need financial support for accommodation and daily living.

Further challenges may include linguistic and socio-cultural barriers, lack of access to services and resources, acculturation issues, social exclusion and men-tal health issues (Grüttner et al., 2021; Lambrechts, 2020; Ramsay & Baker, 2019). Maltese university students with a refugee background for instance, mentioned that while integration is becoming more visible and Maltese society more open and receptive, there is still a need for more positive views of migra-tion, intercultural openness and mutual learning (TandEM, 2019). Although there is little research on online hate in higher education in Malta, the Euro-barometer on immigration (2018a) reported that 63% of Maltese respondents view immigration as a problem, while 64% completely disagree that migrants enrich the cultural life of the country. Fifty-five percent made use of online hate speech – the highest percentage in the EU (Eurobarometer, 2018b). Most of the hate speech appears to be expressed on social media; social media plat-forms are not being regulated unlike online journals (Bayer and Bard, 2021). In a European study on hate crime and hate speech in nine European countries by the Monitoring and Reporting Online Hate Speech in Europe (eMORE, 2018), out of the 123 participants from Malta, 34% reported being the victims of hate speech and hate crime, and only 28% reported never being a victim; 67% reported witnessing hate speech, hate crime or other forms of prejudice. Seven per cent were victims of online hate speech, while 35% witnessed online hate speech. The main reasons for hate speech/crime and prejudice were skin colour/ethnic origin (27%) and nationality (16%) (eMore, 2018).

Measures to facilitate access and provide support

In view of these challenges, there have been increasing calls for universities and higher education institutions to broaden their access through flexible entry pathways, provide more adequate support and create safe, inclusive and enabling contexts for students from RMB (EU, 2019, Naidoo et al., 2018, Ramsay and Baker, 2019).

A recent EU report on the integration of asylum seekers and refugees into Higher Education in Europe (EU, 2019) reported that in almost half of the higher education systems, there is no mention of asylum seekers and/or refugees in top-level policy documents, while amongst those that do mention them, very few include any significant top-level policy. In most member states, higher education institutions have no specific policy approach to the integration of students with RMB. The report, however, identified several good practices in some higher education institutions, such as grants or scholarships and fee exemptions, language training, online programmes for refugees and asylum seekers, personalised guidance, training for staff working with refugees and asylum seekers, and recognition of documents. Linguistic support is the most common identified practice, followed by financial support and staff training. In Malta, support measures include language training in English, information sessions, personal guidance, fee waivers and courses for people working with asylum seekers/refugees. There is also a clear legal requirement on the procedures to be followed in the recognition of qualifications held by students with a refugee background, namely interviews with refugees and efforts by the Qualifications Recognition Information Centre to trace claimed qualifications (EU, 2019).

Alongside these specific measures and procedures, various countries also provide flexible and alternative higher education routes, which may also benefit students from RMB, namely alternative routes to entry qualifications, possibilities of entry without formal entry qualifications and recognition of prior non-formal and informal learning. At Malta university, students can gain admission without formal qualifications (maturity clause for those over 23 years) and in consideration of prior learning (Recognition of Prior Learning policy). Alternative routes to entry qualifications include a foundation preparatory programme in some programmes.

The TandEM report (2019) makes various recommendations for policies and actions to address the challenges in accessing and completing tertiary education. It encourages higher educational institutions to recognise the potential contribution of migrant and refugee students to integration, to acknowledge that their student body represents diversity in the population and to ensure access to higher education. A second recommendation is for higher education institutions to increase policy support for the participation of students with RMB in higher education as a means to promote equity and social integration. The provision of targeted integration funding, in collaboration with the national government and civil society organisations, to facilitate the participation of students from RMB, will ensure that policy actions could be put into actual practice. Another recommendation is to enhance multi-stakeholder, trans-sectoral policy development and implementation, in the development, implementation and evaluation of the inclusion and participation measures provided by the higher education institutions.

Integration is a two-way process, with economic, social and cultural benefits for the host country, and thus measures need to address also the local population. Such measures which may include cultural exchanges and community-based learning approaches also serve to combat negative perceptions and attitudes towards those from RMB. Another recommendation to facilitate access to and participation in higher education is to ensure that migrant and refugee students are given equal treatment as national and EU students in higher education policy and practice (rather than as international, third-country students) and where possible given priority in equity and diversity measures. Another measure is to streamline procedures and address information gaps through targeted, accessible and refugee-friendly information, including outreach initiatives, buddy or mentoring programmes, as well as cultural activities. Ratkovic et al. (2020) underline the role of 'social justice' mentoring to help create safe and inclusive climate at university, serving to 'break traditional patterns of isolation and competition that are typical within higher education' and which pose a challenge for students with a refugee background. This entails formal mentoring programmes with new students paired with peers who have progressed further in their studies, as well as with faculty staff to help them 'navigate' university life and promote their safety, inclusion and sense of belonging. Finally, integration and language courses for migrants and refugees may also be utilised to enhance access to higher education complemented by language and bridging course at higher education institutions (TandEm, 2019)

In a meta-scoping study of 46 papers on RMB students in HE institutions in various parts of the world, Ramsay and Baker (2019) concluded that facilitating access to HE for RMB students has wide-ranging benefits for the students, their families *and* society as a whole. Various strategies facilitate access to HE, such as recognising the experiences of refugees as strengths rather than deficits; providing personalised academic, social and practical support, both in gaining admission and in pursuing their HE studies; helping students to navigate university life; and academic staff training in addressing the needs of RMB students sensitively within an inclusive, strengths-based approach. They also recommend that in view of the impact of their unique pre-migration and post-settlement challenges and experiences, RMB students form a distinct equity group. Furthermore, particular attention should be given to RMB students with intersecting needs, such as female and older students with family responsibilities. Specific areas which need to be investigated further include the intersectional factors that cause disadvantage and marginalisation; the experiences of educators teaching and working with RMB students; and the mechanisms and supports which facilitate success despite language, culture and psychosocial challenges in HE.

Case study: A policy proposal for broadening access and increasing participation for RMB students at the University of Malta

Background

One of the strategic themes in the University of Malta's *Strategic Plan for 2020–2025* (University of Malta, 2019, p. 25) is 'the creation of an inclusive university for an inclusive society . . . to strengthen, develop and synergize the intersections of gender, race, ethnicity, disability and other spheres of diversity in Maltese society'. Over the past years, it has taken various initiatives to facilitate access and support the participation of underrepresented groups, students with disability and students from marginalised and disadvantaged backgrounds. It offers the possibility of programme registration without formal entry qualifications and recognises prior non-formal and informal learning (Recognition of Prior Learning). Registration fees are waived for asylum seekers and refugees, and the Committee on Race and Ethnic Affairs (CREA) monitors and addresses issues related to race and ethnic prejudice, including awareness, access, integration and safety.

Another ongoing initiative is the development of an equality and inclusive policy which seeks to bring into one overarching framework the policies and practices related to gender, disability, race and ethnicity, and other sectors. A recent initiative related to race and ethnicity is the development of a policy to increase access of and participation by students from RMB. The proposed policy has been developed by a working group composed of academic and administrative staff, students and external partners such as NGOs. The policy has been developed following a review of existing policies and good practices, consultations with various bodies and staff at the University, and presentations by invited guests on specific issues such as language requirements, recognition of prior learning, student accommodation, visa permits and stipend. It has also been informed by feedback provided by other involved entities and individuals at the University.

The policy draft is divided into three main sections, namely an introduction, a section on attracting and recruiting students from refugee and migrant background, and another section on improving the support systems to enhance the learning experience of students from RMB. The following section provides the main features of the proposed policy, taken from Cefai et al. (2020).

Introduction

For the University to address the needs of students from RMB, the policy framework recommends that students with RMB need to be considered as a distinct category, separate from local and foreign students. At the same time, it needs to support such students within its broader vision of an inclusive, multicultural community, thus actively combating discourse which may reinforce division and stereotypes. This policy framework recommends that particular attention needs to be given to students with RMB experiencing intersecting vulnerabilities, such as those from low socio-economic background, female, disabled, LGBTIQ and older refugee students. Such students are more likely to face obstacles in pursuing tertiary education.

Attracting and recruiting students from underrepresented refugee background

This policy framework proposes a two-pronged approach to attract and recruit more students from such a RMB, namely an outreach programme in schools, communities and centres, and a flexible entry pathway to allow for a broader intake of such students at the university.

Outreach in schools and communities

Outreach initiatives include reaching out to potential students in schools, communities and migrant centres, as well as organising orientation visits on campus, informing secondary and post-secondary students from RMB about the educational system in Malta and the available opportunities for them at tertiary education level, so that they would be able to make informed choices about their educational pathways. This would include information on the different and varied programmes offered at the University, the multicultural nature of the University, the policy on Recognition of Prior Learning policy and the Flexible Entry Pathways being recommended in this policy. Further outreach initiatives include:

- Working with schools with relatively high numbers of students with RMB to identify the barriers which may be hindering such students from continuing furthering their education and seek to provide support to such students and their families.

- Working with schools and educational authorities to promote the benefits of diversity and interculturalism amongst all school students and combat negative stereotypes and prejudice, whilst providing culturally and linguistically responsive education promoting intercultural diversity and inclusion.
- Targeting disenfranchised and disadvantaged families (low socio-economic level, female students, LGBTIQ) to promote a culture of continuing and lifelong education. Activities may include encouraging such family members to attend short courses or modules as visiting students, foundation courses; organising 'First in Family' initiative; and ensuring that these families have online access and the required technological equipment.
- Education 'enrichment' programme targeting a number of individual children to increase the likelihood of participation in tertiary education, providing mentoring, coaching and other forms of support to both children and families.
- Outreach projects for young people who are disengaged from the mainstream educational system, such as early school leavers, in collaboration with schools, open centres, migrant communities and NGOs working in the field.
- Collaboration with migrant communities, centres and services to promote the programmes at the University, including the varied programmes on offer, the policy on Recognition of Prior Learning, and the proposed Flexible Entry Pathways.
- Orientation programmes where secondary school students from RMB are brought to university to participate in lectures/tours/workshops
- Campus festivals to promote refugees' and migrants' cultures, public ceremonies of recognition of achievements by individuals from RMB, and multicultural symbols on campus to promote and underline the multicultural nature of the university. The multicultural nature of the University, however, needs to be integrated in all events, activities and the core business of the University.
- Provision of campus sports and arts facilities for persons from underrepresented communities such as those from RMB and availability of university facilities for community target groups in evenings and summertime.

- An intersectoral national board to identify and remove the structural barriers in Maltese society which may be preventing children from RMB from continuing their post-secondary and tertiary education.

Flexible entry pathways

Another key strategy in recruiting students from RMB is for the University to open up diverse entry pathways to allow for an increased intake of students from such backgrounds. This will be a natural extension of other such diversification pathways for entry at the University, as in the case of flexible entry pathways for mature students, students with disability and the Policy on the Recognition of Prior Learning. This policy would make provisions for the following actions by the University:

- Flexible entry pathways to allow for a broader intake of students from RMB, including lower qualifications and flexibility in language requirements
- Extension of the RPL policy to students 18–22 years, whilst ensuring comparability of learning outcomes and that applicants can, with the necessary supports, cope with their programme of studies
- Exemption from application fees and course tuition fees for all applicants from a refugee background
- Preparatory admission courses, which include academic writing and English language courses
- Classes in the Maltese language, to help give cultural and academic confidence to students
- Structures and procedures to facilitate the timely evaluation and recognition of qualifications from different countries
- New programmes which may be particularly attractive for students from RMB, in terms of both course content and course structure, such as programmes tapping on multiple intelligences, rather than simply academic learning

Improved support systems to enhance the learning experience and sense of belonging of RMB students

One of the strategic objectives for the coming years at the University (UM, 2019) is to improve support systems that enhance the learning experience and increase the completion rates of students from diverse and underrepresented backgrounds. The following action recommendations would help to university to reach this strategic objective.

One-stop shop

One of the challenges mentioned by previous refugee and migrant students at the University is the lack of a centralised service to facilitate issues related to visa and residence permit, registration, recognition of qualifications, finance and bank accounts, and provision of support to students in their studies. A one-stop shop would have a dedicated team responsible for the coordination of the services and support systems for students with RMB and help address the issue of bureaucratic procedures, one of the top barriers mentioned by previous refugee/migrant students. Besides coordinating the initiatives to recruit students as described in the previous section and support students with the submission of applications and course registration, the one-stop shop would also provide support with visa and residence permit, financial issues and accommodation; ensure access to technological equipment and online communication; guide students on the various types of support they can obtain during their course of studies and liaise with academic, administrative and technical staff about matters related to access and inclusion issues; support students experiencing difficulties in their studies to prevent drop out from the course, possibly through the use of early warning systems; and provide a reference list of services including services outside university. The one-stop shop may also form part of a broader entity at the University to promote diversity and the inclusion of students on campus, including disability, gender issues and socio-economic deprivation, besides students from RMB.

Academic and psychosocial support and mentoring

Adequate support for students such as orientation, mentoring, social and emotional support and support with academic work and language issues in collaboration with the services at the Health and Wellness Centre at the University. Mentors may include personal tutors and peer mentors, including previous migrant students who have successfully completed their studies at the university. A designated campus space where mentors and mentees can meet would be provided. A programme of social and emotional competences for all university students, including migrant ones, may be organised during Freshers' Week

Diversity and inclusion

The University to continue strengthening its international and intercultural ethos, emphasising the benefits of diversity, including the economic, social and cultural benefits of integration for the local students and the host country, and providing safe, inclusive and communal spaces fostering mutual understanding and sense of belonging. In this way, the University will be also taking a leading role in promoting a more open and inclusive society, by virtue of being the only University in the country where most professionals and leaders in the country are trained.

Safe spaces

The University will seek to empower students from RMB to exercise their rights and speak and act against discrimination, bullying, cyberbullying and hate speech. The University's revised Harassment and Bullying Policy (2021) provides guidelines on what action students may take in case of harassment and bullying, including cyberbullying and mobbing.

Stipend

All groups of refugees as defined in this policy (refugee status, subsidiary protection, asylum seekers, temporary humanitarian protection and specific resident authorisation) would receive the university stipend

Inter-faith centre, extended library hours and childcare facilities

Are other measures which will make the campus more responsive to the diverse cultural and ethnic backgrounds.

More active and influential involvement

More opportunity for students from RMB to be represented and appointed on various boards and committees at the University to empower them to participate actively and influentially in the life of the university. The Students' Representative Council may also encourage and welcome more students from RMB on its committees and boards, and support the migrant representation within student organisations.

Postgraduate studies

More possibilities for students from RMB to continue their studies at the postgraduate level. Faculties and Departments may restructure some of their courses so that these are more open to non-Maltese and non-Maltese-speaking students. This would be in line not only with the university's inclusion policy but also with its current policy of internationalisation.

Staff training

All academic and administrative staff at the University will receive training in inclusion and intercultural competences. All staff need to be more aware of a clear code of conduct to ensure there is no discrimination against students from areas with low representation, such as students from RMB.

Advocacy

Together with other entities and stakeholders concerned, both state and NGOs and including the refugee and migrant communities themselves, advocate for the removal of structural barriers faced by refugee and migrant communities.

Transition to the world of work

Given the difficulties which graduates from RMB may encounter in securing employment commensurate with their qualifications, students from RMB would benefit from support in the transition to the world of work, such as internships or field placements.

Conclusion

Students from RMB are an 'underrepresented equity group' necessitating specific policies and actions to facilitate their access to higher education which take into consideration their past experiences and the challenges they face and provide flexible and alternative entry pathways to higher education. They also require a safe, inclusive and enabling learning context with adequate academic, social and psychological supports tailored to their needs. The proposed policy presented in this chapter illustrates how broadening access and providing more inclusive and enabling learning experiences for this target group may be implemented. Considering the needs of this target group within an equity and social justice lens will ensure that young people from RMB will have access to higher education and provided with an enabling empowering learning environment, and consequently are better integrated and in a better position to make a more meaningful contribution to both their host and home countries. Integration, however, also benefits the host country economically, socially and culturally and contributes to evolving national and global needs. The sooner students from RMB are recognised and acknowledged as an asset for their communities, the better will be their integration and contribution.

References

Asylum Information Database (AIDA)/European Council on Refugees and Exiles (ECRE) (2021a). *Statistics country report: Malta.* https://asylumineurope.org/reports/country/malta/statistics/

Asylum Information Database (AIDA)/European Council on Refugees and Exiles (ECRE) (2021b). *Access to education country report Malta.* https://asylumineurope.org/reports/country/malta/content-international-protection/employment-and-education/access-education/

Bayer, J., & Bard, P. (2021). *Hate speech and hate crime in the EU and the evaluation of online content regulation approaches.* www.europarl.europa.eu/RegData/etudes/STUD/2020/655135/IPOL_STU(2020)655135_EN.pdf

Cefai, C., Brown, M., Chizoba Anizoba, P., Downes, P., Galea, N., Mangion, C., Mifsud, F., & Rossi, A. (2020). *Broadening access for, and supporting, students with a migrant and low socio-economic background at the University of Malta.* Unpublished document, University of Malta.

Cefai, C., Keresztes, N., Galea, N., & Spiteri, R. (2019). *A passage to malta. The health and wellbeing of foreign children in Malta.* Malta: Commissioner for Children.

eMore (2018). *An overview on hate crime and hate speech in 9 EU countries towards a common approach to prevent and tackle hatred.* www.rissc.it/wp-content/uploads/2020/06/AN_OVERVIEW_ON_HATE_CRIME_AND_HATE_SPEEC.pdf

Ernest, J., Joyce, A., de Mori, G., & Silvagni, G. (2010). Are universities responding to the needs of students from refugee backgrounds? *Australian Journal of Education, 54*(2), 155–174. https://doi.org/10.1177/000494411005400204

Eurobarometer (2018a). *Integration of immigrants in the European Union.* https://europa.eu/eurobarometer/surveys/detail/2169

Eurobarometer (2018b). *Illegal content online.* https://ec.europa.eu/commfrontoffice/publicopinion/index.cfm/ResultDoc/download/DocumentKy/83669

European Commission/EACEA/Eurydice (2018). *The European Higher Education Area in 2018: Bologna process implementation report.* Luxembourg: Publications Office of the European Union.

European Commission/EACEA/Eurydice (2019). *Integrating asylum seekers and refugees into higher education in Europe: National policies and measures.* Eurydice Report. Luxembourg: Publications Office of the European Union.

Grüttner, M., Schröder, S., & Berg, J. (2021). University applicants from refugee backgrounds and the intention to drop out from pre-study programs: A mixed-methods study. *Social Inclusion, 9*(3), 130–141 https://doi.org/10.17645/si.v9i3.4126

Lambrechts, A. A. (2020). The super-disadvantaged in higher education: Barriers to access for refugee background students in England. *High Education, 80*, 803–822. https://doi.org/10.1007/s10734-020-00515-4

Macrotrends (2022). *Malta refugee statistics 1993–2022.* www.macrotrends.net/countries/MLT/malta/refugee-statistics

Naidoo, L., Wilkinson, J., Adoniou, M., & Langat, K. (2018). *Refugee background students transitioning into higher education: Navigating complex spaces.* Springer Publications

Naidoo, L., Wilkinson, J., Langat, K., Adoniou, M., Cunneen, R., & Bolger, D. (2015). *Case study report: supporting school-university pathways for refugee students' access and participation in tertiary education.* Microsoft Word – LN4Final.docx (westernsydney.edu.au)

National Statistics Office. (2018). *Population statistics (revisions) 2012–2016.* https://nso.gov.mt/en/News_Releases/View_by_Unit/Unit_C5/Population_and_Migration_Statistics/Documents/2018/News2018_022.pdf

National Statistics Office. (2019). *Percentage of foreign students enrolled in pre-primary, primary and secondary education: Academic year 2018–2019.* Unpublished statistics.

OECD (2018). *The resilience of students with an migrant background: Factors that shape well-being.* Paris: OECD Publishing

Ramsay, G., & Baker, S. (2019). Higher education and students from refugee backgrounds: A metascoping study. *Refugee Survey Quarterly, 38*, 55–82.

Ratković, S. O., Woloshyn, V., & Sethi, B. (2020). Reflections on Migration, Resilience, and Graduate Education: Supporting Female Students with Refugee Backgrounds. *Journal of Comparative & International Higher Education, 12*(3), 81–111.

TandEM (Towards Empowered Migrant Youth in Southern Europe) (2019). *Higher education for third country national and refugee integration in Southern Europe.* IOM – International Organization for Migration

UNHCR (2016). *Missing out: Refugee education in crisis.* Geneva: UNHCR

UNHCR (2018). The other one per cent – refugee students in higher education. *DAFI annual report 2017*. UNHCR

UNHCR (2019). *Stepping up: Refugee education in a crisis*. www.unhcr.org/steppingup/

UNHCR (2021). *Malta factsheet October 2021*. https://reliefweb.int/sites/reliefweb.int/files/resources/Malta%20Sea%20Arrivals%20and%20Asylum%20Statistics_UNHCR_Oct2021.pdf

University of Malta (2019). *University of Malta strategic plan 2020–2025*. University of Malta.

19 Cyberbullying in universities

Looking at the growing trends in developing countries

*Joshua Rumo Arongo Ndiege and
Leah Mutanu Mwaura*

Introduction

There is general agreement amongst researchers and practitioners that the use of information technology (IT) has several benefits in the promotion of teaching and learning within academia. (Manca & Ranieri, 2016; Chingos et al., 2017; Henriksen et al., 2021). Consequently, technology has become an even more prevalent factor within institutions of higher learning. Students use technology not only for academic purposes but also for social engagements through social media platforms such as Facebook, Twitter and Instagram, among others. Furthermore, there has been a rise in the use of smart mobile phone devices to enhance these experiences. This online world presents a new environment in which vulnerable university students can fall victim to perpetrators of cyberbullying who find electronic means a perfect avenue to cause acts of harassment.

While continuous exposure to and engagement with online technologies provide convenience, it is equally true that interaction with such technologies exposes students to certain online connections that may at some point put their safety, psychological and emotional well-being at risk. Acts of cyberbullying usually have a tendency to be more manifest within universities as the availability and accessibility of technology are mostly more attainable and the extent of parental authority, as well as the academic institutions' monitoring, is likely to decline as students progress through the system.

Over the years, a large and growing body of literature has continued to focus on cyberbullying, giving it considerable critical attention (Ak et al., 2015; Lee & Chun, 2020; Akbulut & Eristi, 2011; Watts et al., 2017; Aparisi et al., 2021). However, it is worth noting that the prevalence level of this phenomenon is not largely known in developing countries. A significant number of studies have been carried out within institutions of higher learning with the view of understanding the extent of cyberbullying. However, these studies have largely focused on developed countries, (Akbulut & Eristi, 2011; Aparisi et al., 2021; Cénat et al., 2021; Faucher et al., 2014). Consequently, there is very little known regarding cyberbullying in institutions of higher learning in developing countries. Significantly, therefore, a need exists for more understanding of this phenomenon in such institutions due to its profound effects. In this chapter,

DOI:10.4324/9781003258605-24

we look at the growing rise of cyberbullying within universities in developing countries. We describe their level of preparedness to deal with the issue and propose what could be done by putting a case for policies and frameworks that are sensitive to local dynamics. Additionally, we propose several future research agenda in this area.

The rise of cyberbullying within universities in developing countries

Prevalence of cyberbullying

With the increasing use of the internet, new opportunities for negative behaviour have emerged affecting the young and adults alike. One opportunity that has had an adverse effect on society is online harassment, a behaviour propagated by the prevalence of social media and digital forums. The fact that students spend a lot of time on these platforms has in turn negatively affected their mental health and subsequently their academic growth. Cyberbullying results in different mental health issues such as depression, emotional distress, low self-esteem and poor academic achievement, which can affect both the perpetrator and the victim (Watts et al., 2017; Aparisi et al., 2021). This is an increasingly emergent problem even in developing countries as reported in studies from Malaysia (Al-Rahmi et al., 2019), Pakistan (Abbasi et al., 2018) and Kenya (Ndiege et al., 2020) among others.

Smith et al. (2014) attribute the rise of cyberbullying to the prevalence of digital technology in society and the challenges of monitoring it. They point out that the prevalence of smartphone addiction was reported as 48% in Saudi Arabia, 13% in Egypt, 12.5% in Spain, 21.5% in Belgium, 39%–44% in India and 21.3% in China. This evidences the manifestation of the problem in both developed and developing countries. Similar observations have been disseminated by studies in Turkey, United Arab Emirates and Saudi Arabia. Developing countries such as Lebanon, Morocco and Jordan exhibited significantly higher rates ranging from 32% to 47% (Qudah et al., 2019). A cyberbullying study conducted in Kenya (Ndiege, 2020) observed that the prevalence of cyberbullying appeared slightly high in comparison to the majority of findings from developed economies. Qudah et al. (2019) also note that other developing countries experienced an increase in the frequency of cyberbullying among the young but the lack of studies in these areas meant that no accurate statistics existed.

While cyberbullying is on the rise worldwide, data gathered on global cyberbullying statistics, trends and facts between 2011 and 2018 reveal the extent of the problem globally and the lack of statistics in Africa's developing countries (Cook, 2020). The results show that developed countries experienced lower levels of cyberbullying among the young as reported by their parents or guardians. It is worth observing too that the statistics on cyberbullying laws and their perception point towards a link between the effectiveness of the laws and the prevalence of cyberbullying (Cook, 2020).

The same study by Cook (2020) indicates that the Google trends data based on searches for 'cyberbullying' increased threefold since 2004, an indicator of the increased awareness and attention towards cyberbullying. An interesting pattern in the data revealed steep drop-offs during the summer and over the Christmas break, suggesting that cyberbullies are at their worst during the school term. A significant drop was also observed in 2020 when the COVID-19 pandemic forced schools to switch to online learning. All we know is that since this initial dip, search traffic seems to have returned to its usual pattern (Cook, 2020).

The case of universities in developing countries

The heightened awareness of cyberbullying has increased the number of studies on the subject. Although research about cyberbullying among school students is growing day by day, studies on cyberbullying among university students remain scarce. A systematic review of cyberbullying studies conducted between 2015 and 2020 revealed that the highest numbers of studies are from Malaysia, Spain and Turkey (Shaikh et al., 2020). A few studies also occurred in Pakistan, China and the United States.

In developed countries and developing countries with high Gross Domestic Product (GDP), university students still experienced cyberbullying, albeit at lower levels. Students in a university in Spain, for instance, confirmed the existence of cyberbullying and reported the consequences as difficulties with studies and exams (Aparisi et al., 2021). Although developed countries and some developing countries with high GDPs experience lower levels of cyberbullying due to the existence of legislation, these laws are not always effective. University students in Canada, for example, cited frustrations at finding solutions despite reporting them to authorities (Cassidy et al., 2017). Laws should also be context specific. Differences in cyberbullying in some Arab countries emerged from cultural differences. In Qatar, significant associations were found between cyberbullying experiences and gender (Alrajeh, Hassan et al., 2021). A similar study in Saudi Arabia concurred with these findings noting that males indulge more in cyberbullying than females (Qudah et al., 2019).

Studies conducted in upper-middle-income developing countries also reveal the existence of cyberbullying in higher educational institutions and shed more light on the nature of the problem. University students in Malaysia reported that exposure to social media use and cyber engagement amplifies cyberbullying, cyber harassment and cyberstalking (Al-Rahmi et al., 2019). This raises concerns because such tools are important to learning and teaching since they enhance student learning, collaboration and information sharing, especially with online learning. A similar study in Malaysia concluded that psychological factors, including self-esteem, internalising behaviour and anti-social behaviour, play an instrumental role in perpetrating cyberbullying while social media usage plays a moderating role between cyberbullying intention and cyberbullying behaviour (Shaikh et al., 2021).

Studies in lower-middle-income developing countries in Asia and Africa report similar observations. Pakistan university students reported an association between the amount of time spent on the internet and particularly on social networks and cyberbullying (Musharraf et al., 2019). Nigerian university students reported similar findings, noting that the frequent use of social networks enhanced the practice of cyberbullying (Balogun et al., 2018). A different study in Pakistan reported that age and ICT self-esteem significantly reduced cyberbullying hence cyberbullying was prevalent among younger students and those who perceived themselves as having limited ICT skills (Abbasi et al., 2018). Most of these studies revealed that female students faced more cyberbullying than their male counterparts, with male students being twice as likely to perpetrate cyberbullying (Musharraf et al., 2019; Abbasi et al., 2018; Ndiege et al., 2020). Pakistani university students pointed out that the motive for cyberbullying among male students is the desire to appear socially strong, while for women the anonymity offered by cyberbullying was the most prominent motive (Abbasi et al., 2018). The most common forms of cyberbullying include deception or sending rude messages, as reported by university students in Kenya (Ndiege et al., 2020). University students in Myanmar revealed that being a victim of cyberbullying was associated with difficulties in concentrating and substance abuse (Khine et al., 2020). Because these effects are not unique to cyberbullying, it can be difficult to detect a student who experiences cyberbullying and therefore the problem may easily go unnoticed. The study in Myanmar also observed that non-resident students were at a higher risk of cyberbullying victims than their resident peers were. While there is no reason provided, the absence of the university's authority over the behaviour of students who resided outside the university may perpetuate it.

It is worth noting that research in cyberbullying among low-income developing countries hardly exists. Furthermore, most of the developing countries' studies focused on the cyberbullying of students and yet instructors as key stakeholders of universities face cyberbullying too (Smith et al., 2014). A survey conducted on a large online university in a developed country (Minor et al., 2013) revealed the existence of student cyberbullying of instructors which affected their performance and morale. The study revealed that the majority of the victims attempted to handle the situation themselves while the majority of the instructors were unaware of any policies in existence for curbing the practice.

Universities in developing countries preparedness to deal with cyberbullying

As is the case with data on cyberbullying within universities in developing countries, the debate on the level of preparedness of universities in developing countries is similarly constrained by insufficient and sometimes unreliable data on this subject (Chan et al., 2020). While cyberbullying has continued to grow, data on this have remained limited in developing countries. For developed countries, more information remains both available in the mass media and published in scholarly journals. Equally, preventive measures are normally publicly available on university websites. The limited evidence available points to a lack of available regulatory frameworks to curb the issue in institutions of higher learning in developing countries (Shaikh et al., 2020; Ndiege et al., 2020). This notwithstanding, institutions of higher learning and learners in developing countries remain involved in embracing digital technology like developed economies. Traditional and cultural dynamics have also been reported to hinder the discussions and reporting of cyberbullying within such institutions.

In view of the preceding arguments, we propose a sequential approach that takes into consideration values, evidence and policies as a coherent whole. Such a position permits a deeper interrogation of how policies for dealing with the growing culture of cyberbullying can be formulated and implemented in a way that accommodates different cultural, economic and political dynamics prevailing in developing countries. Additionally, there is a need to strengthen the legislative systems as one way of dealing with the issue.

Future agenda

Findings from a systematic review which sought to identify the factors that contributed to cyberbullying revealed that the lack of cyberbullying awareness and poor moral values, information technology literacy and lack of laws were key propagators of cyberbullying (Shaikh et al., 2020). In this section, we look at the priority agenda that should underpin future initiatives for addressing cyberbullying.

Setup cyberbullying centres

The increased prevalence of cyberbullying within institutions of higher education in developing countries and its associated impacts on education call for urgent measures to curb the problem. Educational systems in Africa and other developing economies should therefore create frameworks to deal with the emerging reality of cyberbullying within institutions of higher learning. A study conducted in 74 Canadian universities that examined 465 policies relevant to cyberbullying noted that the majority of the policies were codes of conduct or complaint procedures that did not specifically touch on cyber behaviours (Faucher et al., 2015). This highlights the fact that most institutions do not yet view cyberbullying as a problem that warrants distinctive intervention, thereby limiting options for victims.

Additionally, institutions should establish committees to examine bullying online and set up strategies to create awareness and policies to discourage the practice (Faucher et al., 2020). Existing centres of excellence within higher education institutions should initiate the process through research-based cyberbullying policies and work towards fostering a more respectful online campus culture (Cassidy et al., 2017). The need to consider cyberbullying in its cultural, social and environmental context would provide more tailored and effective solutions. Curricula and pastoral care systems in higher education should address moral disengagement alongside other cultural issues (Myers & Cowie, 2019). In light of this, awareness programs should target the entire community, rather than be confined to higher education institutions only. To this end, there is a need for educators, parents, students and community members to be vigilant in ensuring that students and faculty members are safe both physically and psychologically.

Training programmes on cyberbullying

Education and training are necessary for creating awareness in society on the causes and effects of cyberbullying. In Myanmar, university students highlighted the importance of cyber-safety educational programs and awareness-raising campaigns (Khine et al., 2020). By increasing cyberbullying awareness, users recognise when they are being bullied, identify cyberbullies and report cyberbullies to appropriate authorities (Balogun et al., 2018).

University students in Spain pointed out that students are less likely to be victims and bullies as their ability to adapt to university increases (Aparisi et al., 2021). Therefore, addressing academic adjustment during orientation programs is one way of curbing the practice. Programs that focus on teaching students digital citizenship, communication skills, exercising empathy and coping skills alongside parental involvement significantly reduce cyberbullying and cyber victimisation in youth (Alrajeh et al., 2021). However, studies on such programs have so far occurred in developed countries. More research is required to establish their efficacy in developing countries.

To develop effective programs, those concerned with the welfare of students need to keep abreast of their cyber problems. Some studies have reported that cyber victim students would seek help from a university lecturer and therefore there is a need for lecturers to be trained on how to handle incidents (Wozencroft et al., 2015). Future research should investigate ways of developing context-specific programs that would help university stakeholders to recognise cyberbullying, heighten awareness and take steps towards addressing cyberbullying.

Technology-based solutions

In a bid to enhance cyberbullying interventions, a cyberbullying study in Pakistan recommended the inclusion of ICT-related skills in anti-cyberbullying programs (Musharraf et al., 2019). A study by Faucher et al. (2020) recommended technology-based solutions to help in addressing cyberbullying phenomena. Such solutions should include reducing online anonymity in online platforms, increasing privacy settings, blocking, reporting and monitoring online interactions. A different study conducted in Australia concurred with these findings, stating that blocking the sender of a bullying message was the most common strategy of coping with cyberbullying (Wozencroft et al., 2015). In Nigeria, students recommended the privatisation of social network profiles by users, such that only people known to them and people they give authorisation to can access their profiles (Balogun et al., 2018). These studies highlight the need to use technology to curb technology-related challenges, such as cyberbullying. The need for increased ICT training on how to handle cyberbullies should therefore form part of higher education ICT literacy programs.

Legislation and policy interventions

Many developing countries lack adequate laws to address cyberbullying. A cyberbullying study in Nigeria, noting the absence of legislation relating to cyberbullying in their cybercrime law, recommended enacting laws to punish cyberbullies in the country (Balogun et al., 2018). In countries, such as Qatar, where laws existed the extent of their implementation and effectiveness have not been adequately examined. Examining cyberbullying with a holistic lens to pave the path for developing socio-culturally compatible guidelines and interventions would assist in developing and implementing effective laws (Alrajeh et al., 2021).

Conclusion

Cyberbullying within universities is a phenomenon that has grown as a result of the constant exposure and interaction that students have with online technologies. As the institutions of higher learning continue to embrace technologies and learners demand to embrace them as a tool to enhance their learning experience, students are more likely to expose themselves to certain online connections that may at some point put their safety, emotional and psychological well-being at risk and consequently affect their academic life. The chapter has presented the growing trend of cyberbullying within universities in developing countries. It is evident that these institutions, while operating in unique settings that differ from their counterparts in more developed countries in terms of political, economic and cultural dynamics, have inadequate systems and frameworks to effectively deal with the growing trend of cyberbullying.

The chapter has argued for the design of frameworks and policies that are adapted to different local dynamics prevailing within these institutions. It is imperative that such frameworks and policies be designed in a manner that allows for their effective implementation to ensure that victims of cyberbullying as offered the needed and necessary support while also providing deterrents to the perpetrators of cyberbullying.

References

Abbasi, S., Naseem, A., Shamim, A., & Qureshi, M. A. (2018). An empirical investigation of motives, nature and online sources of cyberbullying. *14th International Conference on Emerging Technologies (ICET)*, (pp. 1–6).

Ak, Ş., Özdemir, Y., & Kuzucu, Y. (2015). Cybervictimization and cyberbullying: The mediating role of anger, don't anger me! *Computers in Human Behavior, 49*, 437–443.

Akbulut, Y., & Eristi, B. (2011). Cyberbullying and victimisation among Turkish university students. *Australasian Journal of Educational Technology, 27*(7), 1155–1170.

Al-Rahmi, W. M., Yahaya, N., Alamri, M. M., Aljarboa, N. A., Kamin, Y. B., & Moafa, F. A. (2019). A model of factors affecting cyber bullying behaviors among university students. *IEEE Access, 7,* 2978–2985.

Alrajeh, S. M., Hassan, H. M., Al-Ahmed, A. S., & Alsayed, H. D. (2021). An investigation of the relationship between cyberbullying, cybervictimization and depression symptoms: A cross sectional study among university students in Qatar. *PLoS ONE, 16*(12), e0260263.

Aparisi, D., Delgado, B., Bo, R. M., & Martínez-Monteagudo, M. C. (2021). Relationship between Cyberbullying, Motivation and Learning Strategies, Academic Performance, and the Ability to Adapt to University. *International Journal of Environmental Research and Public Health, 18*(20), 10646.

Balogun, N. A., Ahlan, A. R., & Awodele, T. A. (2018). Digitalizing bullying: Do Nigerian students get cyberbullied? *2018 International Conference on Information and Communication Technology for the Muslim World (ICT4M),* (pp. 208–212).

Cassidy, W., Chantal, F., & Margaret, J. (2017). Adversity in university: Cyberbullying and its impacts on students, faculty and administrators. *International Journal of Environmental Research and Public Health, 14*(8), 888.

Cénat, J. M., Smith, K., Hébert, M., & Derivois, D. (2021). Polyvictimization and Cyber-victimization Among College Students From France: The Mediation Role of Psychological Distress and Resilience. *Journal of Interpersonal Violence, 36*(17), 9252–9271.

Chan, H. C., Sheridan, L., & Adjorlolo, S. (2020). Stalking and intrusive behaviors in Ghana: Perceptions and victimization experiences. *International Journal of Environmental Research and Public Health, 17*(7), 2298.

Chingos, M. M., Griffiths, R. J., Mulhern, C., & Spies, R. R. (2017). Interactive online learning oncCampus: Comparing students' outcomes in hybrid and traditional courses in the university system of Maryland. *The Journal of Higher Education, 88*(2), 210–233.

Cook, S. (2020). *Cyberbullying facts and statistics for 2020.* Website Comparitech.com.

Faucher, C., Cassidy, W., & Jackson, M. (2015). From the sandbox to the inbox: Comparing the acts, impacts, and solutions of bullying in K-12, higher education, and the workplace. *Journal of Education and Training Studies, 3*(6), 111–125.

Faucher, C., Cassidy, W., & Jackson, M. (2020). Awareness, policy, privacy, and more: Post-secondary students voice their solutions to cyberbullying. *European Journal of Investigation in Health, Psychology and Education, 10*(3), 795–815.

Faucher, C., Jackson, M., & Cassidy, W. (2014). Cyberbullying among university students: Gendered experiences, impacts, and perspectives. *Education Research International,* 698545.

Henriksen, D., Creely, E., Henderson, M., & Mishra, P. (2021). Creativity and technology in teaching and learning: A literature review of the uneasy space of implementation. *Educational Technology Research and Development, 69,* 2091–2108.

Khine, A. T., Saw, Y. M., Htut, Z. Y., Khaing, C. T., Soe, H. Z., Swe, K. K., . . . Hamajima, N. (2020). Assessing risk factors and impact of cyberbullying victimization among university students in Myanmar: A cross-sectional study. *PLoS One, 5*(1), e0227051.

Lee, S., & Chun, J. (2020). Conceptualizing the impacts of cyberbullying victimization among Korean male adolescents. *Children and Youth Services Review, 117,* 105275.

Manca, S., & Ranieri, M. (2016). Facebook and the others. Potentials and obstacles of Social Media for teaching in higher education. *Computers & Education, 95,* 216–230.

Minor, M. A., Smith, G. S., & Brashen, H. (2013). Cyberbullying in higher education. *Journal of Educational Research and Practice, 3*(1), 15–29.

Musharraf, S., Bauman, S., Anis-ul-Haque, M., & Malik, J. A. (2019). General and ICT self-efficacy in different participants roles in cyberbullying/victimization among Pakistani University Students. *Frontiers in Psychology*, *10*, 1098.

Myers, C.-A., & Cowie, H. (2019). Cyberbullying across the lifespan of education: Issues and interventions from school to University. *International Journal of Environmental Research and Public Health*, *16*(7), 1217. https://doi.org/10.3390/ijerph16071217

Ndiege, J. R., Okello, G., & Wamuyu, P. K. (2020). Cyberbullying among university students: The Kenyan experience. *The African Journal of Information Systems*, *12*(1), 24–43.

Qudah, M. F., Albursan, I. S., Hassan, E. M., Alfnan, A. A., Aljomaa, S. S., AL-khadher, M. M., & Bakhiet, S. F. (2019). Smartphone addiction and its relationship with cyberbullying among university students. *International Journal of Mental Health and Addiction*, *17*, 628–643.

Shaikh, F. B., Rehman, M., & Amin, A. (2020). Cyberbullying: A systematic literature review to identify the factors impelling university students towards cyberbullying. *IEEE Access*, *8*, 148031–148051.

Shaikh, F. B., Rehman, M., Amin, A., Shamim, A., & Hashmani, M. A. (2021). Cyberbullying behaviour: A study of undergraduate university students. *IEEE Access*, *9*, 92715–92734.

Smith, P. K., Thompson, F., & Davidson, J. (2014). Cyber safety for adolescent girls: Bullying, harassment, sexting, pornography, and solicitation. *Current Opinion in Obstetrics and Gynecology*, *26*(5), 360–365.

Watts, L. K., Wagner, J., Velasquez, B., & Behrens, P. I. (2017). Cyberbullying in higher education: A literature review. *Computers in Human Behavior*, *69*, 268–274.

Wozencroft, K., Campbell, M., Orel, A., Kimpton, M., & Leong, E. (2015). University students' intentions to report cyberbullying. *Australian Journal of Educational & Developmental Psychology*, *15*, 1–12.

20 The rise of the #MeToo movement in Croatia, Serbia, Bosnia and Herzegovina

Renata Miljević-Riđički

Introduction

This chapter shows how the social media can become a powerful tool to confront historical abuse and bad behaviour. It highlights several case studies which influenced university policies on sexual misconduct in the present while giving a dramatic voice to survivors from the past. It is almost impossible to write about this topic as a piece of academic and scientific literature in the usual manner. Some survivors are ready to talk about their traumatic experiences straightaway, some open up after a decade and others will remain silent. This chapter draws on several sources, including various personal accounts and social media platforms, alongside traditional academic literature. The **#MeToo** movement, the focus of this chapter, has other identities in the countries presented here. In Bosnia and Herzegovina, the **#MeToo** movement is called 'I didn't ask for it!', while in Croatia and Serbia it is also known as 'You're not alone' and 'I didn't report it'. In Serbia, the movement is known as 'No means no!' and 'You're not alone'. Like the **#MeToo** movement, it first arose among celebrities. It was started by a famous Serbian actor, Milena Radulović, who accused her former acting coach, also a high-profile person in acting circles, of sexual abuse. However, the actor herself noted that there was a big difference between **#MeToo** and 'You're not alone'. **#MeToo** aims first and foremost to strengthen the rights of women. It also endeavours to achieve equality between women and men. It was launched by white, famous, privileged women in the United States from positions of power, not as victims (Lazard, 2020). Powerful women in the United States wanted to lead by example to disclose sexual abuse and harassment. By contrast, the 'You're not alone' movement focuses predominantly on victims, especially those who are underage, encouraging them to talk about their experiences of sexual abuse.

The rise of #MeToo

Encouraged by the momentum **#MeToo** gained overseas, three actors from Sarajevo, Matea Mavrak, Nadine Mičić and Ana Tikvić, and playwright Asja Krsmanović, launched a similar movement in Bosnia and Herzegovina

DOI:10.4324/9781003258605-25

in January 2021. In an interview, Matea Mavrak described how the movement came about and what had happened the year before. The movement was launched when the four women opened a Facebook group. They did not know precisely where to start, but they knew that they wanted to change something in the sense of protecting women from sexual predators, violence and sexual harassment. They decided to set up a Facebook page that would be open to everyone. In the initial stages, they focused on high-profile members of the public because their stories mostly enter the public sphere. As soon as the platform became available to the public, they began to hear from girls and women from various walks of life who narrated stories about their families, school environment, stories from their work and experiences with friends. It immediately became clear that the platform was for all women. In its first 48 hours, the group received more than 3,000 posts. They heard from women of all ages. Some of them realised what had happened to them and why they were experiencing psychological problems only later in life, in their 60s and 70s.

Problems with the Facebook page soon arose. After 48 hours, it was blocked because Facebook had received disinformation reports. They were sent by abusers who recognised themselves, although the stories were published anonymously, and they also began to threaten the victims. The creators of the group did not expect such a response and were not aware that women were so willing to talk about what had happened to them.

One of the posts was accidentally published with the full name of the abuser, a university professor. In a private message to one of the founders, he demanded that the post be removed or otherwise he would sue. The media launched an investigation of its own. They wanted to know who was behind it all. The founders then went public with the names, taking a big risk and exposing themselves to all sorts of attacks. They received ugly comments, such as: 'Idle actresses with time on their hands!' Some comments were highly derogatory and vulgar. They presumed the comments were from abusers or people who condone violence.

The next step was to create a website and a new Facebook page managed by themselves. In addition to user stories, they began to publish useful information to help victims of violence. Although they still experience difficulties, the founders believe that the movement has gained momentum and that this problem will never again be discussed in the same way as before the movement began. The initiative **#nisamtražila** has raised awareness of sexual harassment and abuse, victims receive space in various forms of media, on shared portals and, most importantly, they receive instructions and support in legal proceedings.

The platforms provide practical information about institutions, addresses and telephone numbers where victims can seek help. Some victims are still not ready to report their abusers, but at least they are ready to tell their stories anonymously. The more stories there are on the #nisamtrazila portal, the more encouragement there is for women who have not dared to speak out to date to come forward to do so. The stories demonstrate that girls and women find it hard to report sexual abuse, whether within the family or at university or in the workplace.

Indeed, Mamula, the founder of the Women's Room, gives the following examples to explain why there is a potential failure to disclose.

1   **Personal reasons** include fear of the perpetrator and believing his threats, fear of how people closest to the victim will react, insufficient support for the survivors of sexual violence and fear of the outcome of court proceedings (Stakor, 2021). Another reason is the fear of losing one's job.

2   **Powerful patriarchal values** in institutions, in healthcare systems and in the legal system prevent victims from speaking out by humiliating and denigrating them when they do report abuse.

'I reported it but then I wished hadn't because the police pulled the dress I had worn from the evidence bag and said: "No wonder, look what she was wearing"'

A social worker about the abuse of a 14-year-old girl:

'We cannot do anything about her, she has been promiscuous before'.

A psychiatrist in a hospital (without empathy) to the patient:

'Why didn't you report it [sexual abuse] earlier?'

Sometimes it is hard to find legal protection:

Hello, dear women . . . I cannot describe the sorrow I felt yesterday when I remembered an experience from early last year (attempted rape) and from eight years ago (rape) and the fact that nothing came of my report because the coronavirus had complicated matters and the deadline for the appeal had expired. A few months ago, I even contacted an association, but no, nothing came of that either. The same answer, I was late. Where exactly was I late, at the wrong time or on the wrong planet, and is there a legal institution that will actually help, take steps, and not just engage in empty talk? I am totally listless, still on antidepressants, but I'm not happy with the therapy because I'm tired all the time (I have a small child, so this is even harder for me) and then I ask, where is justice and why is my rapist still at large? Maybe it's my fault because I went to his place (as many ignorant people say) and will justice ever be served? The worst thing is that I don't think I'm the only victim.

3)   **Strong emotional reactions** There have been reports about immediate reactions.

After *the initial shock, it became clear that this was a manipulator and sexual predator and I tried to cut our conversation short so I could leave as soon as possible, which I succeeded in doing. For days, I experienced a mix of feelings ranging from unease, shame to anger and back to unease directed at him, but also at myself because I had been so naïve. I feel sorry for the women who perhaps were not strong and confident enough and with whom his 'examination' might have gone a step further.* Some reactions are delayed: *One day, I simply snapped after spending months believing I was depressed or sick and I realised what was going on. I understood that it was easier for me to believe and live thinking that it had been my fault (although it wasn't) than to accept the fact that they were sick. I think that it is for this reason that people often do not believe victims' stories. For them, just like for us, it is easier to believe that someone is exaggerating than that sick people live in our midst. It took a long while to tell all this to my friends and eventually to my family as well, to whom I am eternally grateful for their support. I think I was lucky that everyone to whom I told this believes that I'm telling the truth.*

There is also the long-lasting psychological damage inflicted on these women over their lifespan. Many of them report problems in their relationships with men, avoiding sex and intimacy:

The trauma made me convince myself that it wasn't true, that it was all a figment of my imagination, a dream. . . . It was only when I entered my first relationship that I realized how damaged I was. . . . I didn't know how to behave, how to love, how to partake of such wonderful feelings, I was a figurine, a statue. . . . A beautiful statue gazed on by many, but I was merely a piece of stone . . . cold and lifeless.

The spread of the movement

The movement soon spread to other countries in the region. It has raised awareness about the types of conduct that are regarded as sexual harassment notably within the higher education sector. Indeed, the first serious response was from the Academy of Drama in Zagreb. It was the first educational institution in the region to react publicly to posts connected with the 'I didn't ask for it' movement and dedicated a space on its premises to deal with sexual harassment and cases of abuse. This was very brave because the dean at that time says she 'experienced some very nasty reactions, comments, threats, even court suits' (Mitrović, 2021, p. 57). Many reports were received. The dean says with respect to the victims that to file a 'report is simultaneously a liberating and traumatising experience' (Mitrović, 2021, p. 57). The Academy founded a working group responsible for collecting reports and a commission to conduct internal investigations on the grounds of the reports of sexual harassment and abuse, on violations of the principle of gender equality and on related forms of discrimination and harassment. On the recommendation of the commission, the new dean of the Academy suspended three professors and reports were submitted to the police and the Public Prosecutor's Office. The head of the Department of Theatre and Radio Directing told his students that 'any form of violence, harassment, chauvinism and homophobia is wholly unacceptable, especially in academic circles, and certainly in artistic pedagogy, which is an environment that should encourage creativity and the widening of horizons, and not provoking withdrawal and fear' (Miljuš and Gotal, 2021, p. 8).

Criminal law protection against sexual harassment is regulated by law, but there are deficiencies. For example, the statute of limitations is ten years, which means that someone who was abused at 18 years of age and decides to speak at 29 years of age can no longer harm the abuser (except indirectly by encouraging victims whose deadline for reporting is still not barred by the statute of limitations). Further, case law is not uniform; there are still only a small number of reports and court proceedings compared to the actual situation. There are the so-called dark figures, and the whole range of possible legal sanctions is not used so it is necessary to ensure a more uniform interpretation of the existing forms of this criminal act (Munivrana, 2021).

Across the various countries, some victims, encouraged by the movement, started court proceedings against their abusers on their own on the grounds of sexual orientation, sexual harassment, mobbing, belittlement, abuse of position and attending class in an inebriated or drunken state. In some cases, legal action was initiated and disciplinary procedures for serious breach of duty and damage to the reputation of the university were taken against perpetrators. Examples include sexual comments and invitations to engage in physical contact, emotional harassment, inappropriate non-verbal signs like staring and encroachment of personal space, and other unpleasant types of conduct.

One student reported:

> The professor told me at the university that he would help me with my absences from class if I helped him to get over his wife.

Another described the behaviour of a professor about whom there had been over one hundred complaints from women students:

> I do not feel safe in the classroom with the professor.

Numerous complaints were soon documented, including:

- asking a student to go out with him to a porno movie theatre
- putting his hand on the hip of a new student asking: 'Will you get horny if I move my hand up?' (The student began to cry.)
- taking a bagel from a student's mouth and putting it in his mouth
- commenting on students' looks, make-up
- touching a student's hair, hand, décolletage
- getting too close (physically)
- during consultation with a student, commenting that her work reminds him of a penis and vagina, putting his hand on the student's hip (she refused him and received a bad mark)
- hugging, touching the face, moving hair from the face

- once inserting a pornographic slide in a PowerPoint presentation
- suddenly approaching and kissing on the face.

Female students claimed that the authorities knew about this behaviour. Some stated that they asked the professor's assistant to protect them, but the assistant replied that this was none of his business. Today, when several cases have come out, it is now covered on several web pages and newspapers, and the universities have acted. Students hope that their collective effort will end in success and that perpetrators will face due process. It also demonstrates the power of the internet as a tool to help victims to both expose and cope with inappropriate conduct and highlights the importance of online platforms to get the messages across. The **#MeToo** movement has global reach.

University action

The system of support, especially legal and psychological support, is still underdeveloped. This is particularly seen in Bosnia and Herzegovina. The founders of the 'I didn't ask for it' movement believe that this is only the beginning and that a lot more must be done. Many women keep their stories secret because of victim stigmatisation and the inadequate system of support. As opposed to Bosnia and Herzegovina, in Serbia and Croatia there are several NGOs and associations engaged in prevention and in the protection of victims of violence (e.g. the Autonomous Women's Centre in Belgrade, Incest Trauma Centre in Belgrade, the Women's Room and the Centre for Education and Counselling and Research (CESI) in Zagreb). In Croatia, one of the most active is The Women's Room – Centre for Sexual Rights. It is a feminist, non-profit, civil society organisation established in 2002 with the aim of preventing and combating sexual violence, providing direct support and assistance to persons who survived sexual violence as well as promotion and protection of sexual rights (www.zenskasoba.hr/). The Women's Room became involved in professor and student education at the Academy of Drama in Zagreb. Following the Academy, they began to cooperate with several other faculties in organising education and they provide advice on the development of procedures. The Women's Room with The Centre for Victims of Sexual Violence works directly with women who have experienced sexual violence. The work involves advisory and therapeutic work regarding traumatic experiences. They also inform and advise persons close to the victims of sexual violence (Stakor, 2021).

The National Plan for the Elimination of Sexual Violence and Sexual Harassment is being developed at the Ministry of Labour, Pension System, Family and Social Policy (Directorate for Family and Social Policy) on the initiative of the Women's Room. They participated in the working group for amending the Criminal Code and drafted some amendments. They provide support in the procedure of reporting sexual violence (escorting victims to the police, hospital, public prosecutors' offices, the court, social welfare centres) and publish materials intended for the survivors of sexual violence (Stakor, 2021).

CESI is a female, feminist, non-profit association that launched a campaign called #nijeuredu (It is not OK.) that aims to show the harmful consequences of gender prejudices against women. Its website highlights its mission: CESI is a feminist organisation that advocates for the advancement of women in society and for the realisation of gender equality, and for the full implementation of all laws and international mechanisms for the protection of human rights (www.cesi.hr/). They point to various prejudices against women, amongst them sexist statements that are still prevalent in society. They receive support from various institutions, including the University in Rijeka, which is known as one of the first institutions whose senate adopted the Gender Equality Plan. They work on raising awareness in various ways – posters, websites, social media platforms and magazines, and they also have an SOS telephone for women victims of violence, and they offer legal counselling. They have implemented various projects (e.g. 'Silence is not golden') and conduct research documenting various injustices in society. The purpose of the initiative 'I can say no' is to contribute to the elimination of sexting and gender-conditioned violence in intimate partner relationships between young people. Once again highlights the positive initiatives that can and are being developed. Although the internet can be a space that causes harm, it can also be a space to help report and record it.

Some faculties, such as the Faculty of Teacher Education in Zagreb, have developed and adopted a Gender Equality Plan for the next five years. The plan involves several lines of work on gender equality. One of them is to prevent sexual harassment and abuse by raising awareness amongst employees and students and by providing support and advice to the victims of sexual harassment www.ufzg.unizg.hr/wp-content/uploads/2021/12/Plan-spolne-ravnopravnosti-UF-a_12-2021_potpisan.pdf. The public is becoming more aware of the problem. For example, in interviews with famous Croatian actors in daily newspapers, responses to the question 'How important is the **#MeToo** movement for raising awareness of the problem of sexual violence in Croatian acting circles?' included the following:

> It is important to raise awareness of any violence, regardless of the place and form it takes. I hope that actors and directors will not become known as sexual predators.
>
> Sexual violence is completely unacceptable, and I see no difference between sexual violence and violence of any other type and form. Therefore, there must be zero tolerance for all forms of violence. The #MeToo movement is very important because there is finally public talk about violence that has been around for years but would always end up brushed under the carpet.

There was a belief that the perpetrator is always provoked to commit violence. The greatest success of the movement is that it has managed to show that the victims of violence are not to blame for the fact that they were made to endure this form of violence, that the perpetrator has a name and surname, and that the perpetrator must be held accountable for his conduct.

The **#MeToo** movement is important from several perspectives, globally. Victims have been made to feel that they are not alone and that they receive support. Publicly they have the right to articulate their pain and demand their legal right to protection and the legal prosecution of the perpetrators. There are boundaries in relationships and in attempts to create one. Everyone has rights. Violence is not part of a relationship based on love. Rather, courage is part of any relationship. There is now more awareness of the view that patriarchal relationships with women should not be assumed, whether between friends or at work. All human beings have the right to create a relationship that suits them in agreement with their partner (Novak Starčević, 2022).

Such public statements by famous actors are important because these people act as a behavioural model for their audience. It is now becoming more common to see celebrities opening up and publicly disclosing their previous bad experiences. Since the movement has become public, universities are responding quickly to reports of sexual harassment. The University of Zagreb has changed its policy and appointed a person to whom students can turn for help. The same has happened at some universities in Serbia. The victims of violence are supported through various portals, which has a therapeutic effect and is in line with initiatives that are discussed elsewhere within this volume.

Scientific and professional gatherings are also being organised to address the topic of sexual abuse and harassment. For example, the Department of Labour and Social Law of the Faculty of Law of the University of Zagreb held a scientific-professional conference on 'Legal Protection against Harassment and Sexual Harassment' in March 2021 (Grgurev & Potočnjak, 2021). One of the main conclusions was that there are many laws but that it is too complicated to apply them. The procedure should be simplified to provide quick legal protection against sexual harassment. There is also a need for more preventive measures (Grgurev & Potočnjak, 2021).

The movement 'I didn't report it' was created as a follow-up to the mentioned movements in late 2021 and was launched by a political scientist from Belgrade, Nina Stojaković, who described on Twitter how her sister had been beaten and bullied by her former boyfriend. After they reported it to the police, they were informed that the police could do nothing because there was no evidence. The movement was supported by a human rights activist and educator Dejana 'Dexi' Stošić, a student at Belgrade's Faculty of Humanities and Social Sciences, in her posts on Twitter. Just like the movement 'No means no', which also began in Serbia, this movement has also spread rapidly to neighbouring countries. On the Twitter platform, victims publish their experiences of abuse and harassment, mostly physical or sexual, and reasons why they failed to report it to the authorities. They express their distrust in the legal system and fear of further victimisation. So far there have been more than 20,000 testimonies. Often the environment in which the victim lives imposes a sense of guilt or shame. Therefore, it has been so important to use the power of the internet to expose abusers. Victims can find mutual support which will be followed by initiatives in society as well as by legal action. Those who are afraid can remain anonymous.

Conclusion

It appears that the movements discussed have led to narratives that are just the tip of the iceberg of the problem. There are so many more stories that remain untold, and therefore many more unprocessed than processed cases. Many victims talk about secondary victimisation, caused even by those people who should be helping as part of their job (including criminal justice and healthcare professionals). The climate in the mentioned countries is still patriarchal, especially in Bosnia, where women often dare not speak out or push back against the perpetrators in some other way. Those who do dare often face a lack of understanding in their immediate surroundings, even by persons closest to them (parents, partners). The founders of the movement have also had to live through various unpleasant experiences. Still, the 'iceberg' has shifted, and changes are taking place, facilitated by online social movements.

All of this would not have happened without multiple connections through social media sites such as Facebook, Twitter, Instagram and similar platforms. The chance to tell their own story, to receive positive feedback and to conclude that they 'are not alone' has helped many victims to open up, reduce their trauma and find useful advice and support at different levels, including peer support, legal guidance, information about psychological help and group interaction. The initiatives are now too strong to be ignored and the internet as a source of support against harm is only going to grow.

References

Grgurev, I., & Potočnjak, Ž. (Eds.) (2021). *Pravna zaštita od spolnog uznemiravanja (Protection against sexual harassment through law)*. Zagreb: Pravni fakultet Sveučilišta u Zagrebu.

Lazard, L. (2020). *Sexual harassment, psychology and feminism: #MeToo, victim politics and predators in neoliberal time*. Cham: Springer Nature/Palgrave Macmillan.

Miljuš, D., & Gotal, V. (2022). Suspendirani profesor Prohić: "Ne znam o kakvoj suspenziji govorite" (Suspended professor Prohić: I do not know which suspension you are talking about). *Jutarnji List*, 5. 11. 2021.

Mitrović, M. (2021). FRANKA PERKOVIĆ GAMULIN Prijavljeni zlostavljači ne vide u čemu je problem (FRANKA PERKOVIĆ GAMULIN Reported abusers do not see what the problem is). *Večernji list*, 19. 12. 2021.

Munivrana, M. (2021). Kaznenopravna zaštita o spolnog uznemiravanja (Protection against sexual harassment through criminal law). In I. Grgurev & Z. Potočnjak (Eds.), *Pravna zaštita od spolnog uznemiravanja (Protection against sexual harassment through the law)* (pp. 119–151). Zagreb: Pravni fakultet Sveučilišta u Zagrebu.

Novak Starčević, L. (2022). Tri mušketira i 10 pitanja (Three musketeers and 10 questions). *Jutarnji List*, *23*, 1–2.

Stakor, K. (2021). Maja Mamula Ženska soba: "Kao društvu potrebna nam je edukacija o seksualnom nasilju (Maja Mamula, Women's Room: As a society we need education about sexual harassment). *Elle*, *25*, 4.s

Index